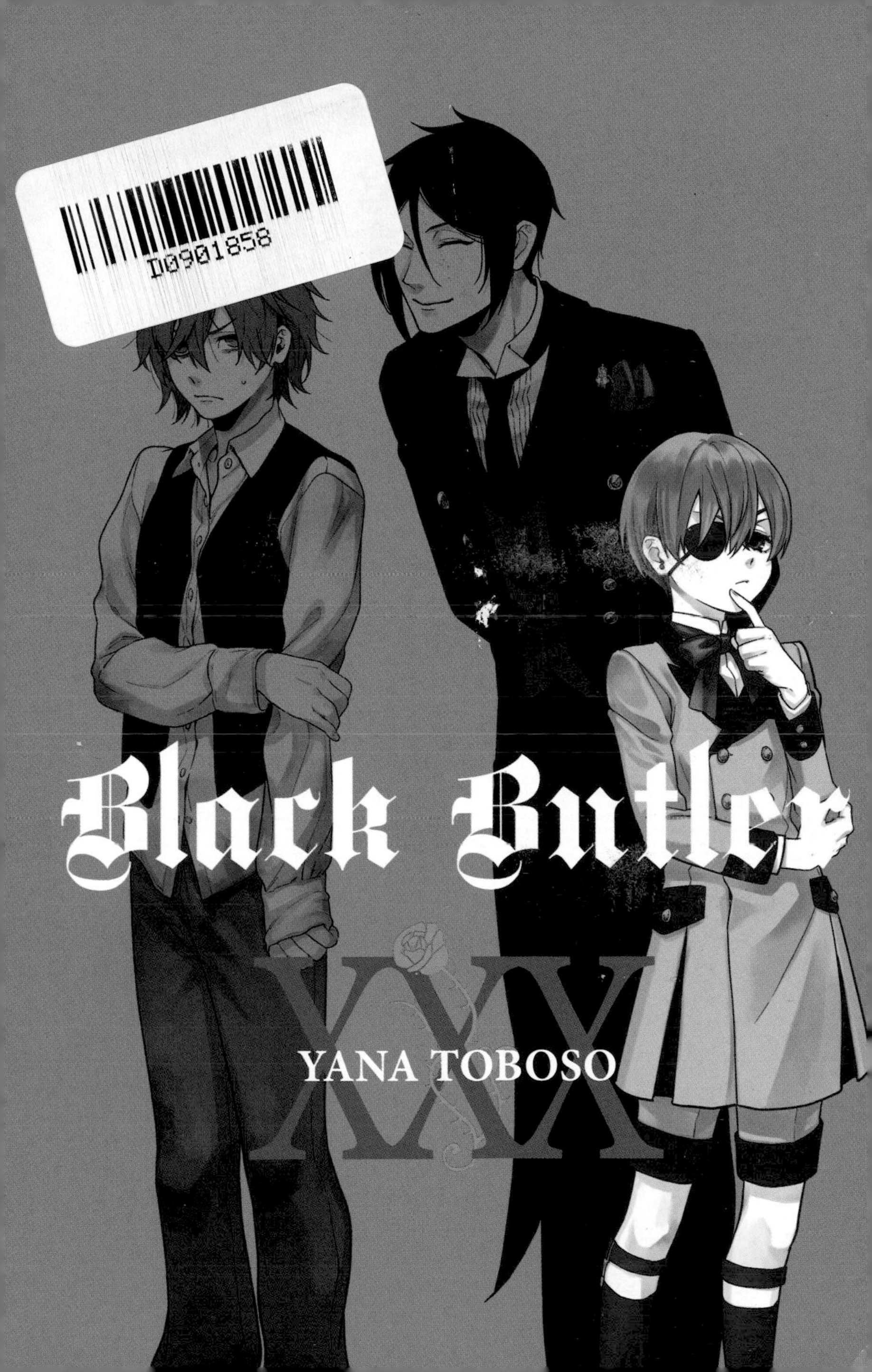
Black Butler
XX
YANA TOBOSO

Contents

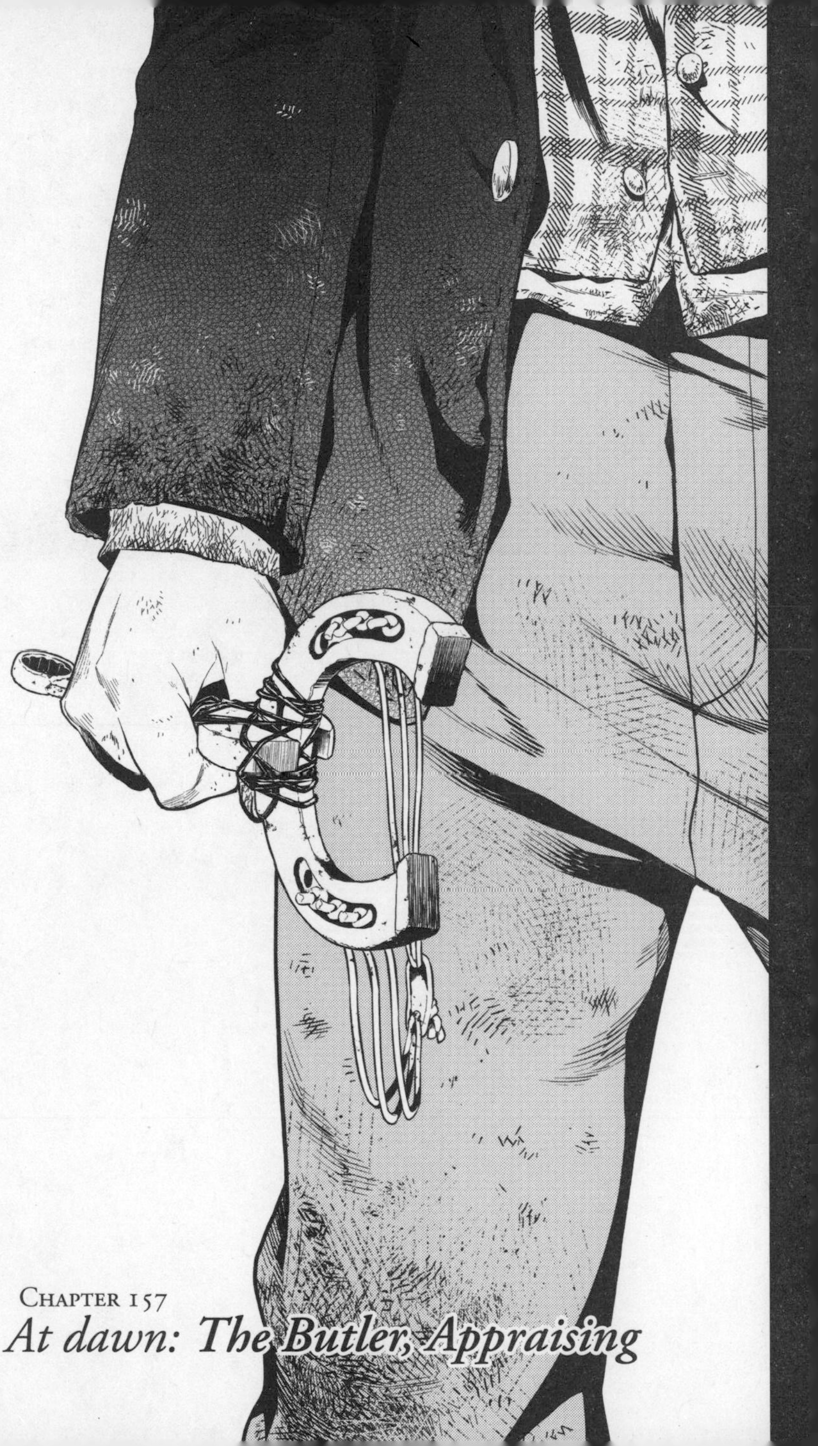

Chapter 157

At dawn: The Butler, Appraising

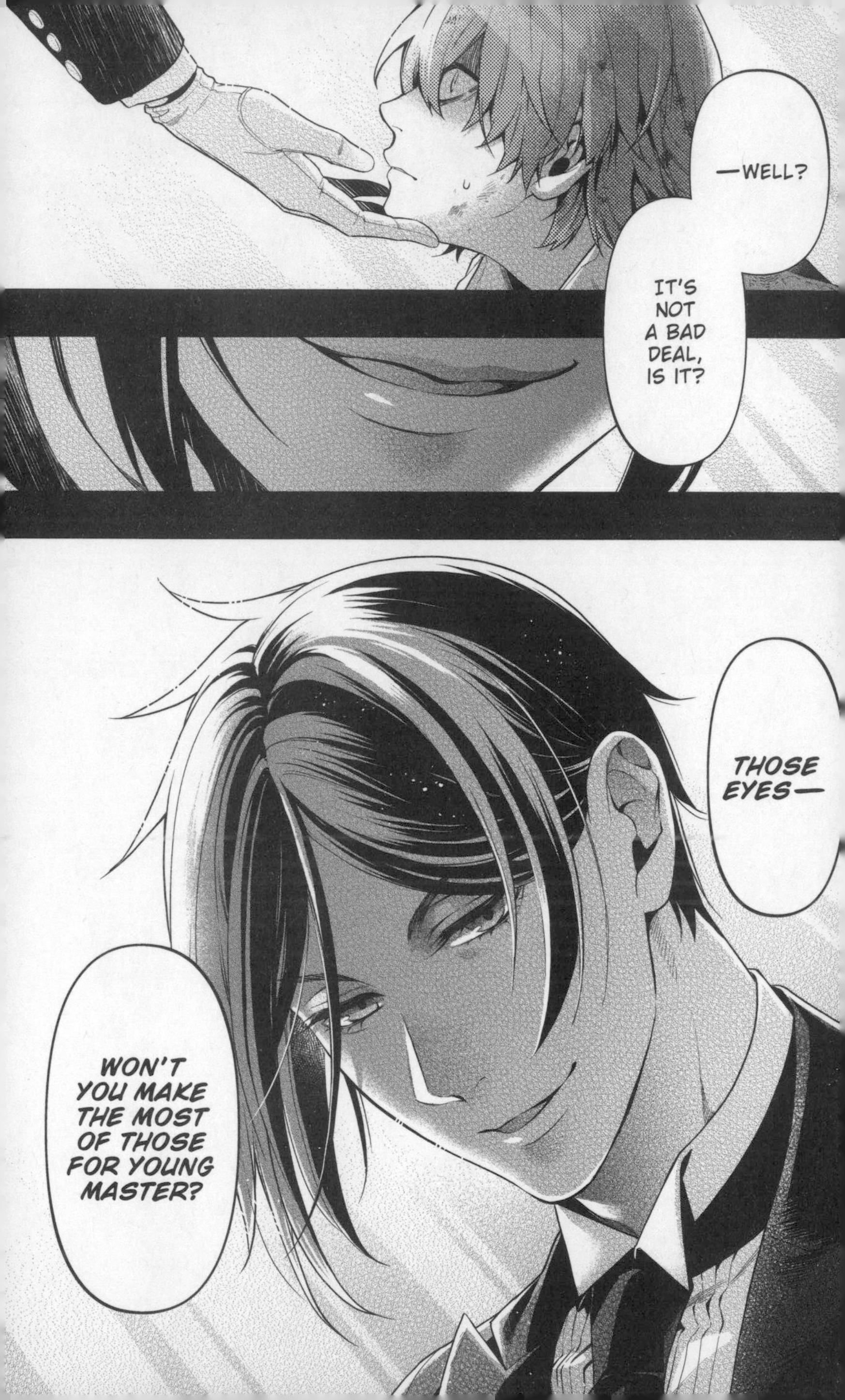
—WELL?
IT'S NOT A BAD DEAL, IS IT?
THOSE EYES—
WON'T YOU MAKE THE MOST OF THOSE FOR YOUNG MASTER?

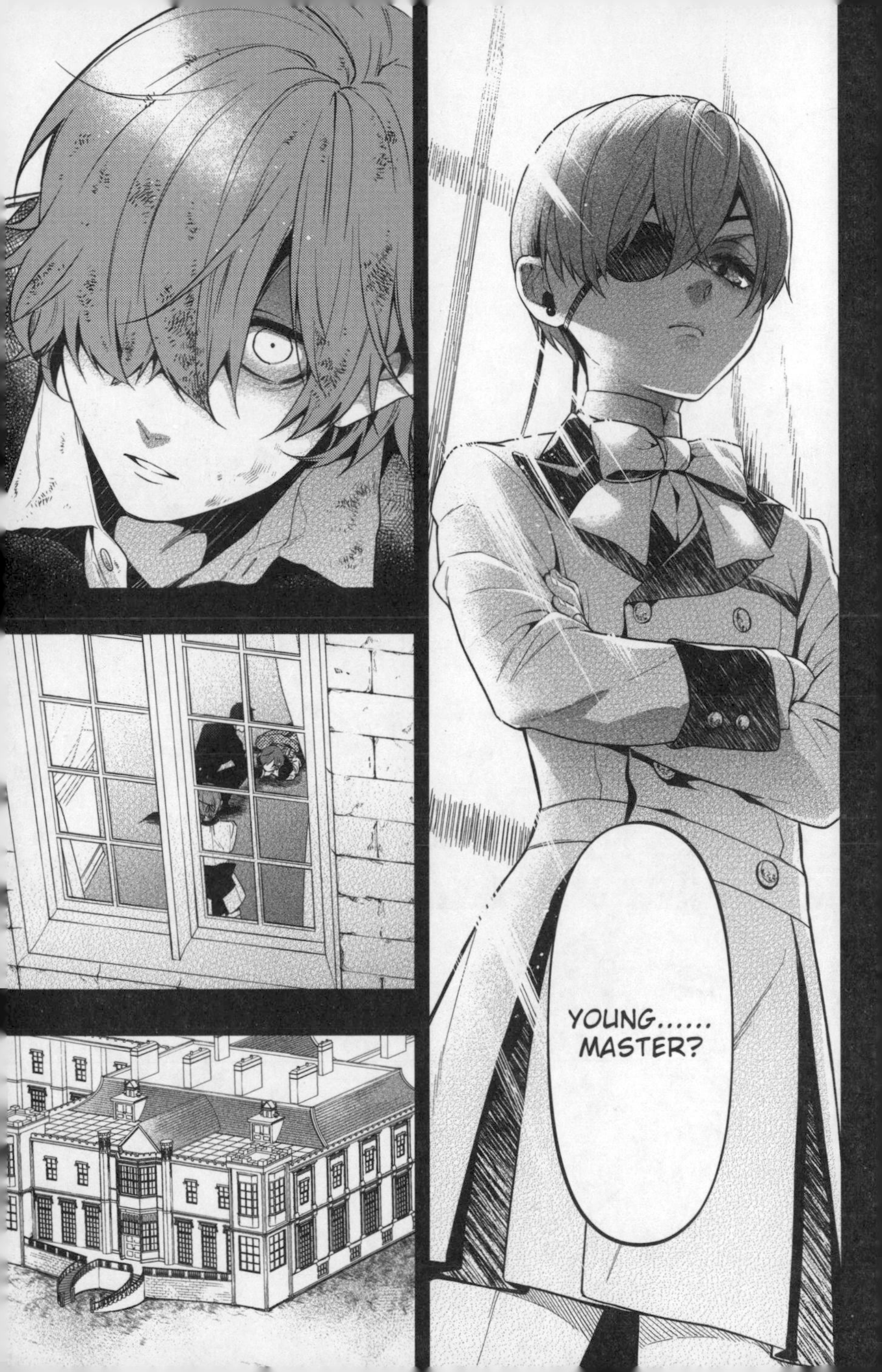
YOUNG...... MASTER?

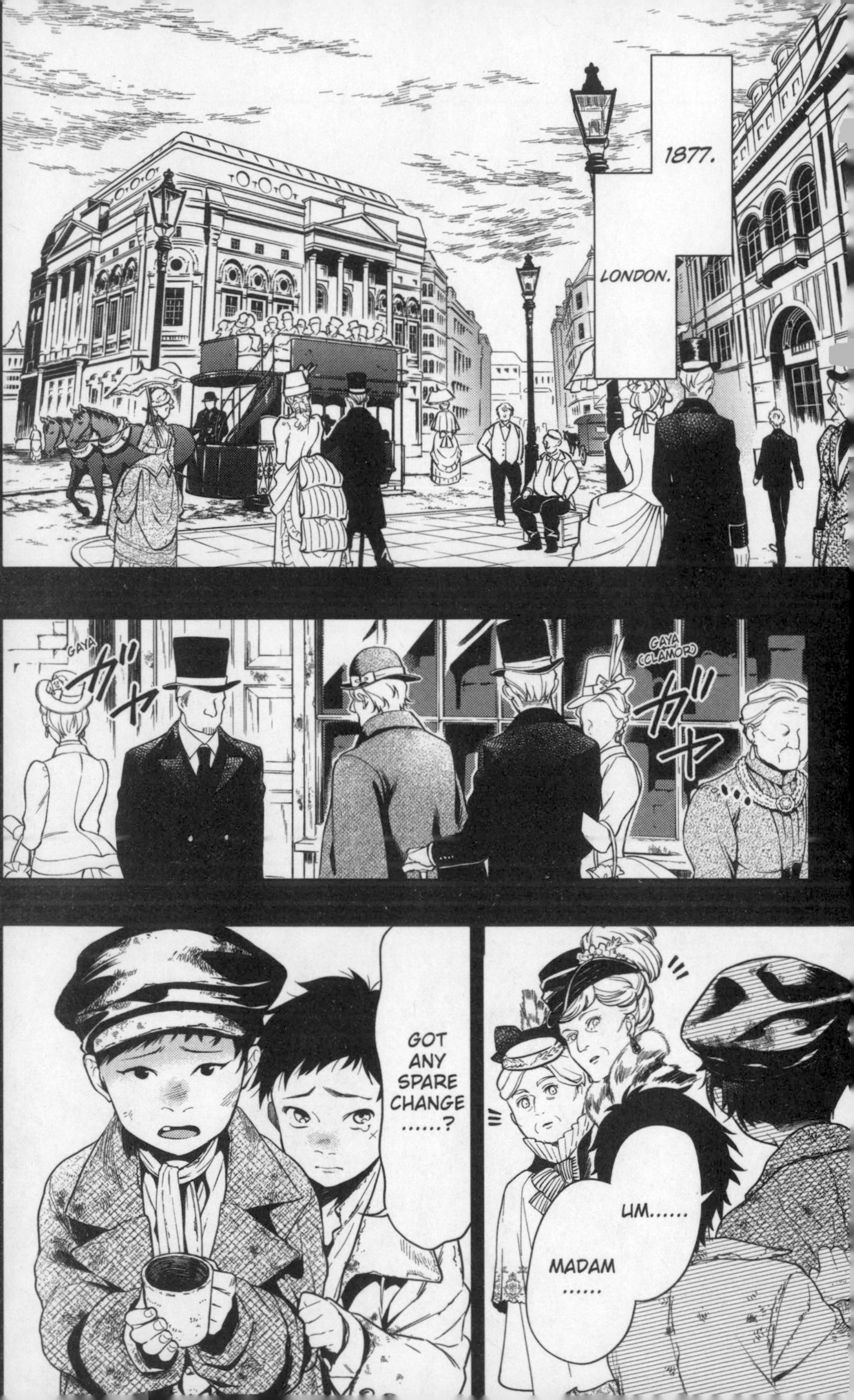

1877.
LONDON.
GAYA (CLAMOR)
ガヤ
GAYA
ガヤ
UM......
MADAM ......
GOT ANY SPARE CHANGE ......?

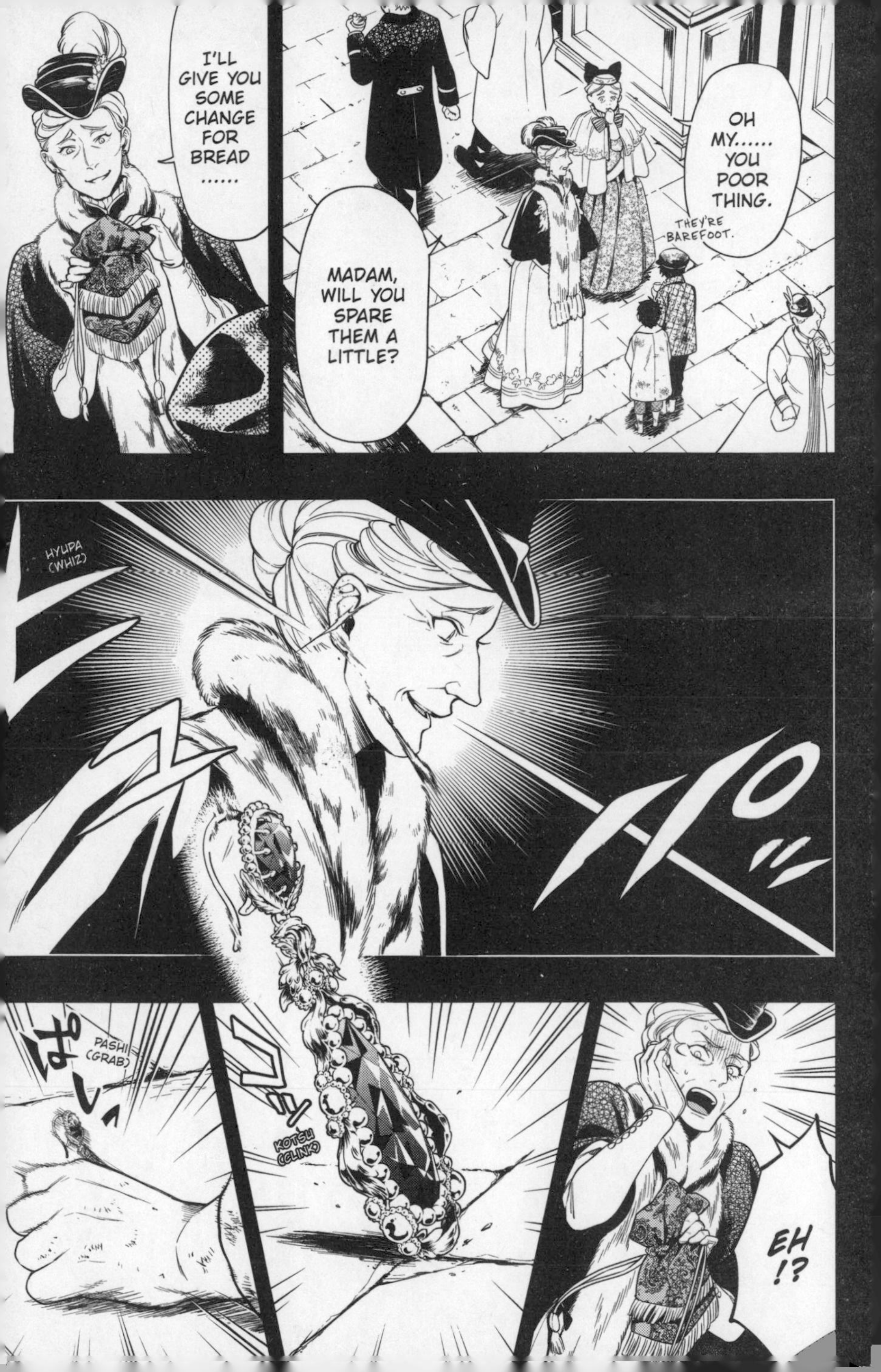
OH MY...... YOU POOR THING.
THEY'RE BAREFOOT.
MADAM, WILL YOU SPARE THEM A LITTLE?
I'LL GIVE YOU SOME CHANGE FOR BREAD ......
HYUPA (WHIZ)
EH !?
KOTSU (CLINK)
PASHI (GRAB)

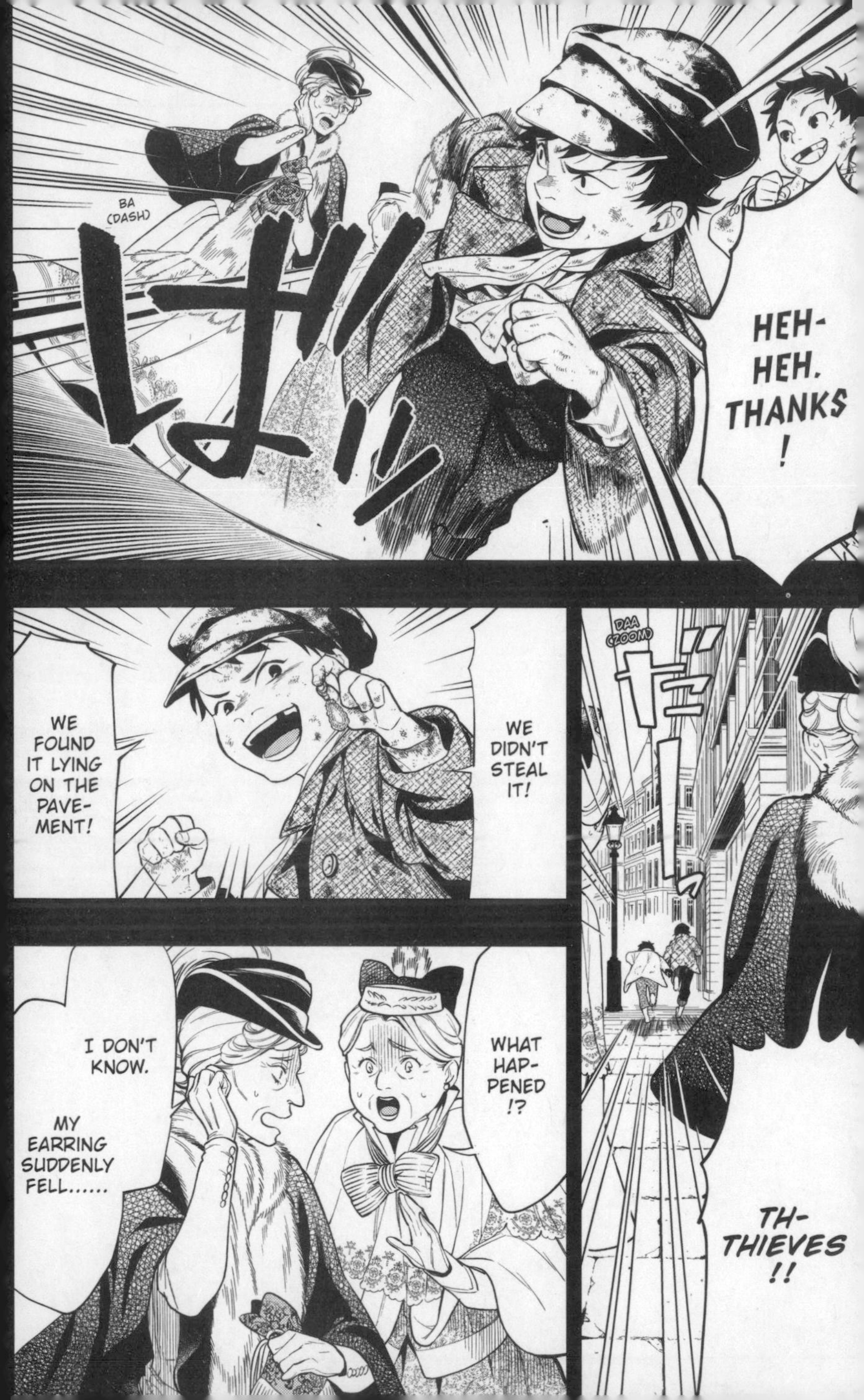
HEH-HEH. THANKS!
BA (DASH)
DAA (ZOOM)
TH-THIEVES!!
WE DIDN'T STEAL IT!
WE FOUND IT LYING ON THE PAVEMENT!
WHAT HAPPENED!?
I DON'T KNOW.
MY EARRING SUDDENLY FELL......

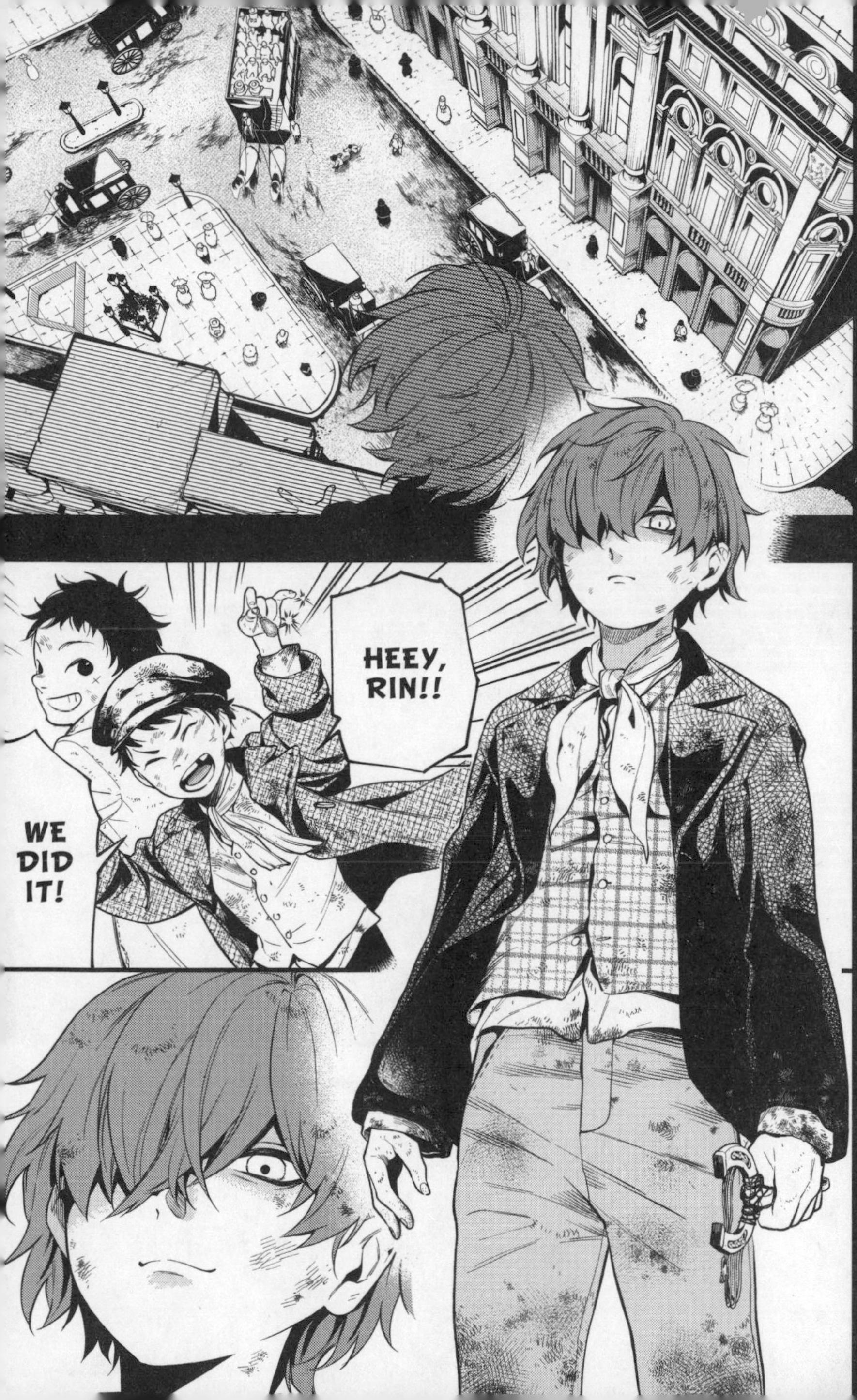
HEEY, RIN!!
WE DID IT!

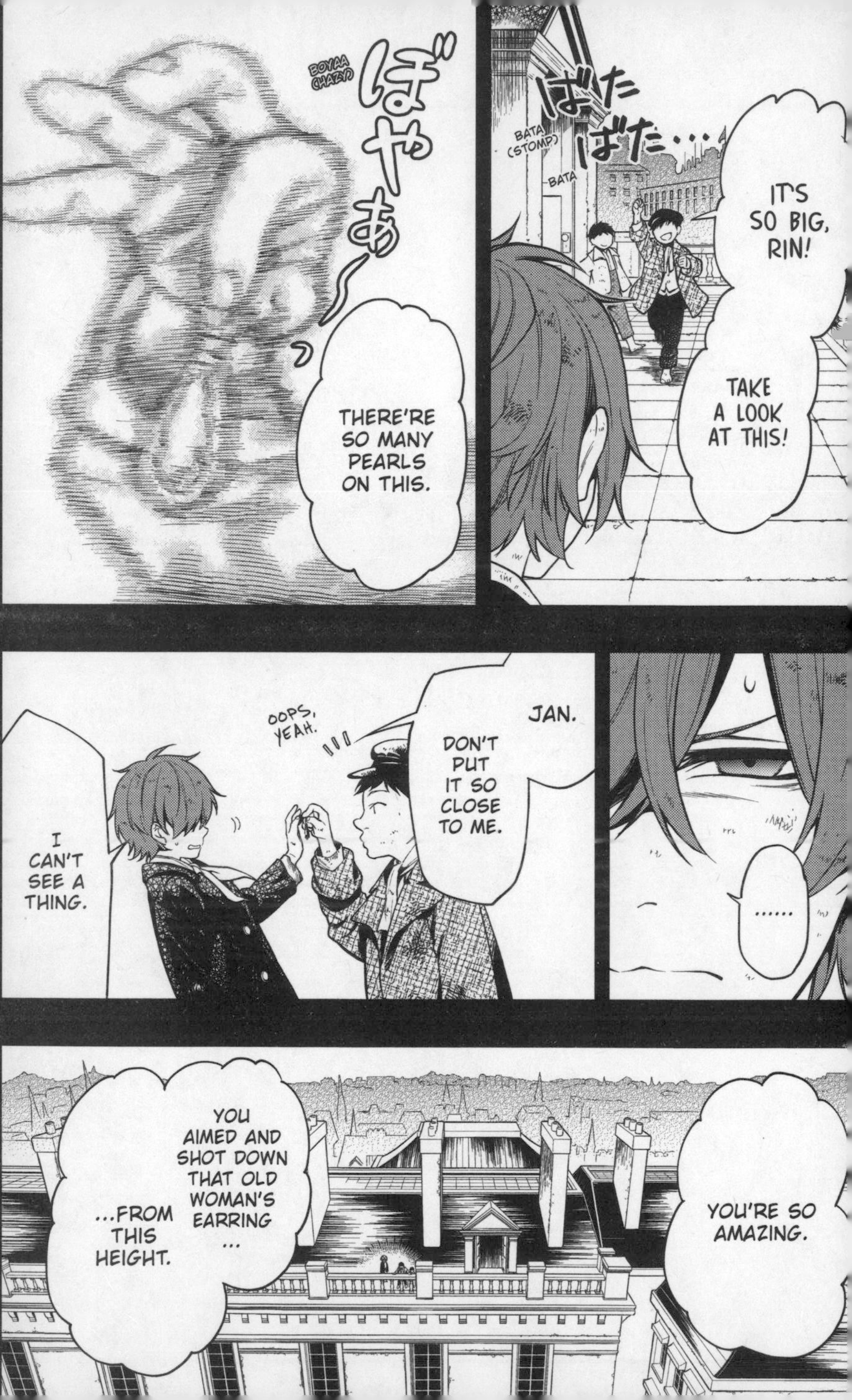
ばた ばた…
BATA (STOMP) BATA
IT'S SO BIG, RIN!
TAKE A LOOK AT THIS!
ぼやぁ~っ
BOYAA (HAZY)
THERE'RE SO MANY PEARLS ON THIS.
......
JAN.
DON'T PUT IT SO CLOSE TO ME.
OOPS, YEAH.
I CAN'T SEE A THING.
YOU'RE SO AMAZING.
YOU AIMED AND SHOT DOWN THAT OLD WOMAN'S EARRING ...
...FROM THIS HEIGHT.

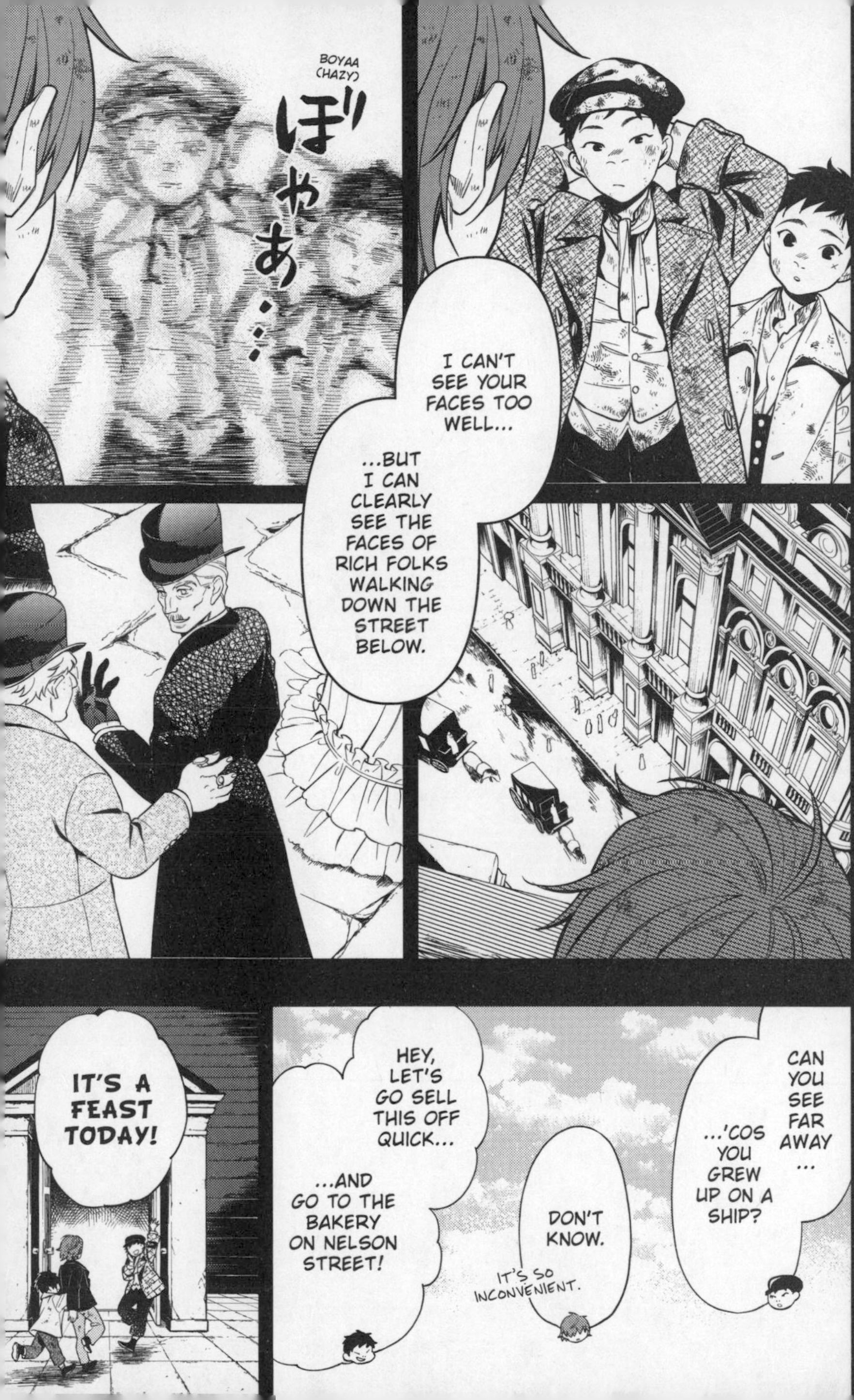
I CAN'T SEE YOUR FACES TOO WELL...
BOYAA (HAZY)
ぼやあ…
...BUT I CAN CLEARLY SEE THE FACES OF RICH FOLKS WALKING DOWN THE STREET BELOW.
CAN YOU SEE FAR AWAY...
...'COS YOU GREW UP ON A SHIP?
DON'T KNOW.
IT'S SO INCONVENIENT.
HEY, LET'S GO SELL THIS OFF QUICK...
...AND GO TO THE BAKERY ON NELSON STREET!
IT'S A FEAST TODAY!

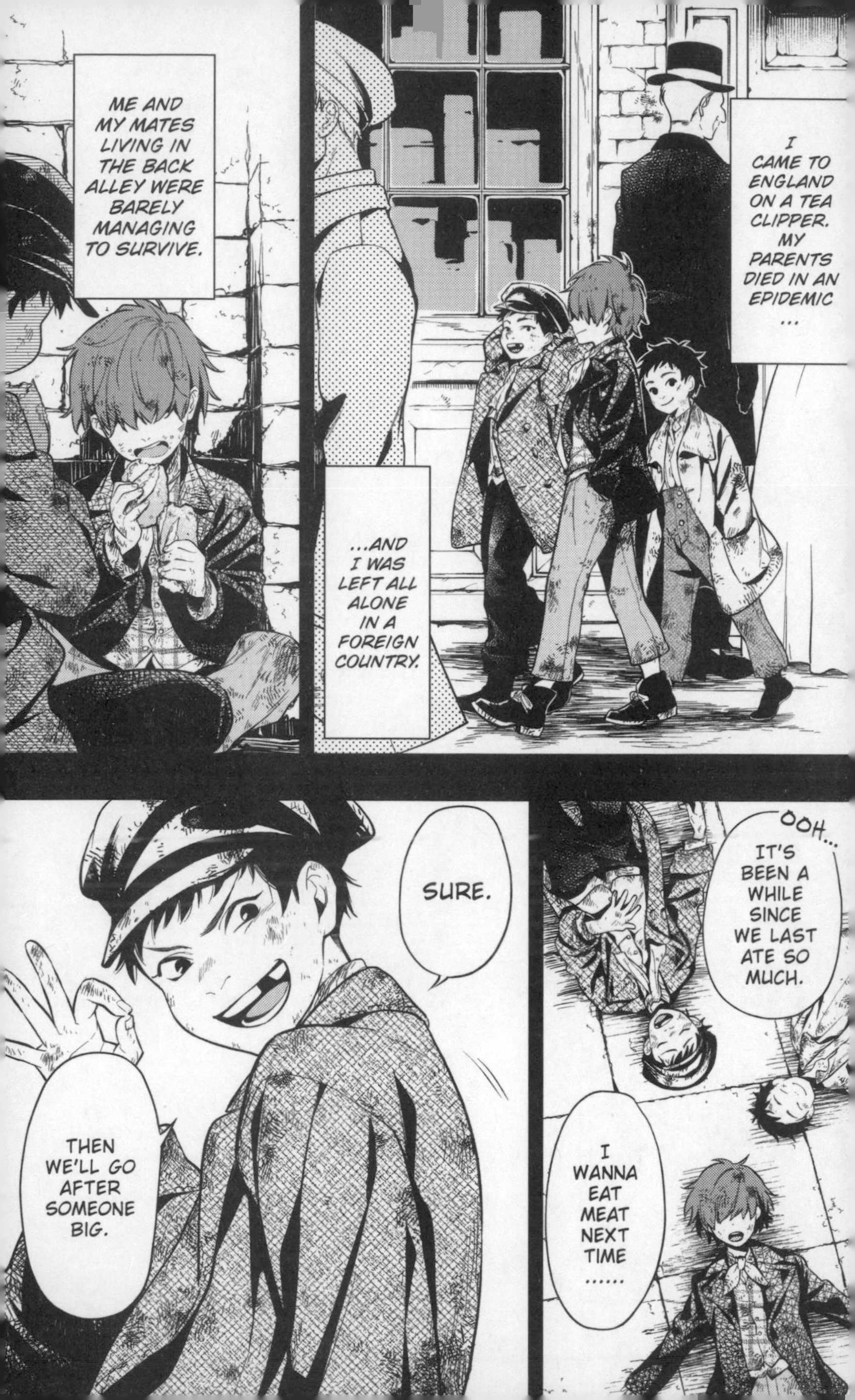
I CAME TO ENGLAND ON A TEA CLIPPER. MY PARENTS DIED IN AN EPIDEMIC ...
...AND I WAS LEFT ALL ALONE IN A FOREIGN COUNTRY.
ME AND MY MATES LIVING IN THE BACK ALLEY WERE BARELY MANAGING TO SURVIVE.
OOH... IT'S BEEN A WHILE SINCE WE LAST ATE SO MUCH.
I WANNA EAT MEAT NEXT TIME ......
SURE.
THEN WE'LL GO AFTER SOMEONE BIG.

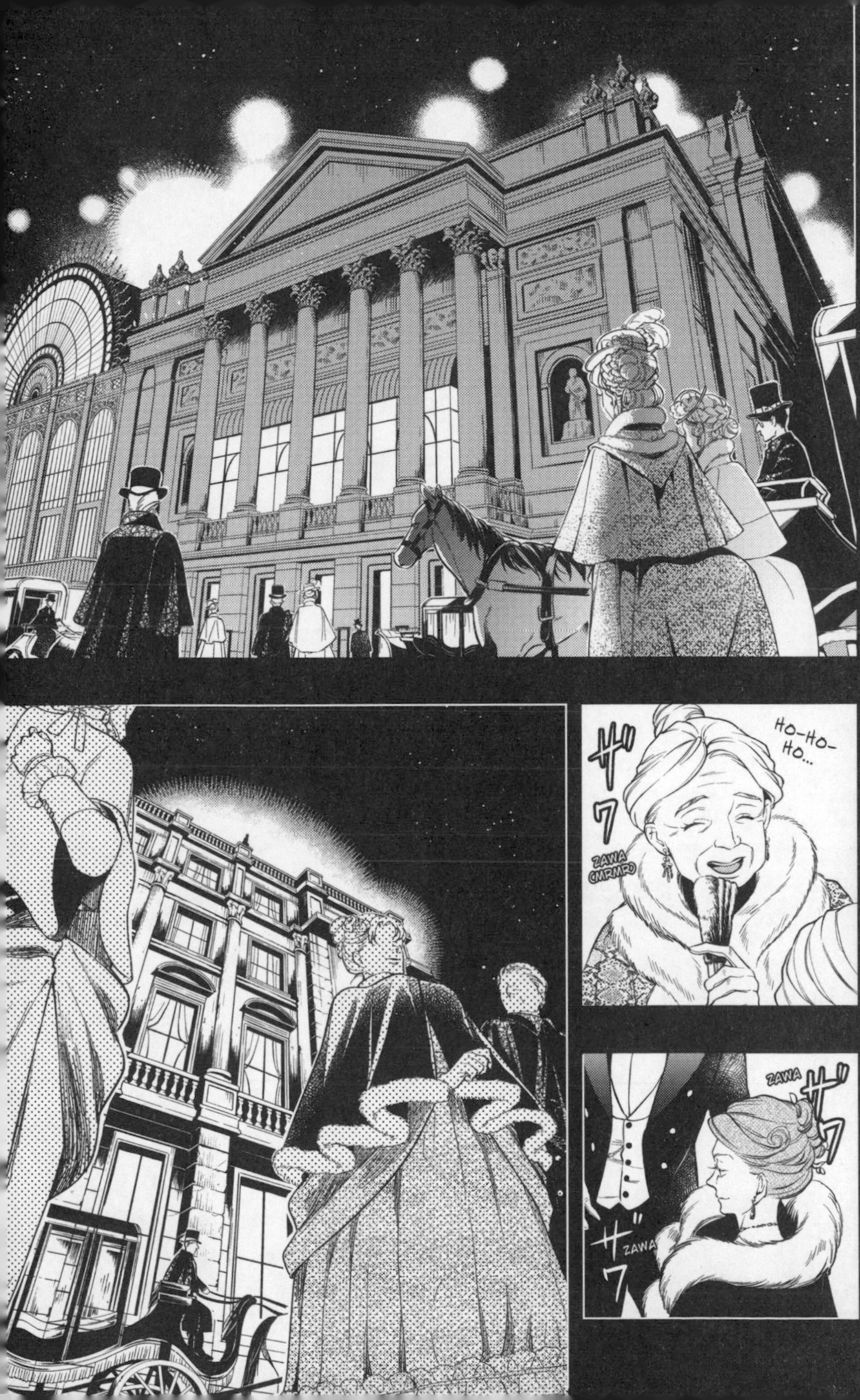
HO-HO-HO...
ZAWA (MRMR)
ZAWA
ZAWA

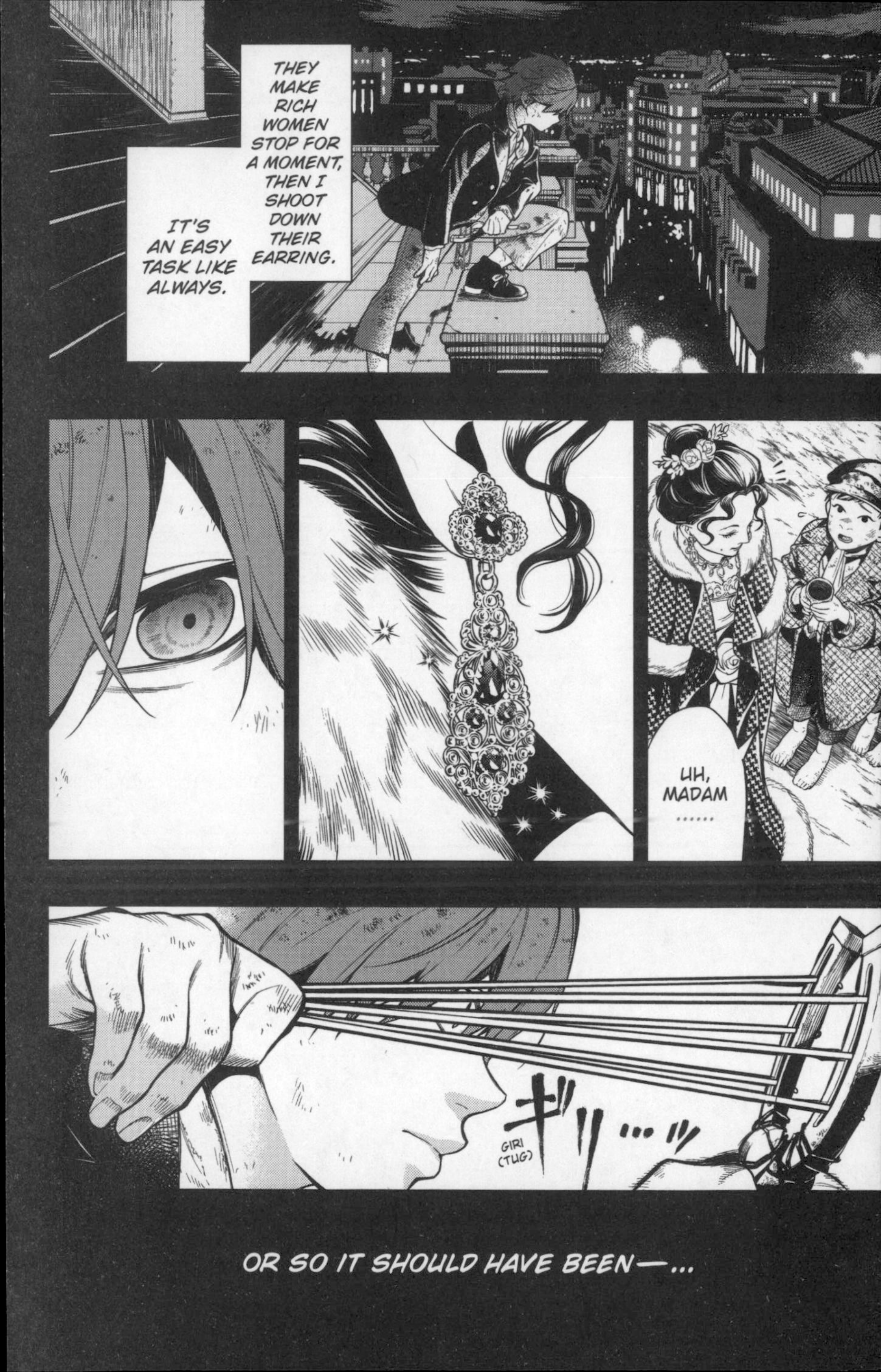
THEY MAKE RICH WOMEN STOP FOR A MOMENT, THEN I SHOOT DOWN THEIR EARRING.
IT'S AN EASY TASK LIKE ALWAYS.
UH, MADAM ......
GIRI (TUG)
OR SO IT SHOULD HAVE BEEN—...

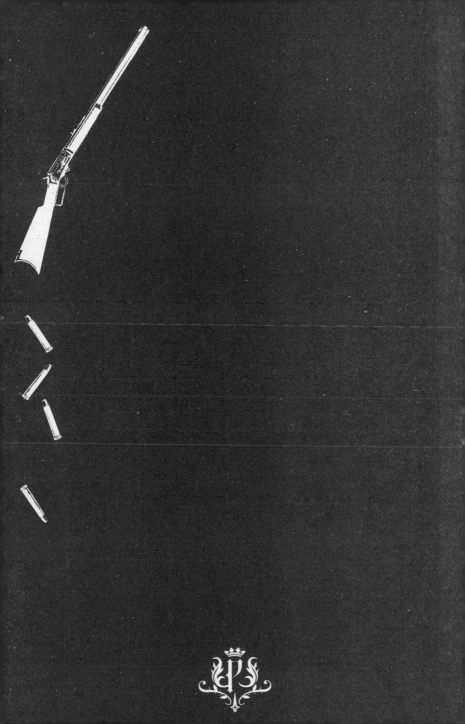

Black Butler

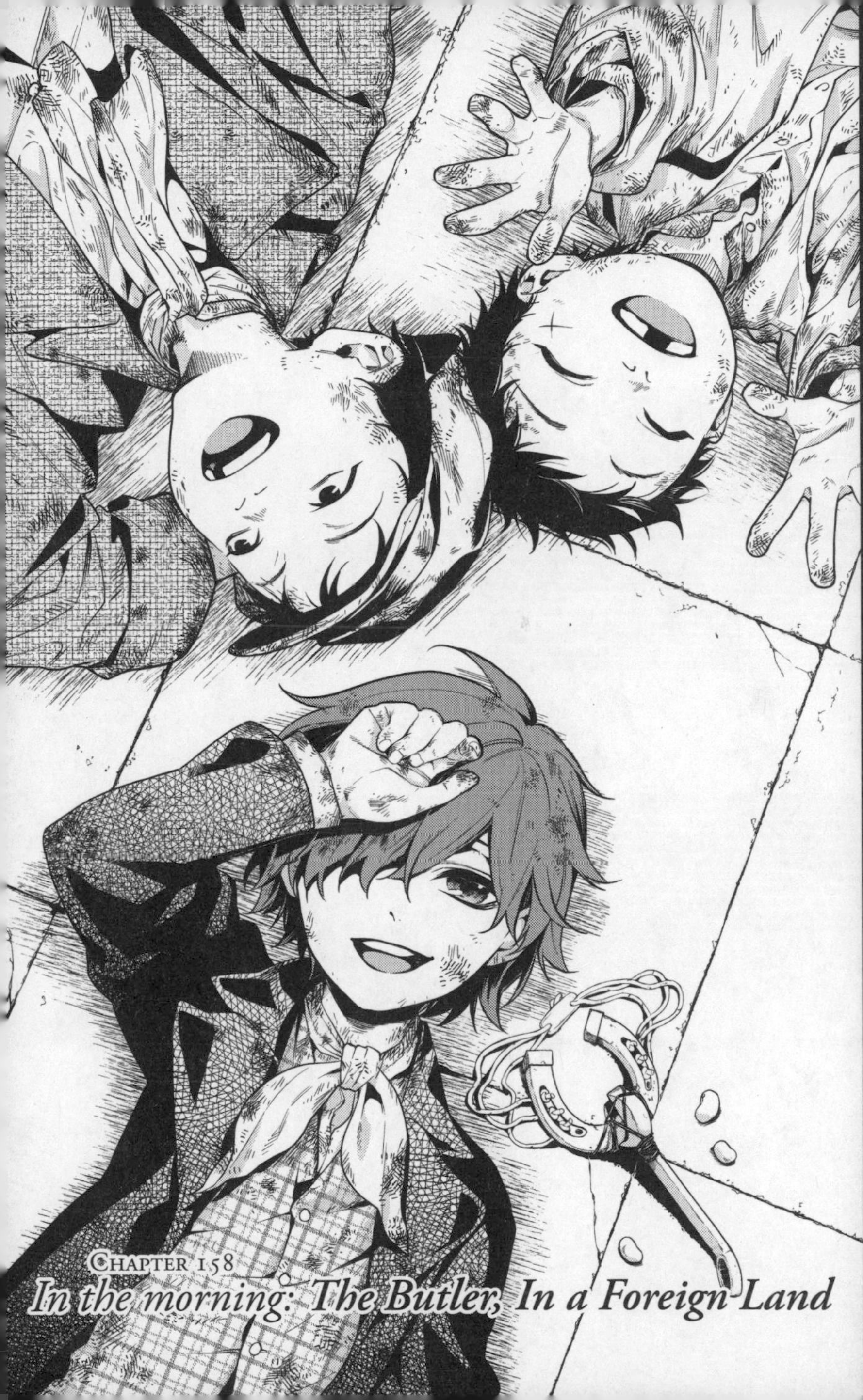
Chapter 158
In the morning: The Butler, In a Foreign Land

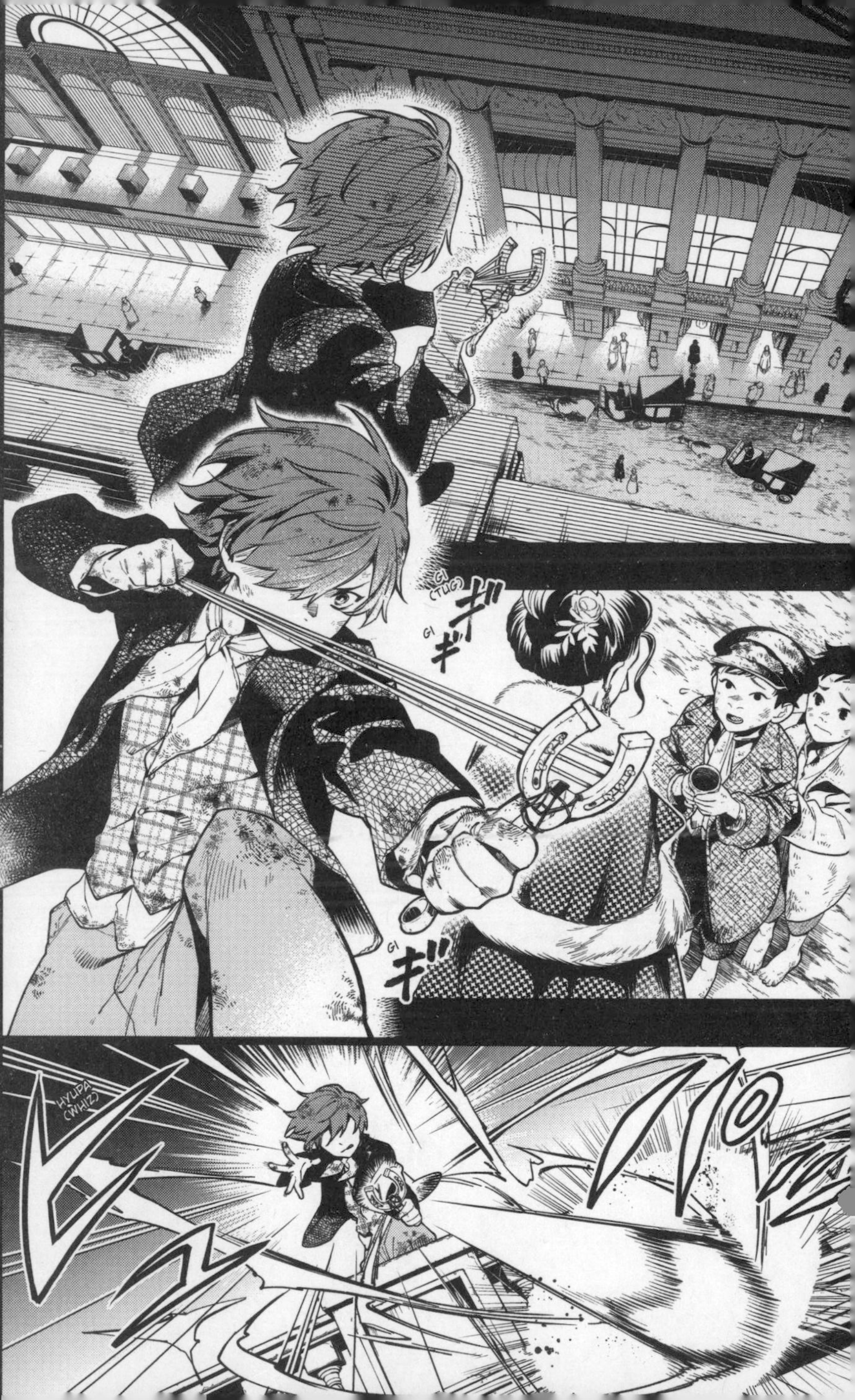
GI (TUG)
ギ
GI
ギ
GI
ギ
HYUPA (WHIZ)

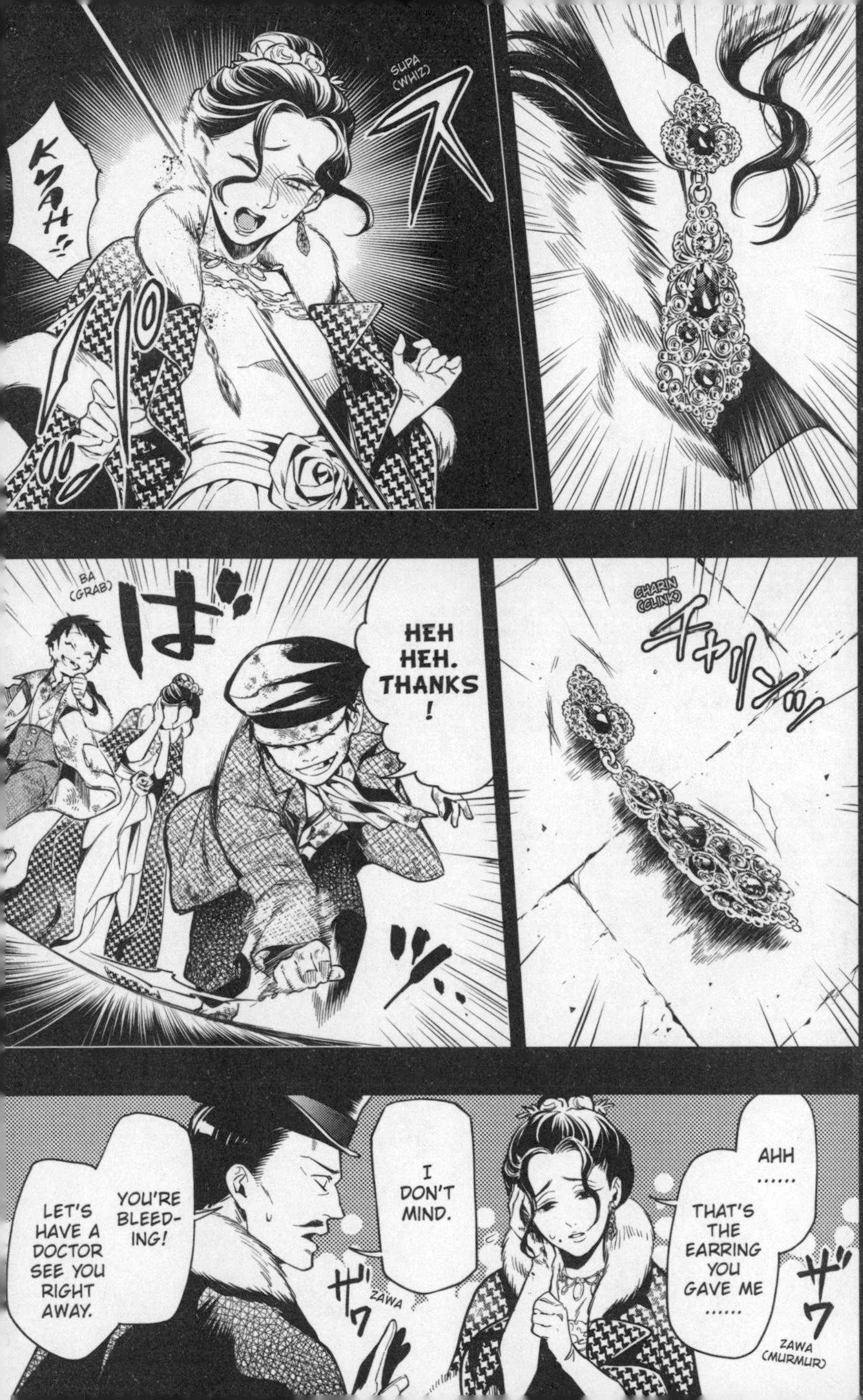
SUPA (WHIZ)
KYAAH!?
CHARIN (CLINK)
BA (GRAB)
HEH HEH. THANKS!
AHH ...... THAT'S THE EARRING YOU GAVE ME ......
ZAWA (MURMUR)
I DON'T MIND.
ZAWA
YOU'RE BLEED-ING!
LET'S HAVE A DOCTOR SEE YOU RIGHT AWAY.

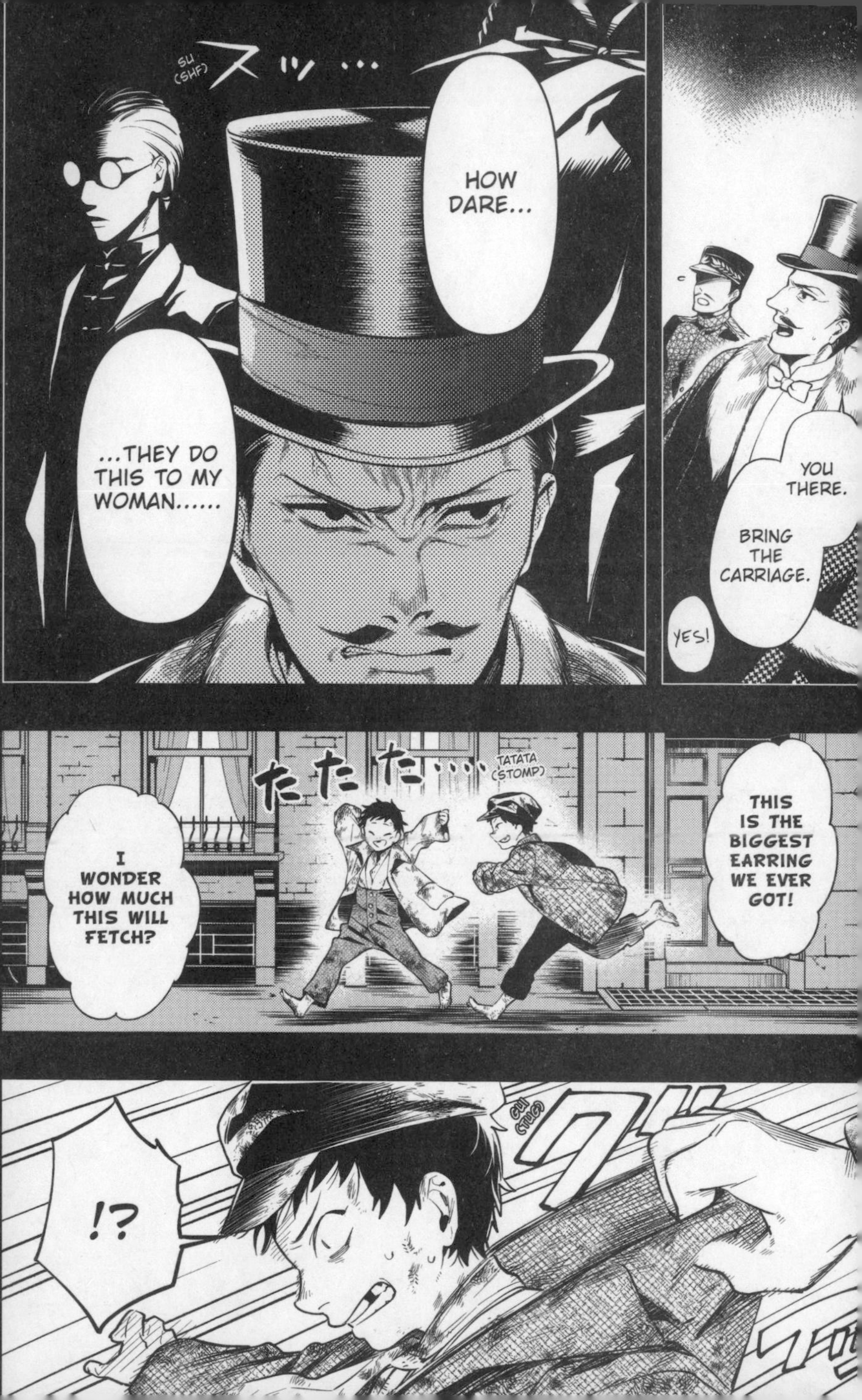
YOU THERE.
BRING THE CARRIAGE.
YES!
SU (SHF)
HOW DARE...
...THEY DO THIS TO MY WOMAN......
THIS IS THE BIGGEST EARRING WE EVER GOT!
TATATA (STOMP)
I WONDER HOW MUCH THIS WILL FETCH?
GUI (TUG)
!?

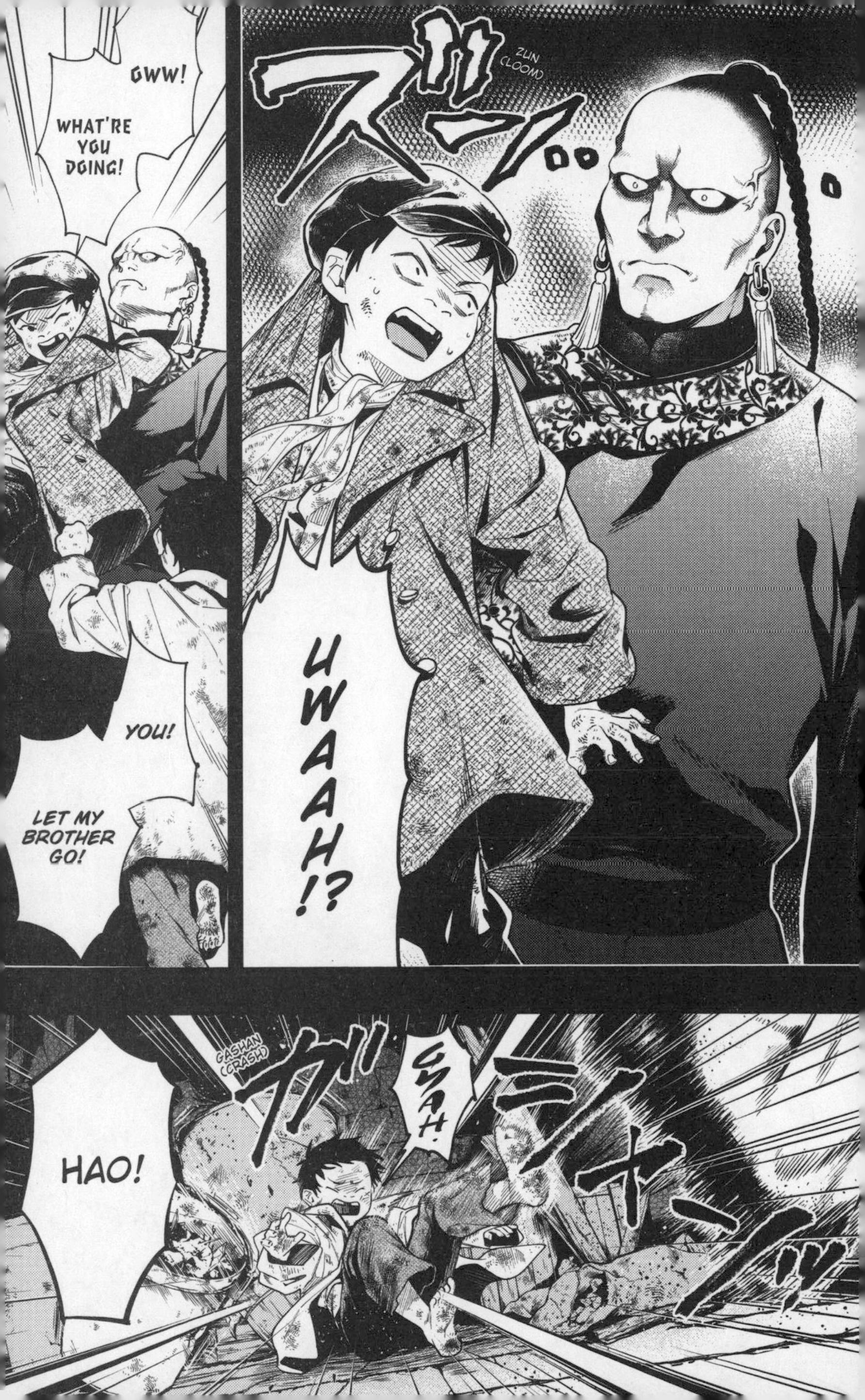
ZUN (CLOOM)
UWAAAH!?
GWW!
WHAT'RE YOU DOING!
YOU!
LET MY BROTHER GO!
GUAH!
GASHAN (CRASH)
HAO!

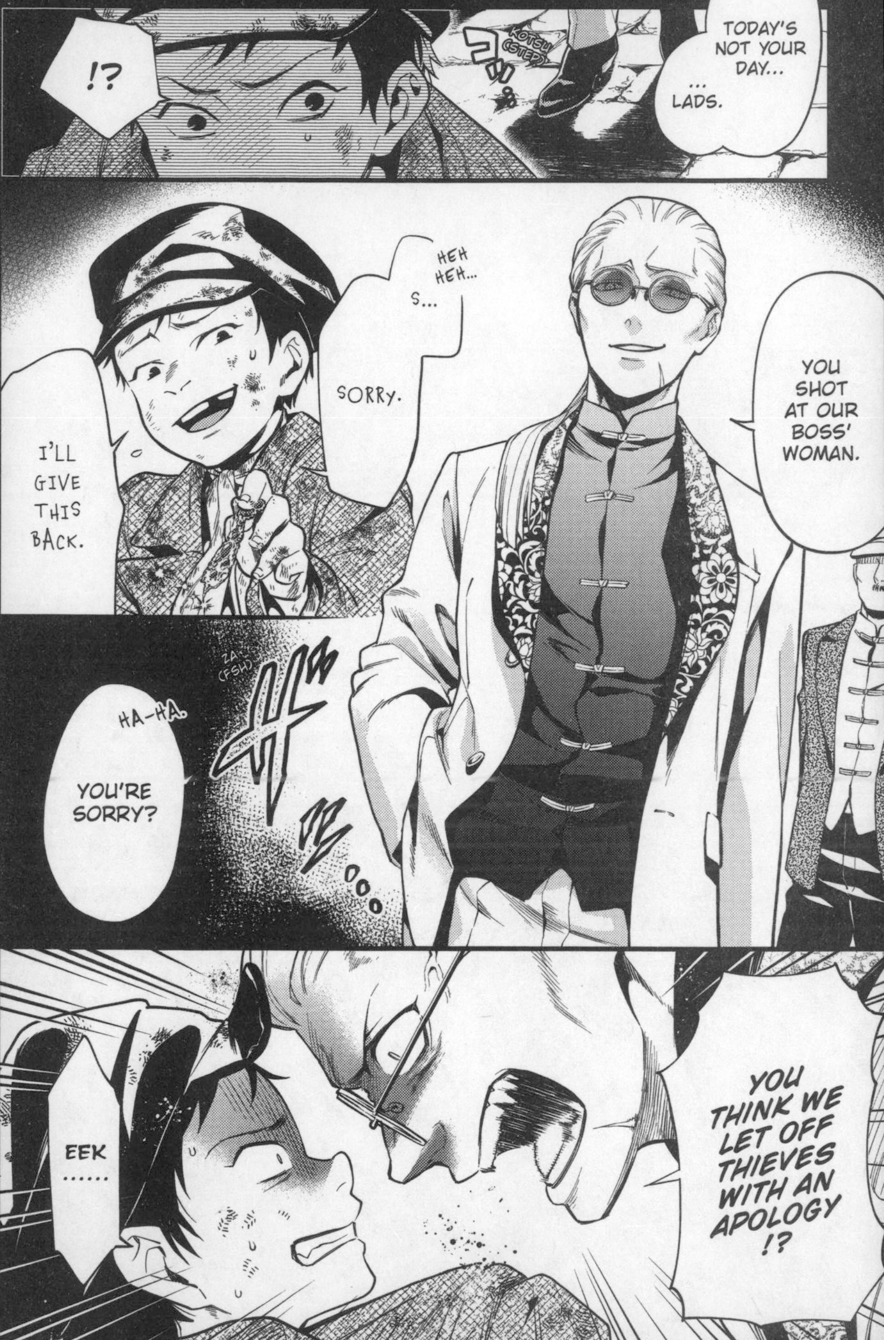
TODAY'S NOT YOUR DAY... ...LADS.
KOTSU (STEP)
!?
YOU SHOT AT OUR BOSS' WOMAN.
HEH HEH... S...
SORRY.
I'LL GIVE THIS BACK.
ZA (FSH)
HA-HA.
YOU'RE SORRY?
YOU THINK WE LET OFF THIEVES WITH AN APOLOGY!?
EEK ......

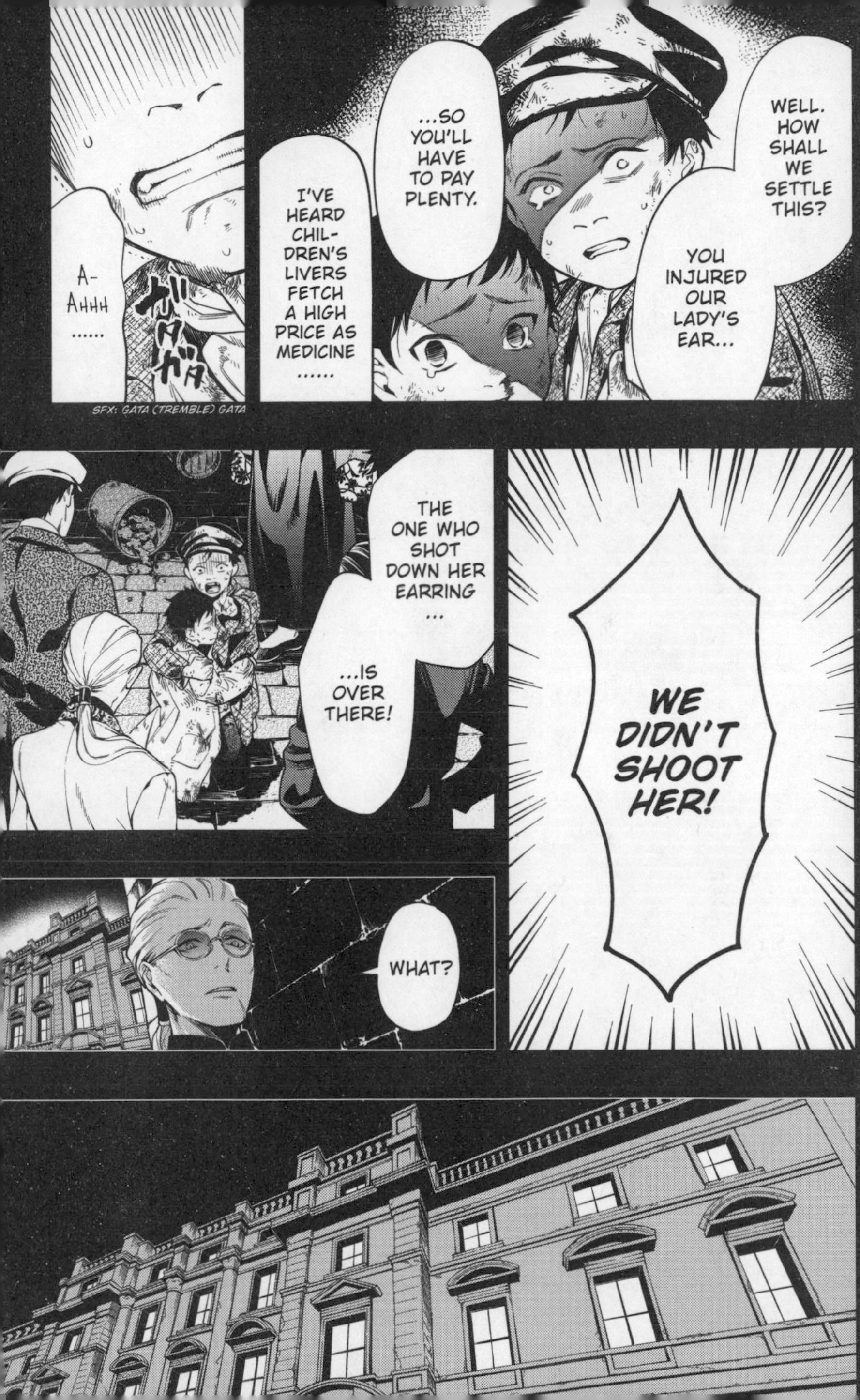
WELL. HOW SHALL WE SETTLE THIS?
YOU INJURED OUR LADY'S EAR...
...SO YOU'LL HAVE TO PAY PLENTY.
I'VE HEARD CHIL-DREN'S LIVERS FETCH A HIGH PRICE AS MEDICINE ......
A-AHHH ......
SFX: GATA (TREMBLE) GATA
WE DIDN'T SHOOT HER!
THE ONE WHO SHOT DOWN HER EARRING ...
...IS OVER THERE!
WHAT?

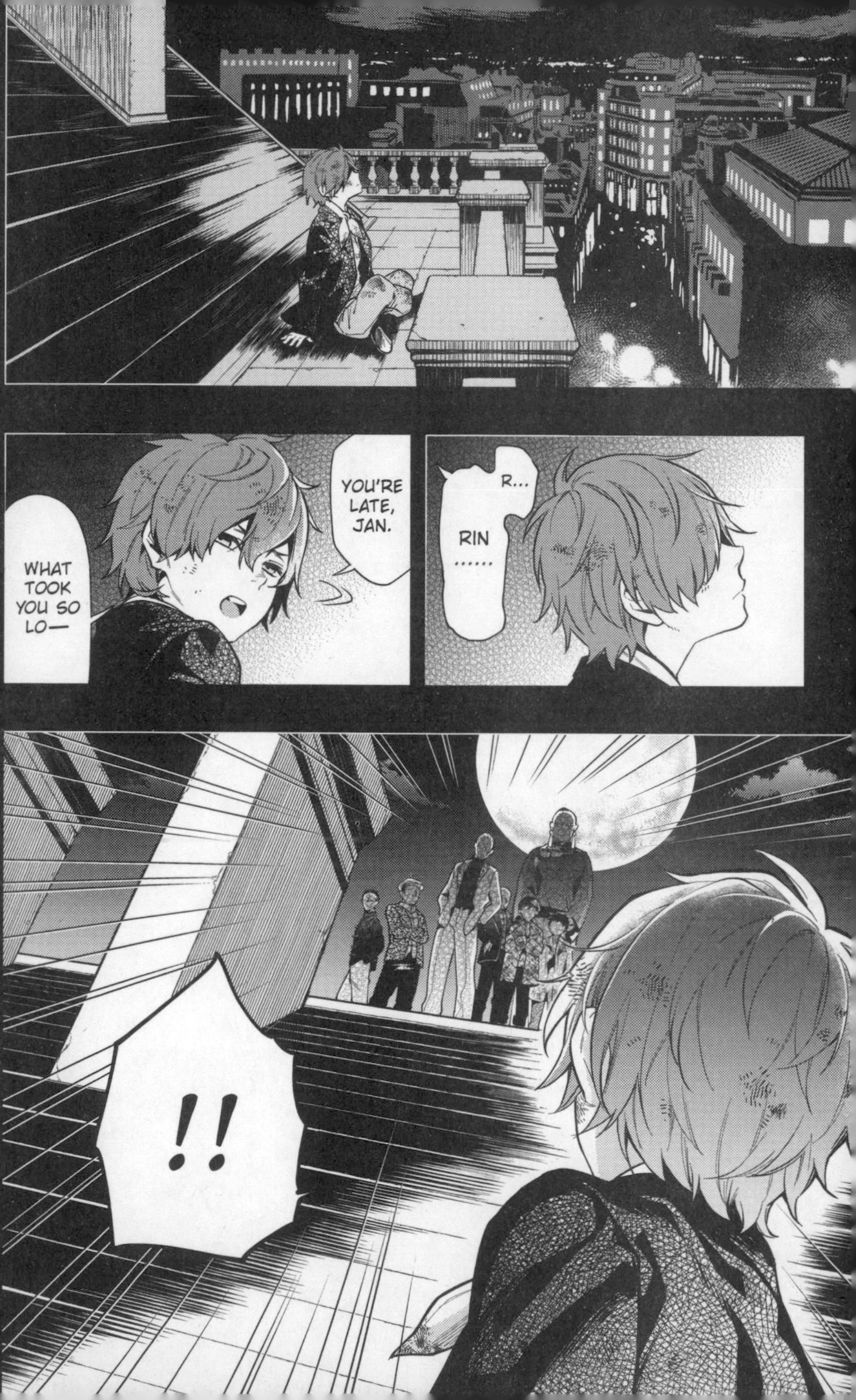
R...
RIN ......
YOU'RE LATE, JAN.
WHAT TOOK YOU SO LO—
!!

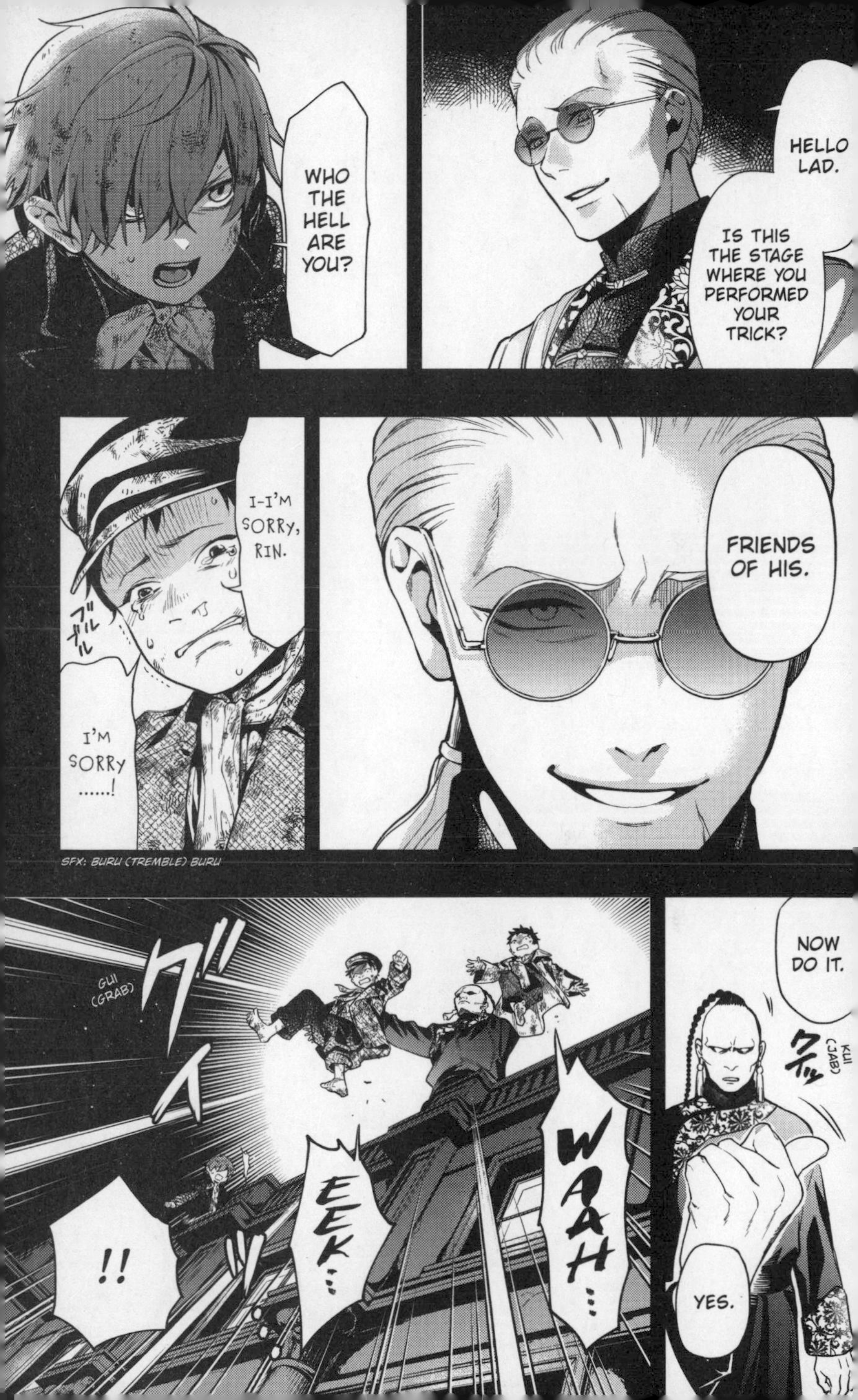
HELLO LAD.
IS THIS THE STAGE WHERE YOU PERFORMED YOUR TRICK?
WHO THE HELL ARE YOU?
FRIENDS OF HIS.
I-I'M SORRY, RIN.
ブルブル
I'M SORRY ......!
SFX: BURU (TREMBLE) BURU
NOW DO IT.
クイッ
KUI (JAB)
YES.
グイ
GUI (GRAB)
WAAH...
EEEK...
!!

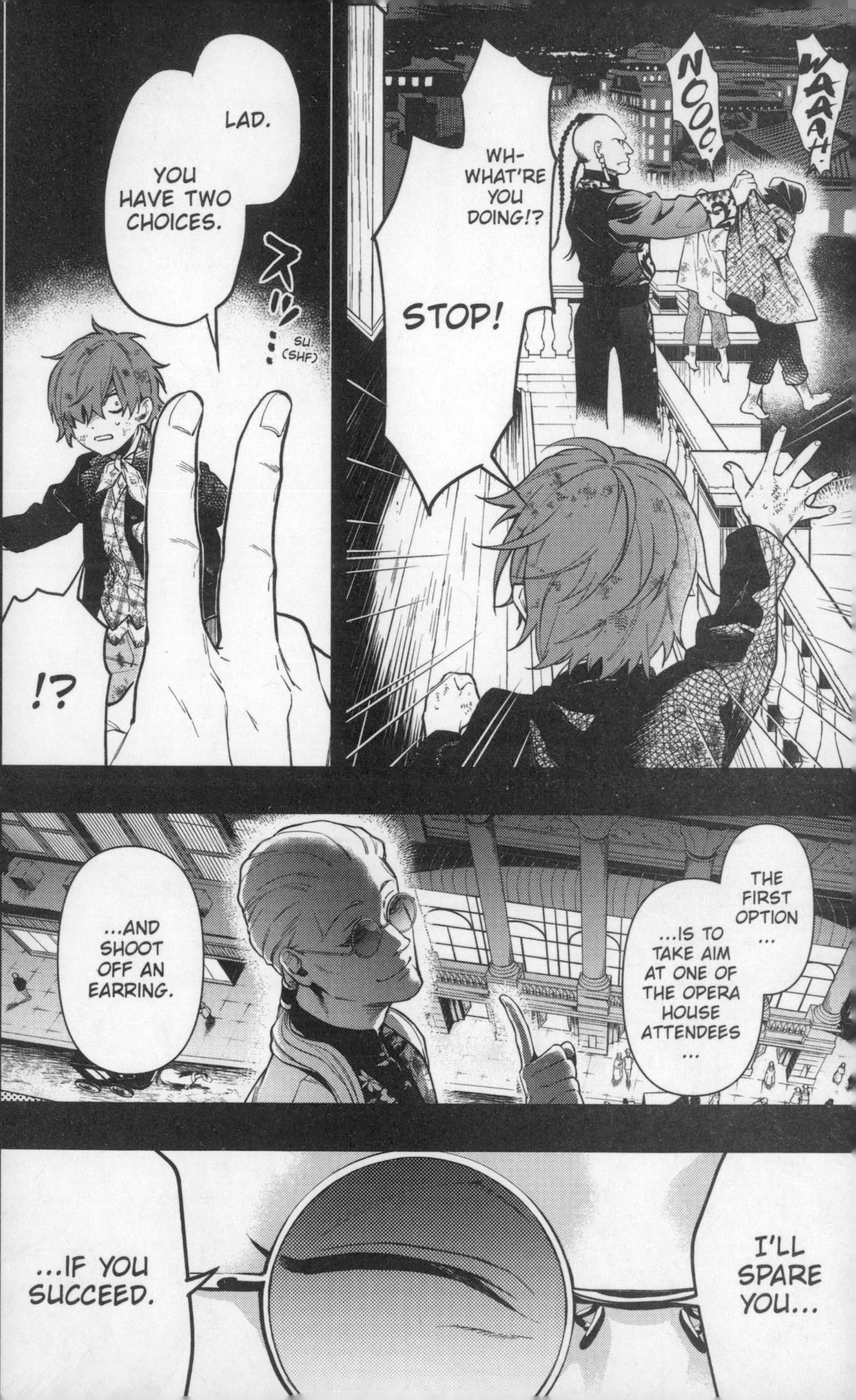
WAAAH.
NOOO.
WH-WHAT'RE YOU DOING!?
STOP!
LAD.
YOU HAVE TWO CHOICES.
スッ
SU (SHF)
!?
THE FIRST OPTION ...
...IS TO TAKE AIM AT ONE OF THE OPERA HOUSE ATTENDEES ...
...AND SHOOT OFF AN EARRING.
I'LL SPARE YOU...
...IF YOU SUCCEED.

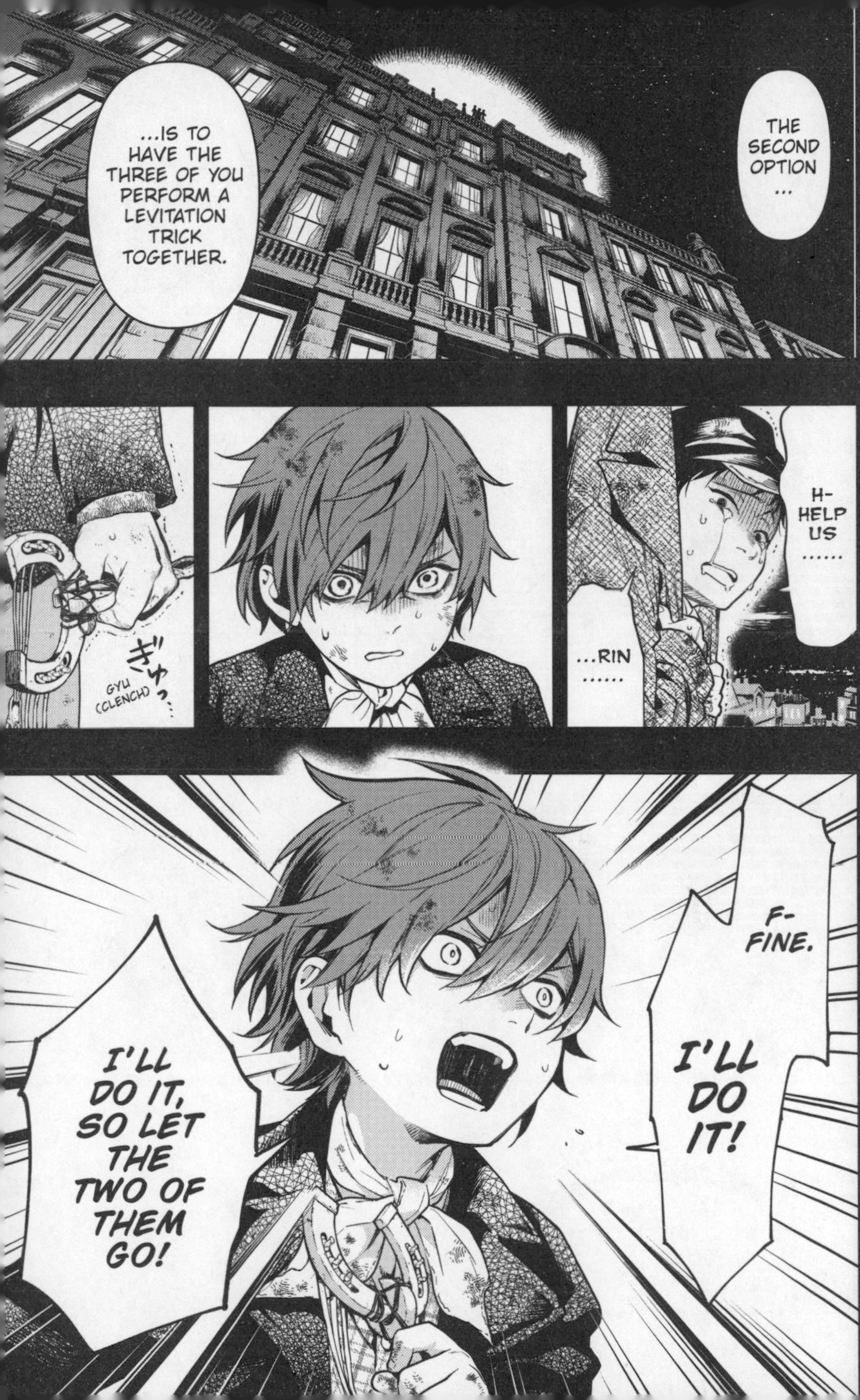
THE SECOND OPTION ...
...IS TO HAVE THE THREE OF YOU PERFORM A LEVITATION TRICK TOGETHER.
H- HELP US ......
...RIN ......
ぎゅっ
GYU (CLENCH)
F- FINE.
I'LL DO IT!
I'LL DO IT, SO LET THE TWO OF THEM GO!

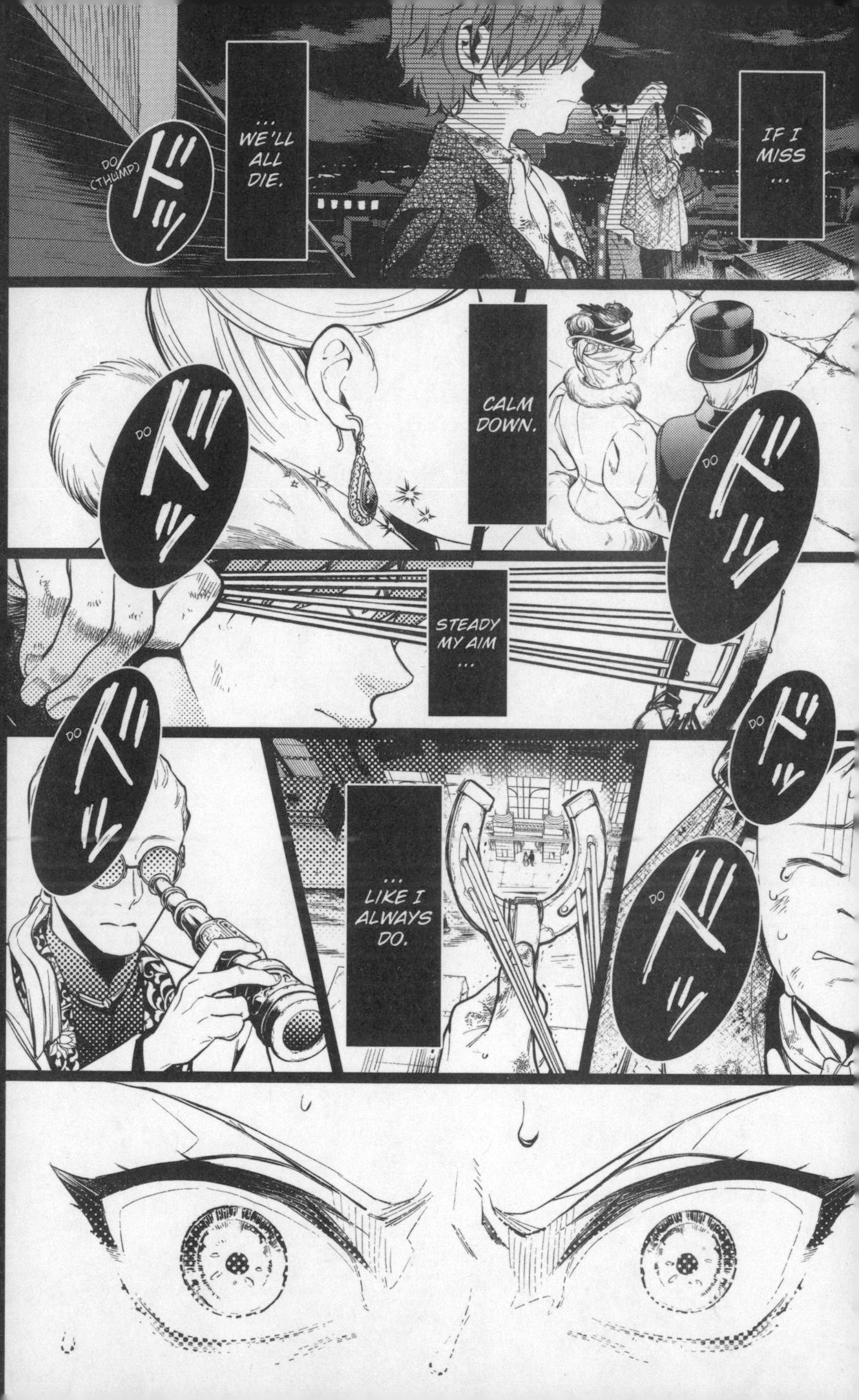
IF I MISS ...
... WE'LL ALL DIE.
DO (THUMP) ドッ
DO ドッ
CALM DOWN.
DO ドッ
STEADY MY AIM ...
DO ドッ
DO ドッ
... LIKE I ALWAYS DO.
DO ドッ

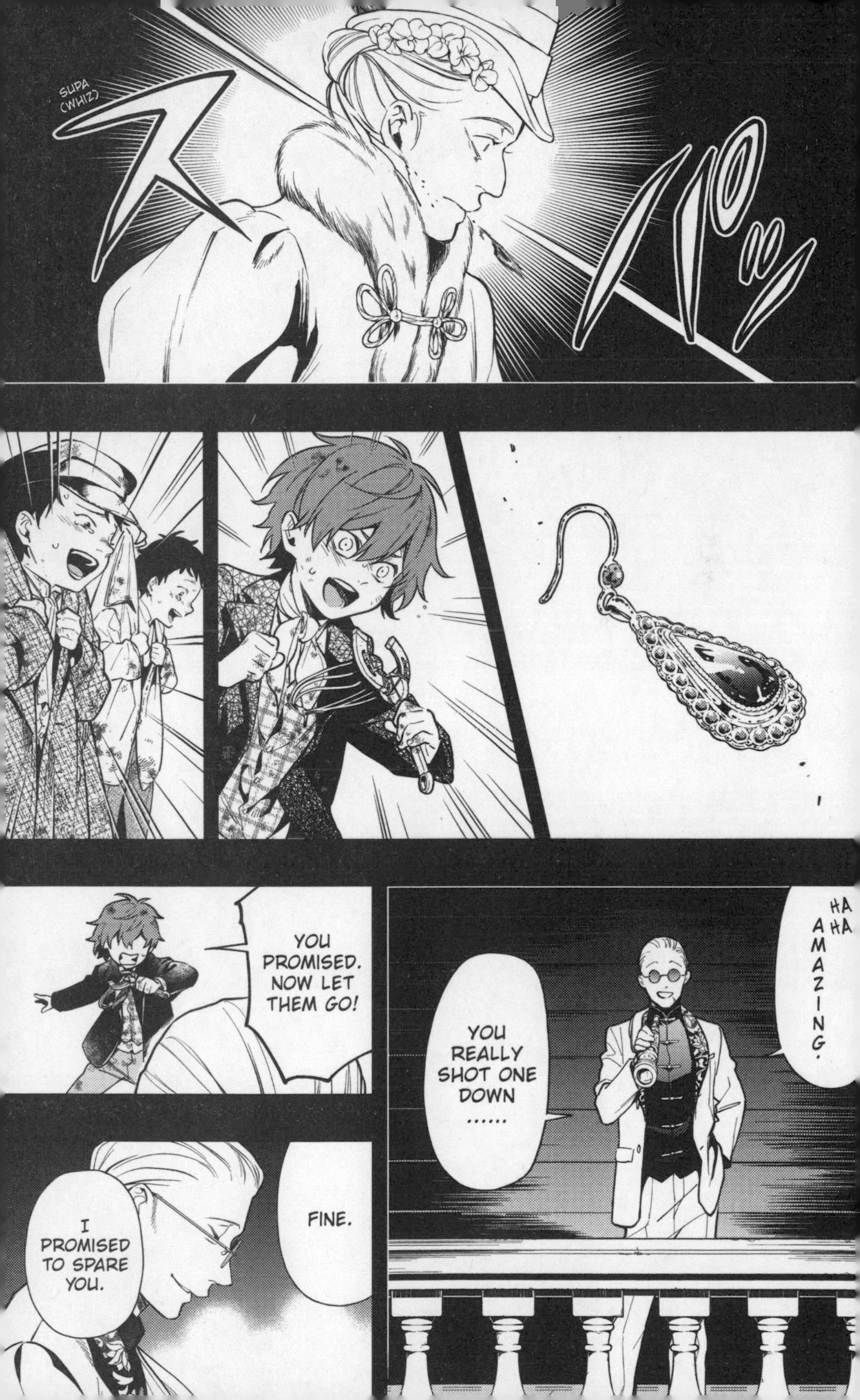
パッ
SUPA (WHIZ)
HA HA
AMAZING.
YOU REALLY SHOT ONE DOWN ......
YOU PROMISED. NOW LET THEM GO!
FINE.
I PROMISED TO SPARE YOU.

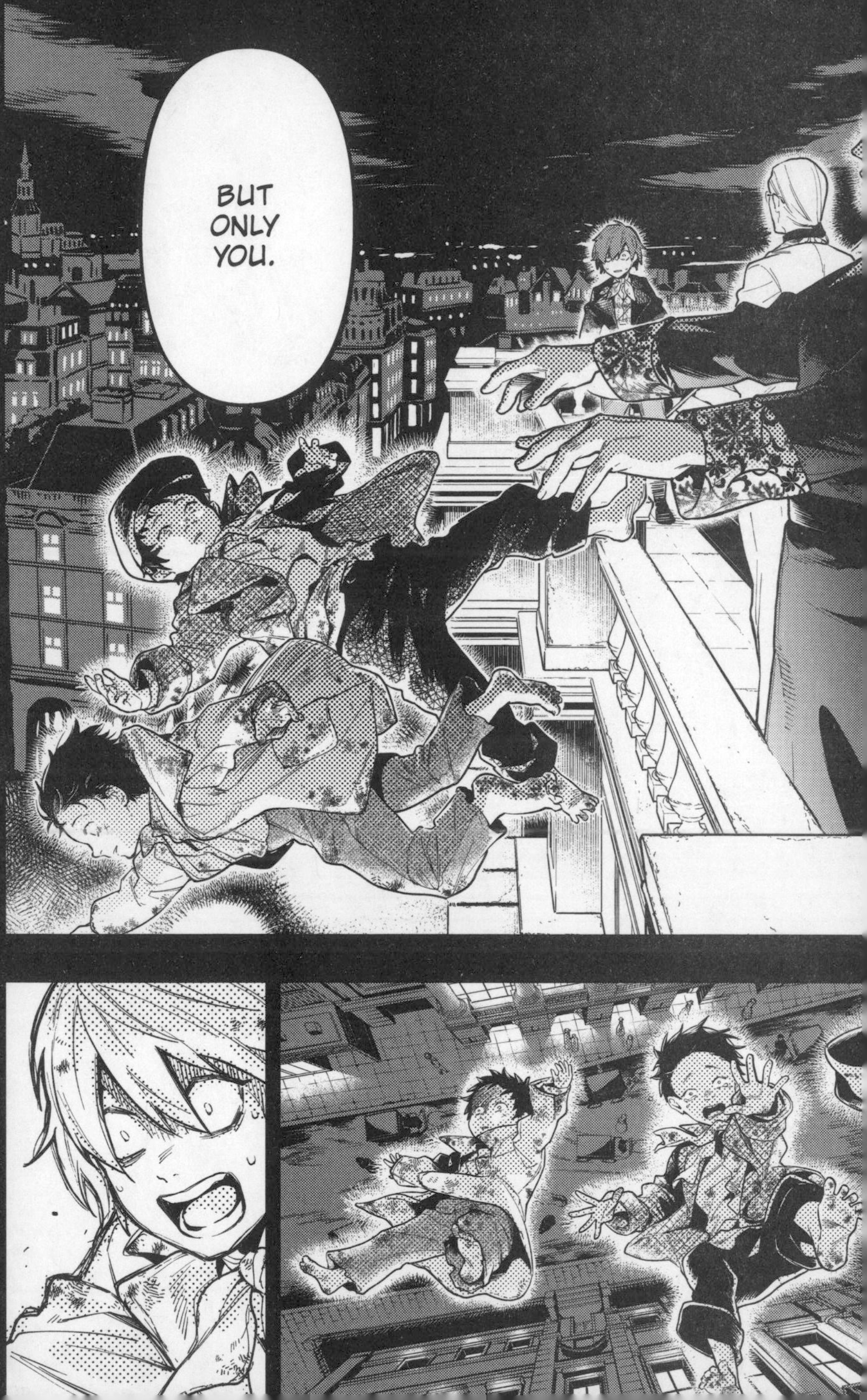
BUT ONLY YOU.

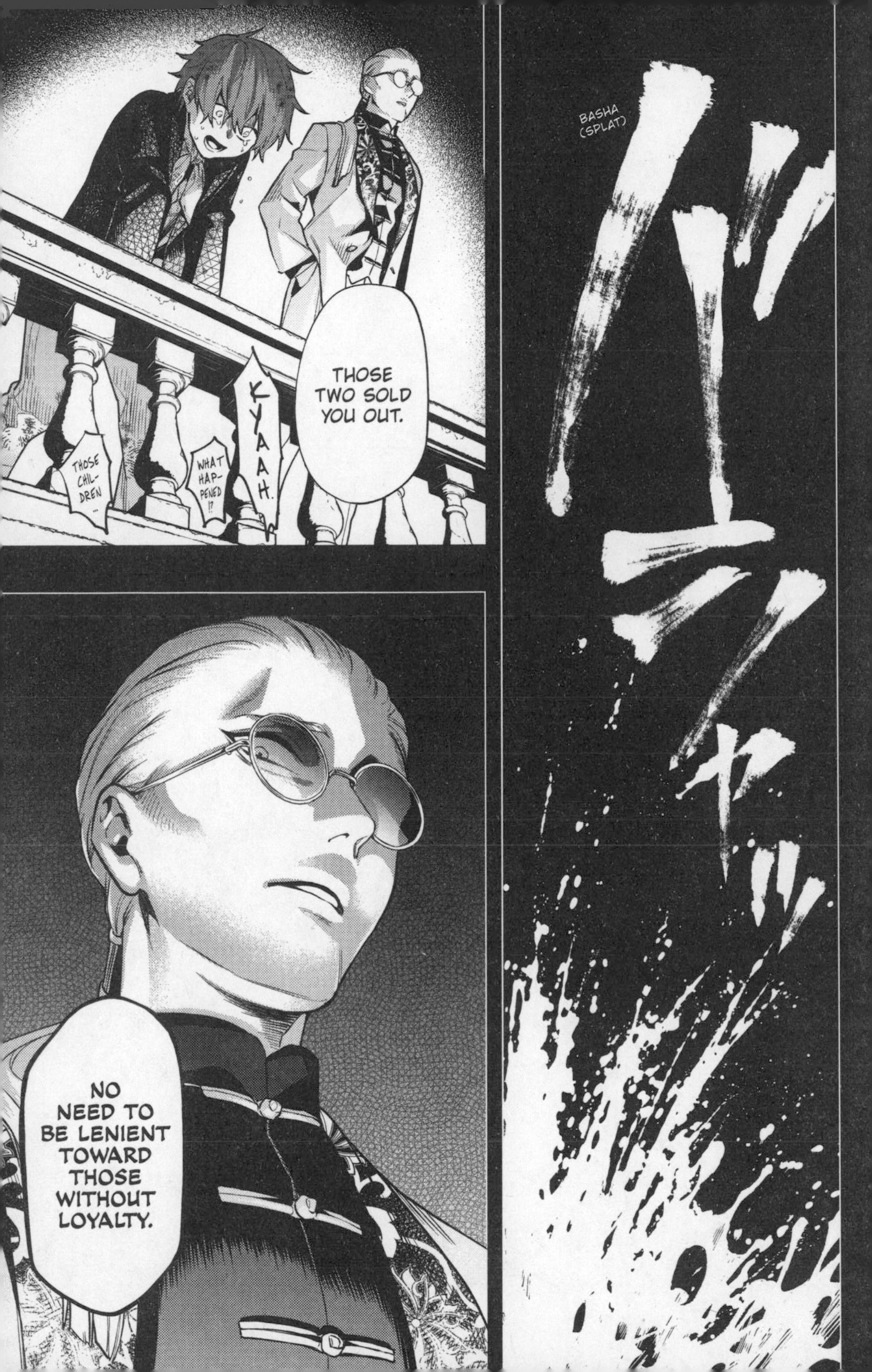
BASHA (SPLAT)
THOSE TWO SOLD YOU OUT.
KYAAH.
WHAT HAPPENED!?
THOSE CHILDREN...
NO NEED TO BE LENIENT TOWARD THOSE WITHOUT LOYALTY.

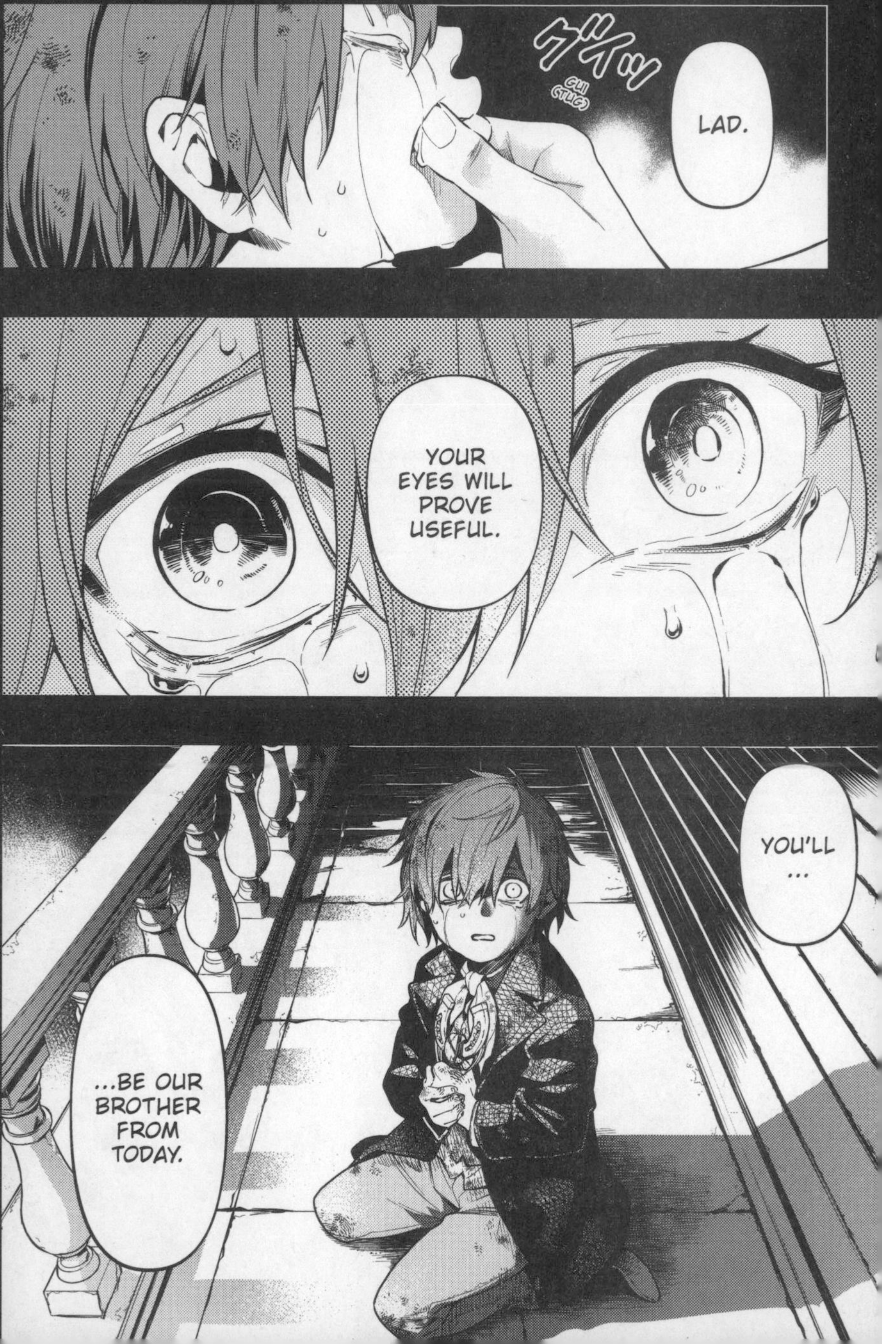
LAD.
グイッ
GUI (TUG)
YOUR EYES WILL PROVE USEFUL.
YOU'LL ...
...BE OUR BROTHER FROM TODAY.

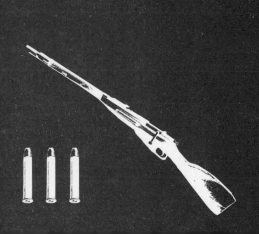

Black Butler

Chapter 159
At noon: The Butler, Delivery

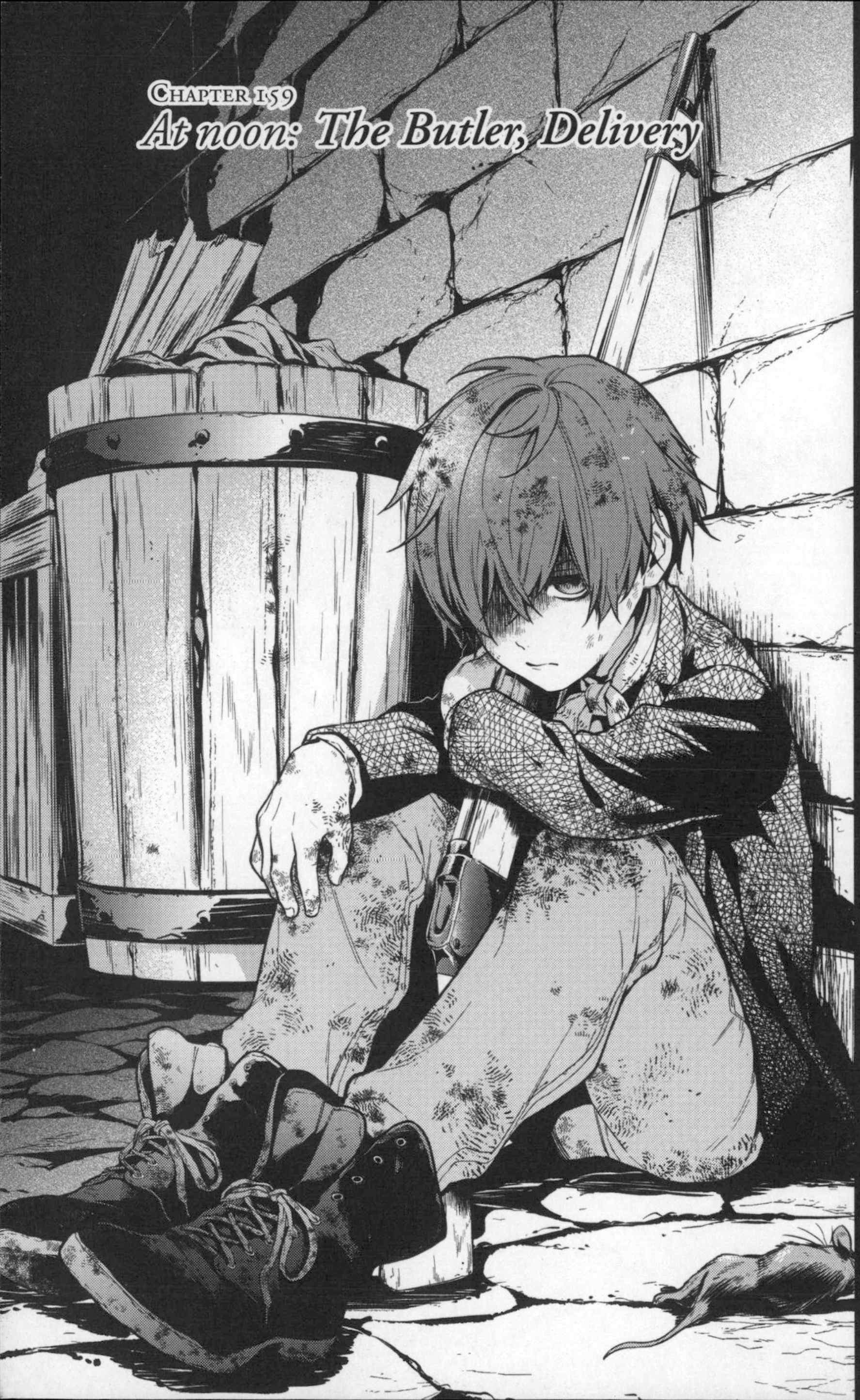

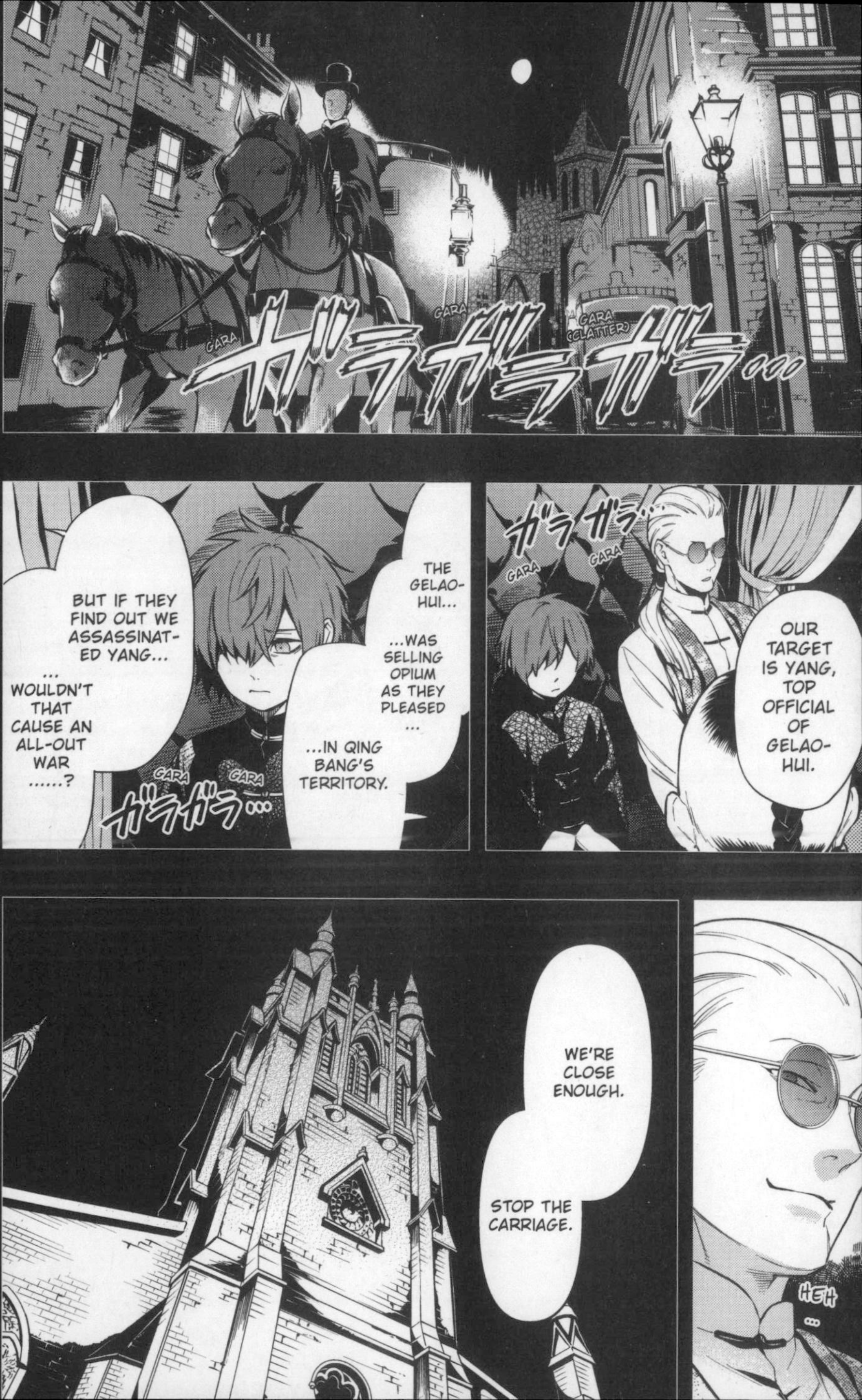
ガラガラガラ…
GARA GARA GARA (CLATTER)
ガラガラ…
GARA GARA
OUR TARGET IS YANG, TOP OFFICIAL OF GELAO-HUI.
THE GELAO-HUI...
...WAS SELLING OPIUM AS THEY PLEASED...
...IN QING BANG'S TERRITORY.
BUT IF THEY FIND OUT WE ASSASSINATED YANG...
...WOULDN'T THAT CAUSE AN ALL-OUT WAR ......?
ガラガラ…
GARA GARA
HEH...
WE'RE CLOSE ENOUGH.
STOP THE CARRIAGE.

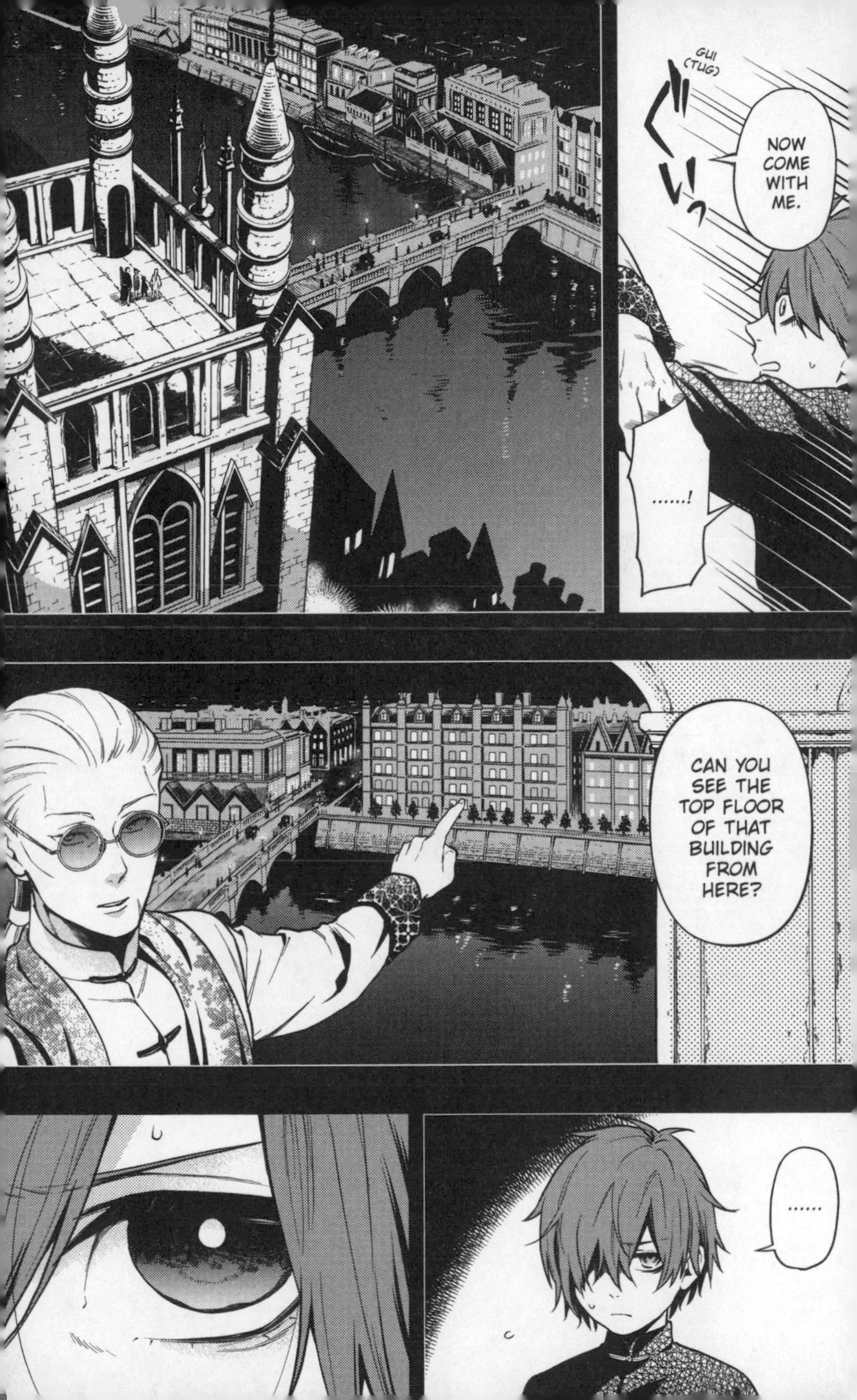
GUI (TUG)
NOW COME WITH ME.
......!
CAN YOU SEE THE TOP FLOOR OF THAT BUILDING FROM HERE?
......

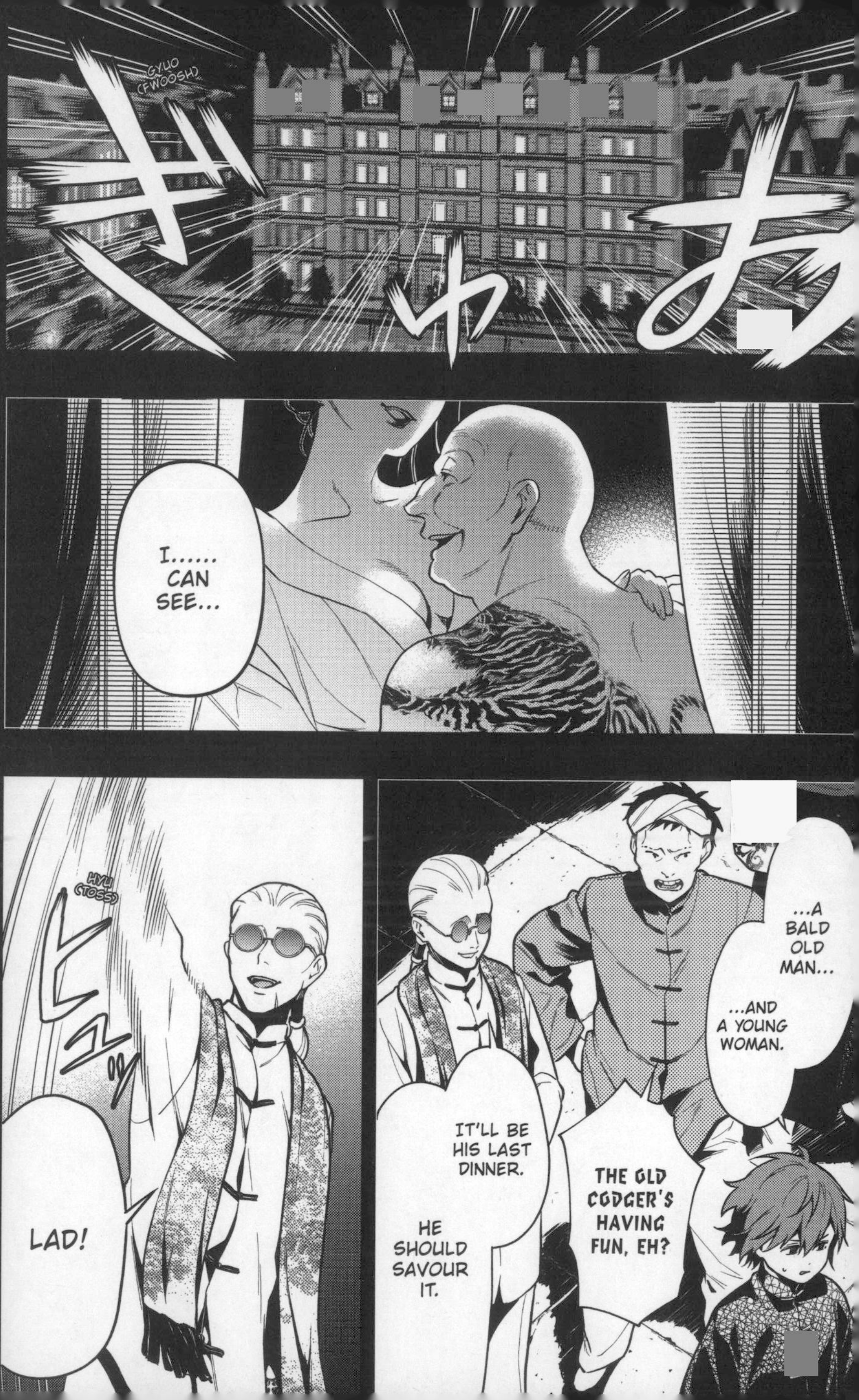
GYUO (FWOOSH)
I...... CAN SEE...
...A BALD OLD MAN...
...AND A YOUNG WOMAN.
THE OLD CODGER'S HAVING FUN, EH?
IT'LL BE HIS LAST DINNER.
HE SHOULD SAVOUR IT.
HYU (TOSS)
LAD!

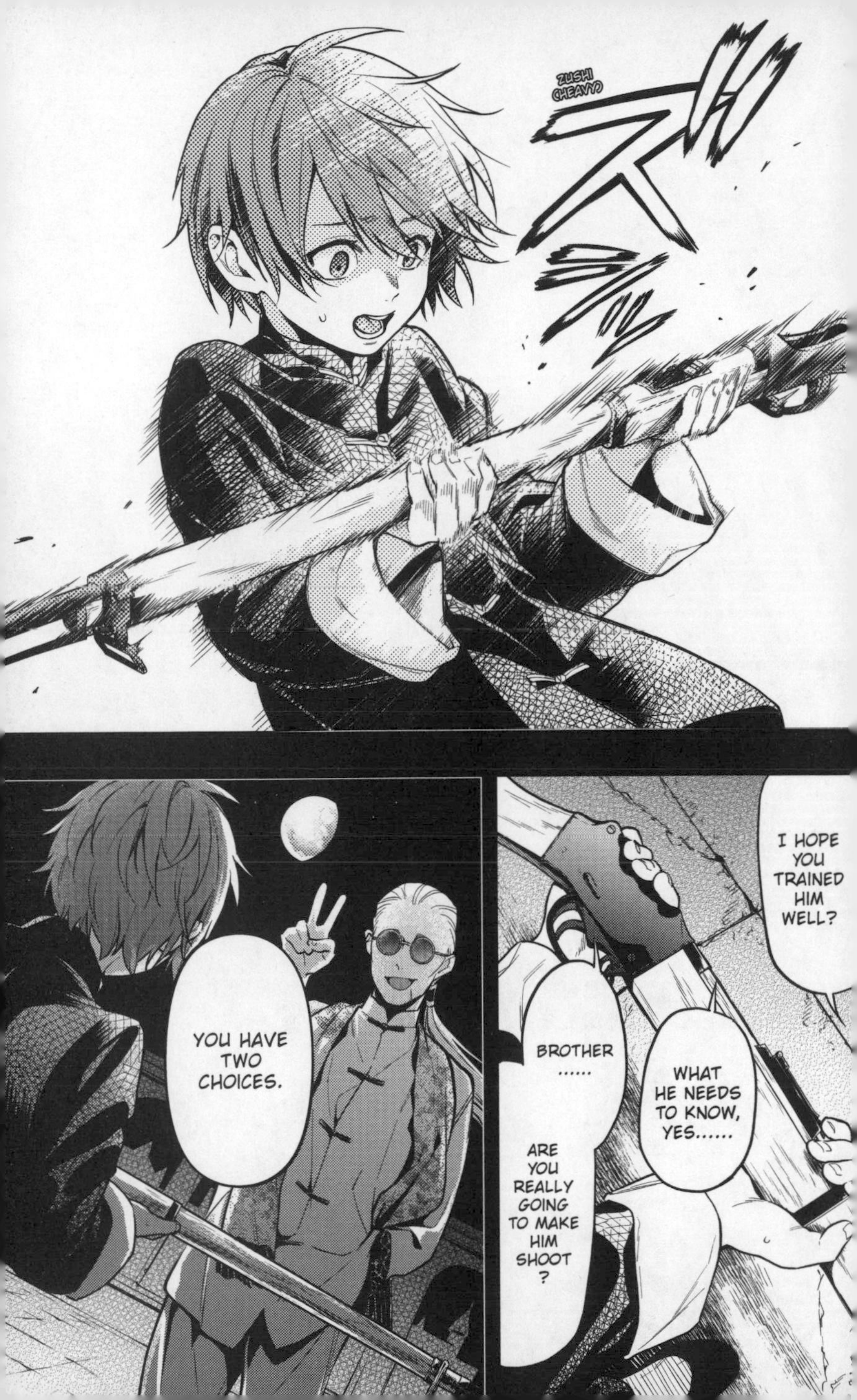
ZUSHI (HEAVY)
I HOPE YOU TRAINED HIM WELL?
WHAT HE NEEDS TO KNOW, YES......
BROTHER ......
ARE YOU REALLY GOING TO MAKE HIM SHOOT?
YOU HAVE TWO CHOICES.

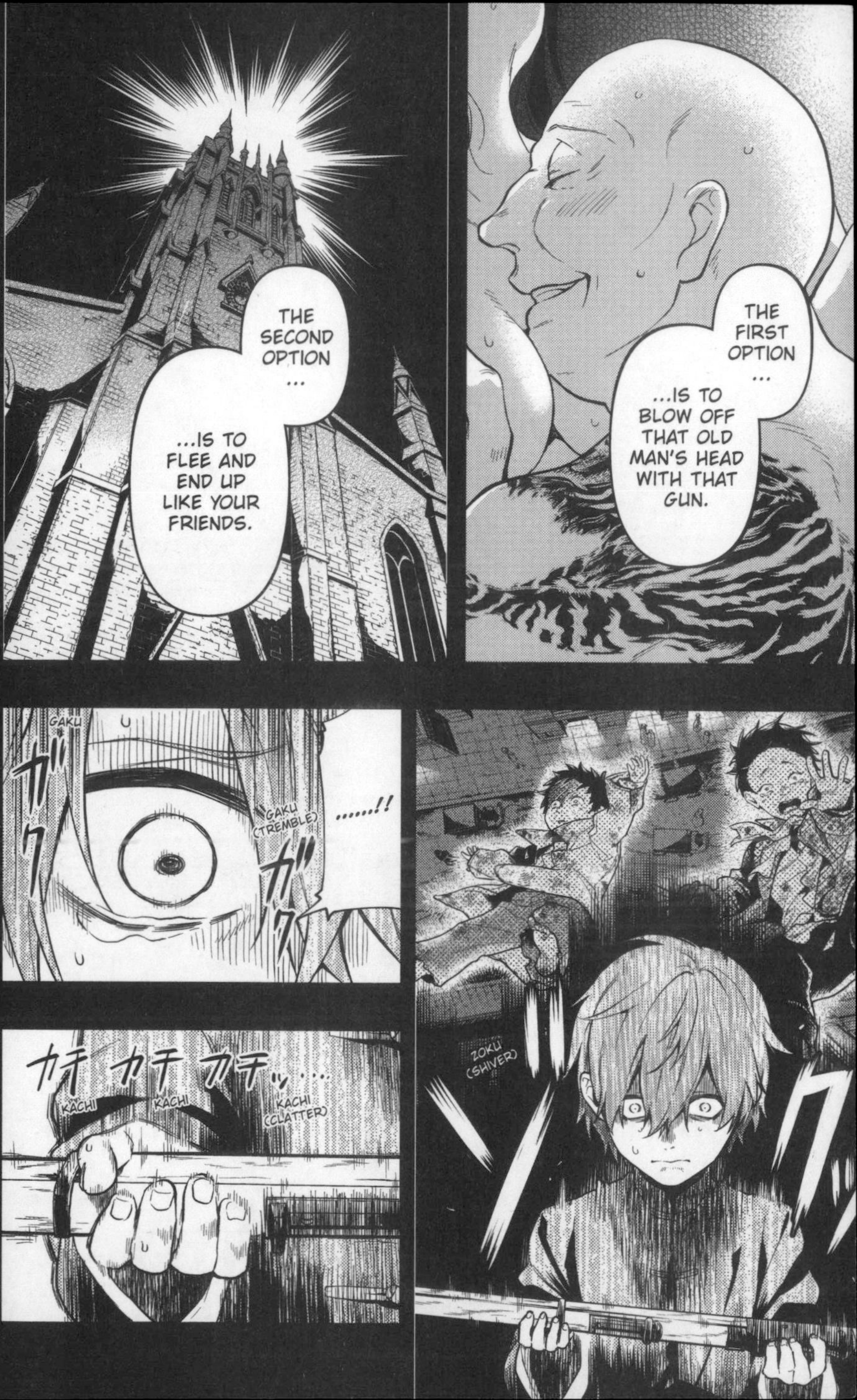
THE FIRST OPTION ...
...IS TO BLOW OFF THAT OLD MAN'S HEAD WITH THAT GUN.
THE SECOND OPTION ...
...IS TO FLEE AND END UP LIKE YOUR FRIENDS.
ZOKU (SHIVER)
ガク
GAKU
GAKU (TREMBLE)
ガク
......!!
カチ カチ カチッ...
KACHI
KACHI
KACHI (CLATTER)

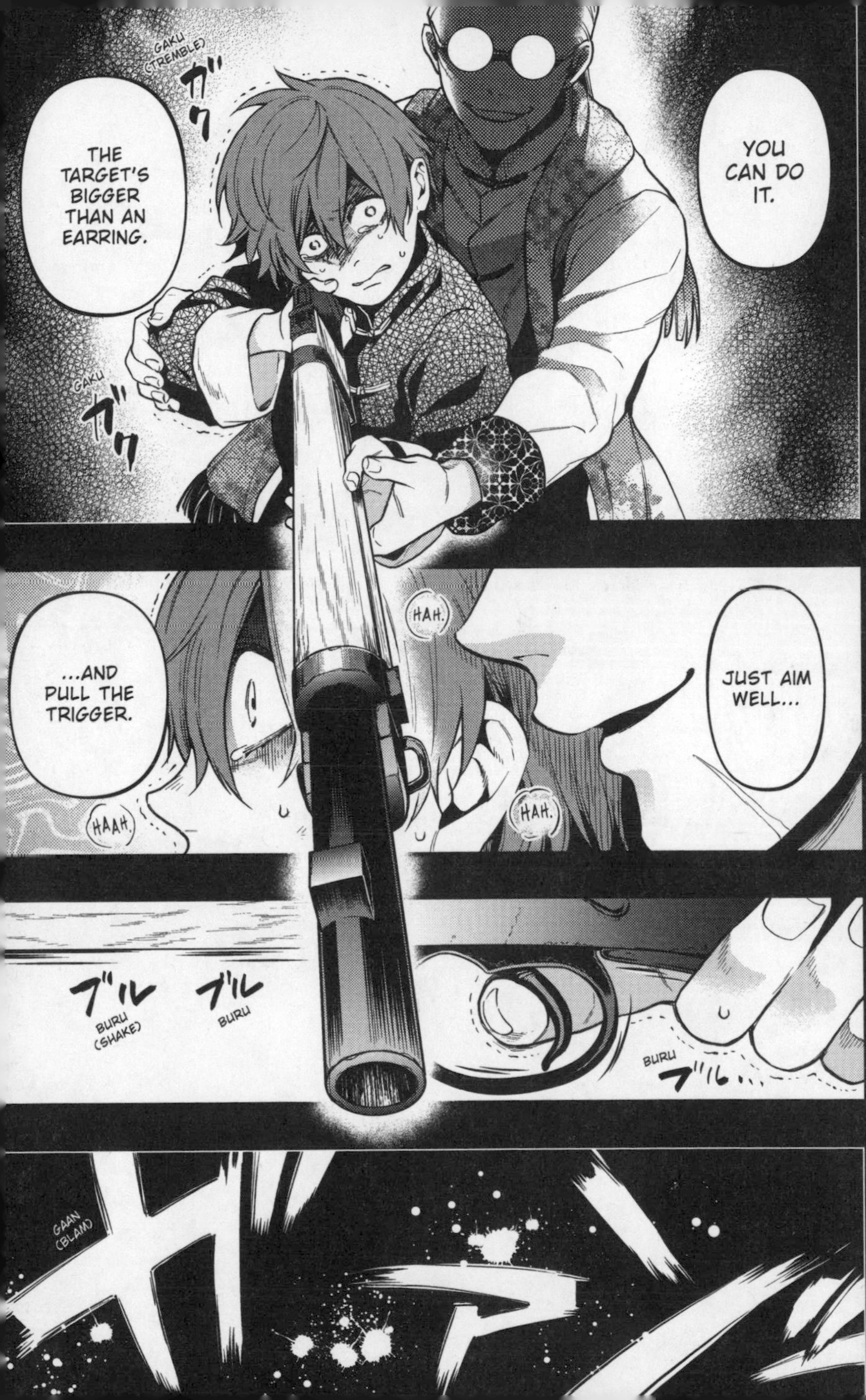
YOU CAN DO IT.
GAKU (TREMBLE)
ガク
THE TARGET'S BIGGER THAN AN EARRING.
GAKU
ガク
JUST AIM WELL...
HAH.
HAH.
...AND PULL THE TRIGGER.
HAAH.
BURU
ブル…
ブル
BURU
ブル
BURU (SHAKE)
GAAN (BLAM)

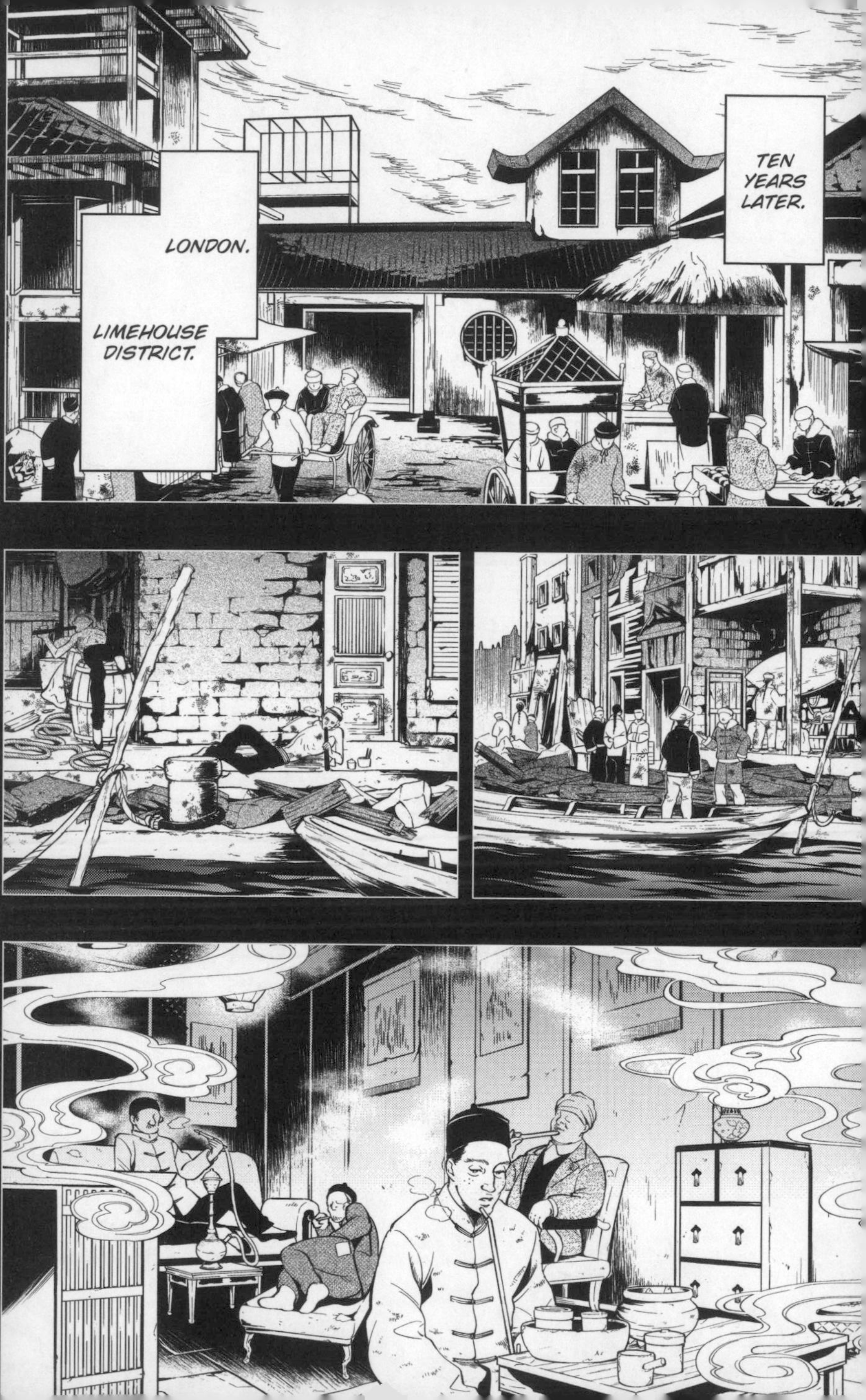
TEN YEARS LATER.
LONDON.
LIMEHOUSE DISTRICT.

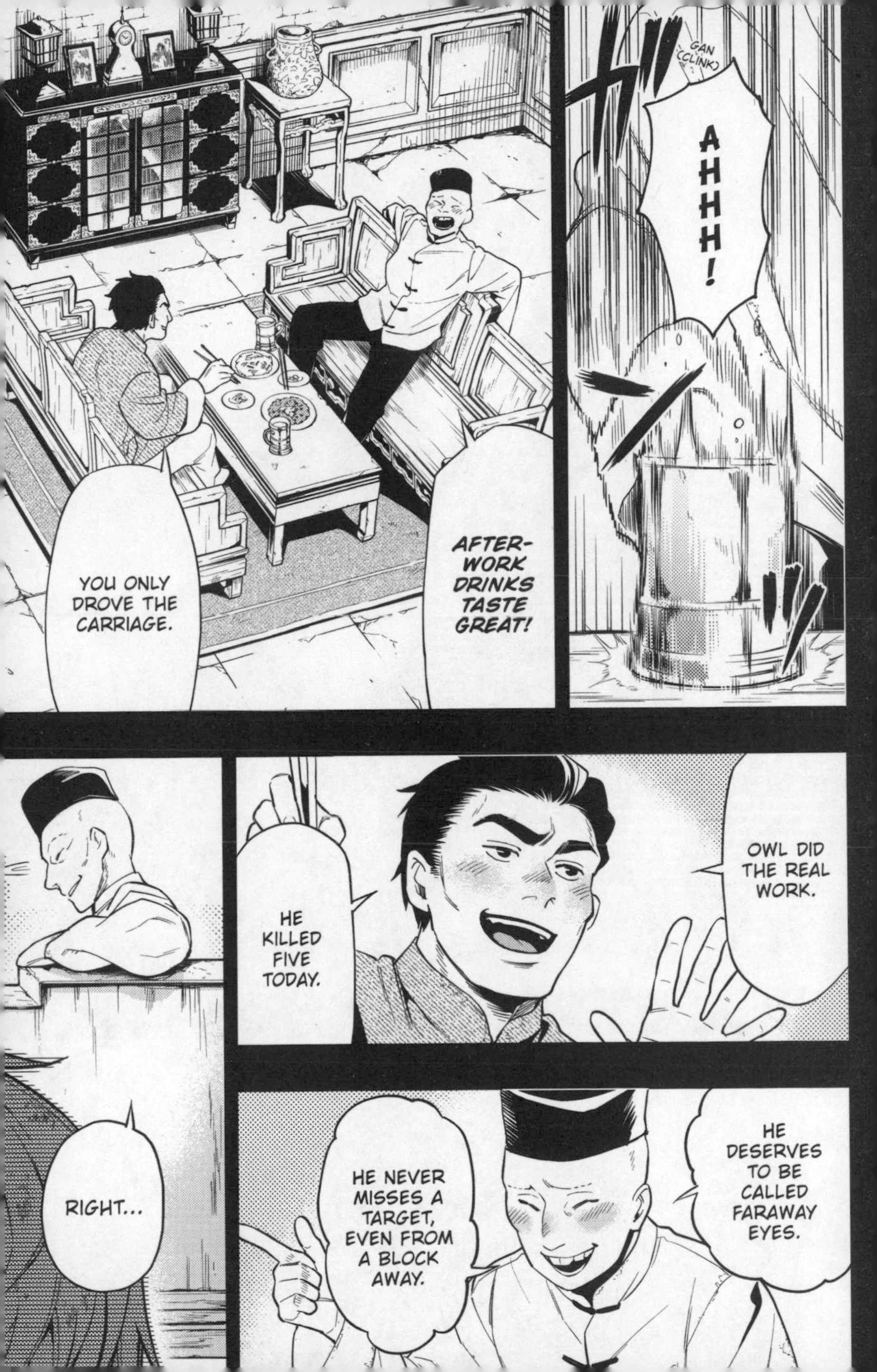
GAN (CLINK)
AHHHH!
AFTER-WORK DRINKS TASTE GREAT!
YOU ONLY DROVE THE CARRIAGE.
OWL DID THE REAL WORK.
HE KILLED FIVE TODAY.
HE DESERVES TO BE CALLED FARAWAY EYES.
HE NEVER MISSES A TARGET, EVEN FROM A BLOCK AWAY.
RIGHT...

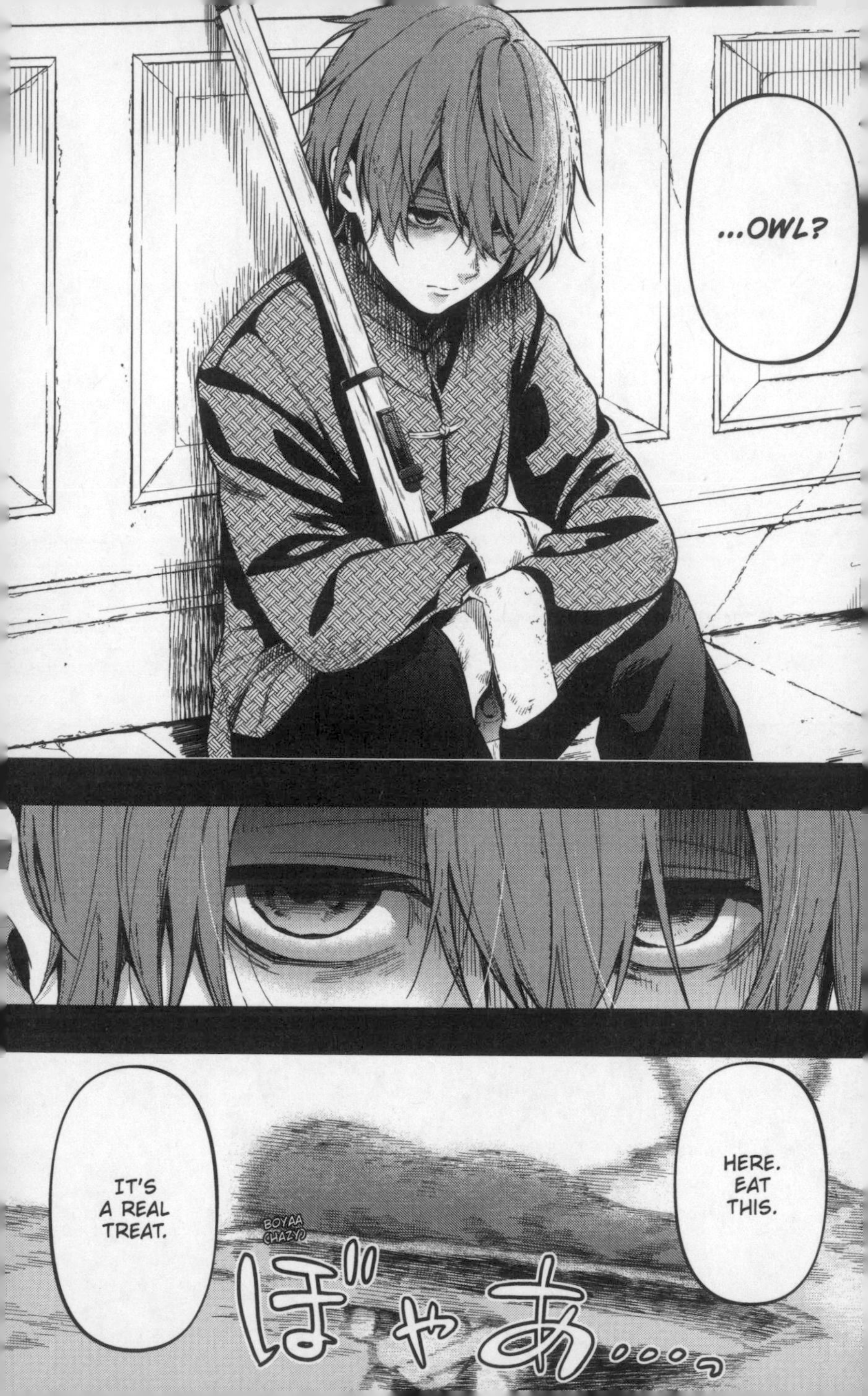
...OWL?
HERE. EAT THIS.
IT'S A REAL TREAT.
BOYAA (HAZY)
ぼゃあ。。。。

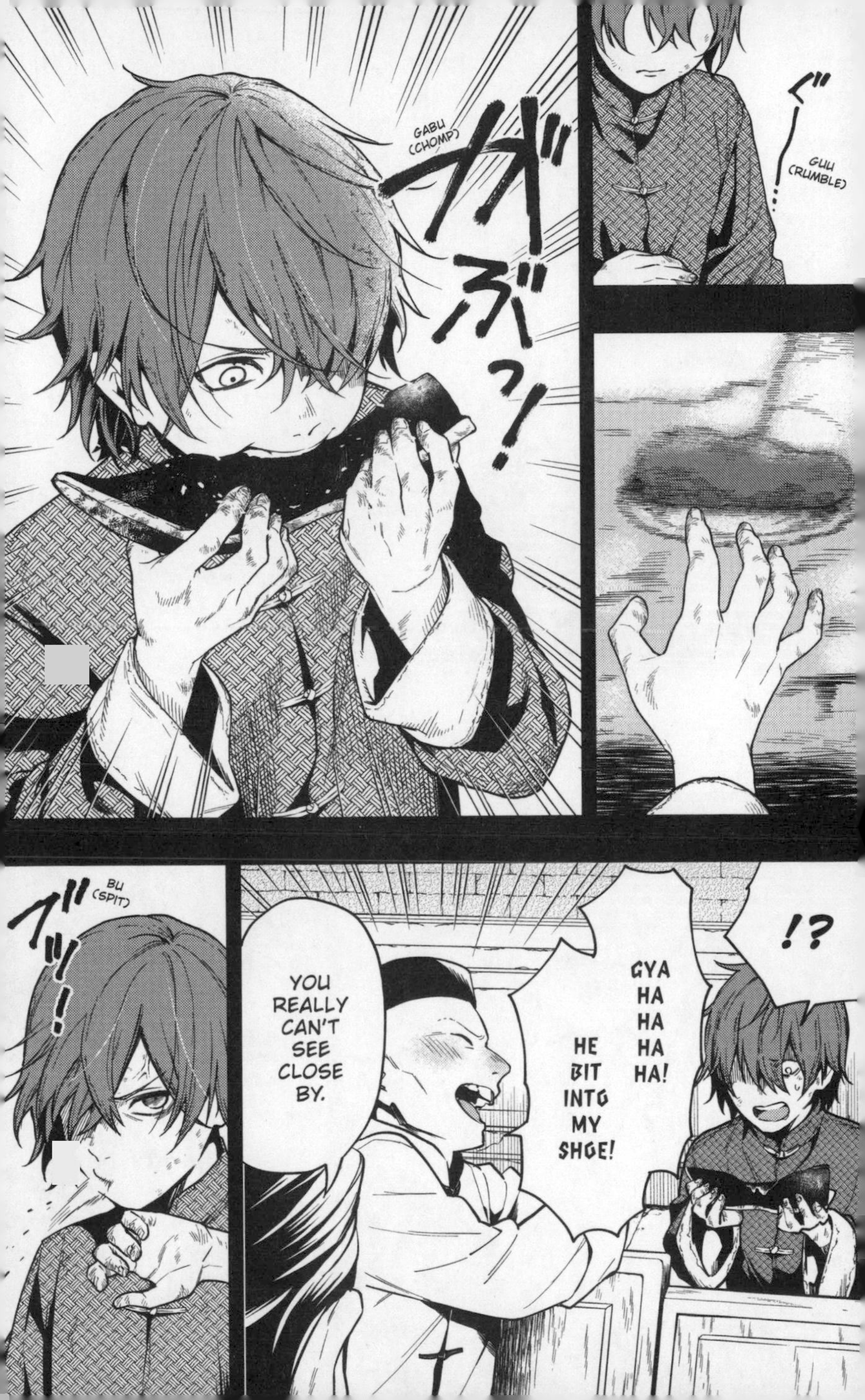
ぐー…
GUU (RUMBLE)
ガブッ!
GABU (CHOMP)
!?
GYA HA HA HA HA!
HE BIT INTO MY SHOE!
YOU REALLY CAN'T SEE CLOSE BY.
ブッ!
BU (SPIT)

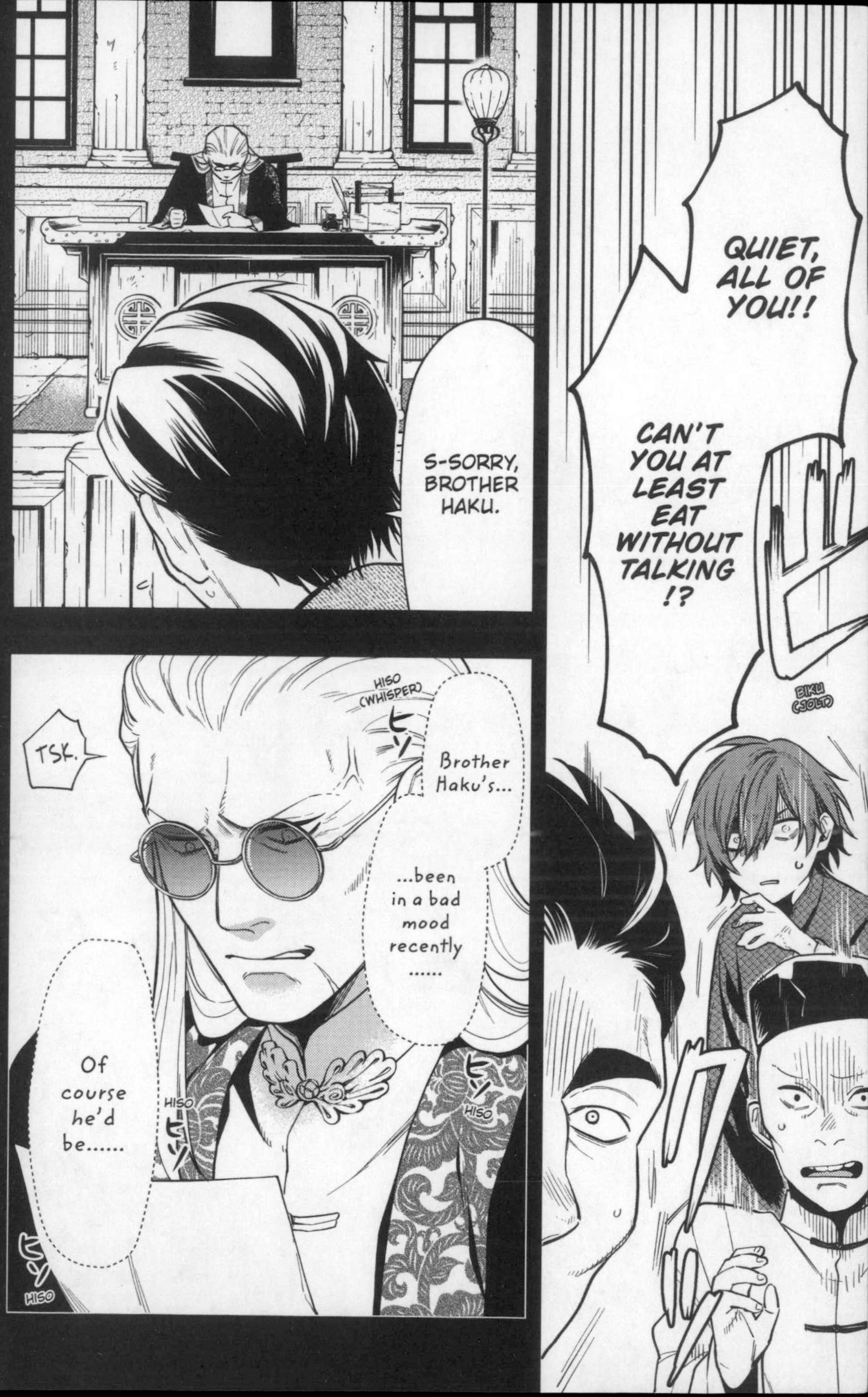
QUIET, ALL OF YOU!!
CAN'T YOU AT LEAST EAT WITHOUT TALKING!?
BIKU (JOLT)
S-SORRY, BROTHER HAKU.
HISO (WHISPER)
Brother Haku's...
...been in a bad mood recently......
TSK.
HISO
HISO
Of course he'd be......
HISO

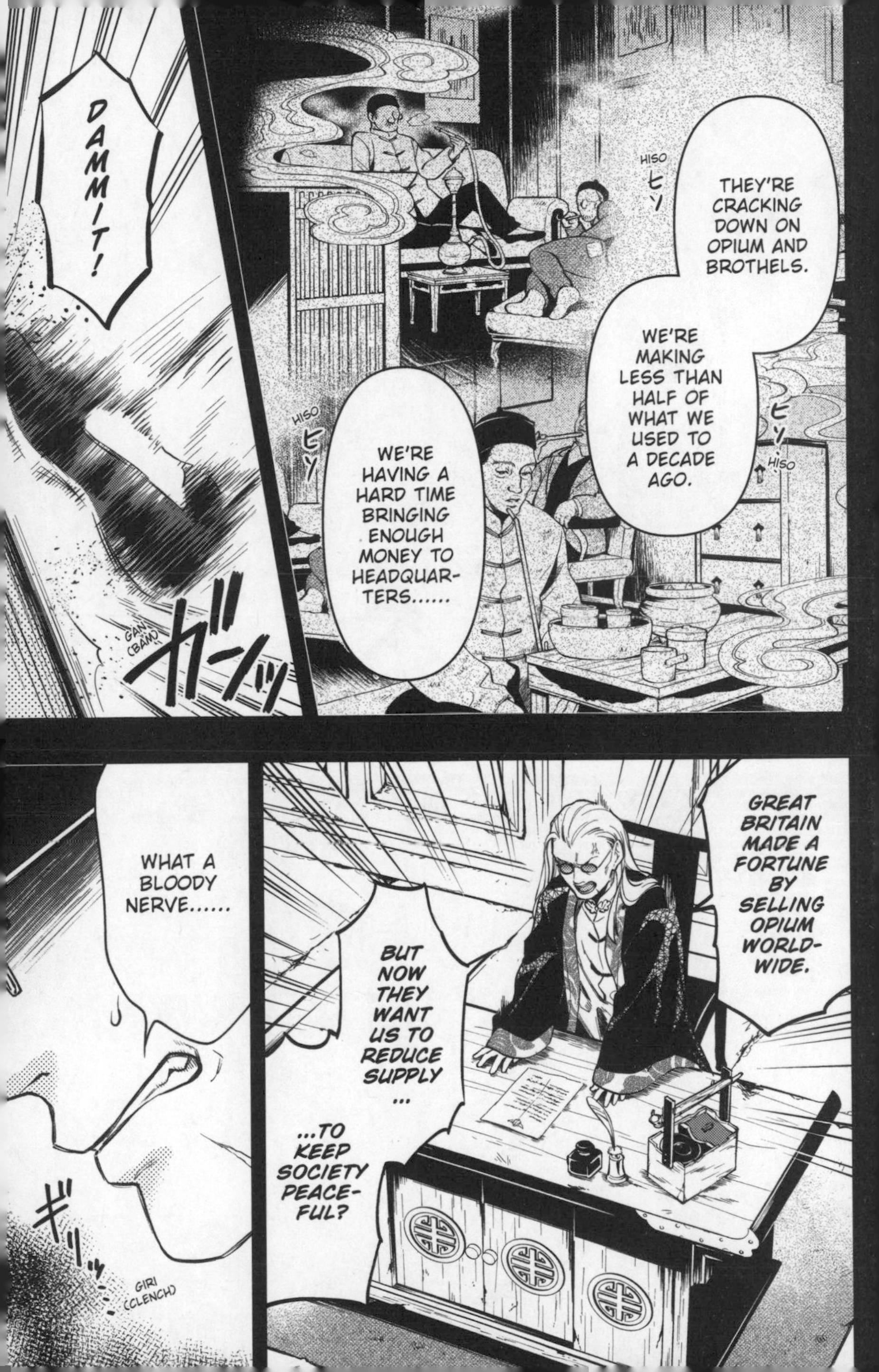
HISO ヒソ
THEY'RE CRACKING DOWN ON OPIUM AND BROTHELS.
WE'RE MAKING LESS THAN HALF OF WHAT WE USED TO A DECADE AGO.
ヒソ HISO
WE'RE HAVING A HARD TIME BRINGING ENOUGH MONEY TO HEADQUAR-TERS......
HISO ヒソ
DAMMIT!
GAN (BAM) ガンッ
GREAT BRITAIN MADE A FORTUNE BY SELLING OPIUM WORLD-WIDE.
BUT NOW THEY WANT US TO REDUCE SUPPLY ...
...TO KEEP SOCIETY PEACE-FUL?
WHAT A BLOODY NERVE......
ギリッ GIRI (CLENCH)

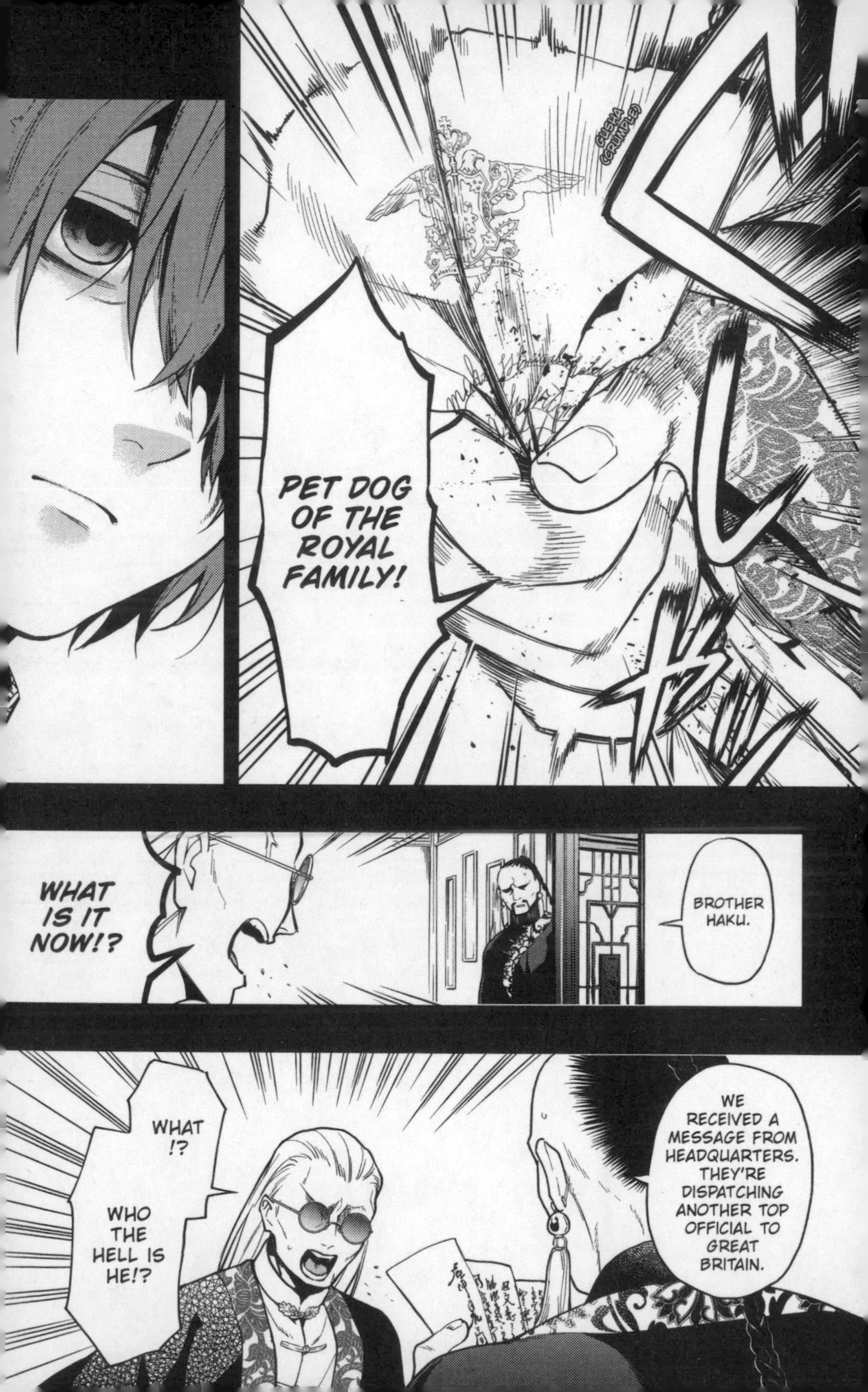
GUSHA (CRUMPLE)
PET DOG OF THE ROYAL FAMILY!
BROTHER HAKU.
WHAT IS IT NOW!?
WE RECEIVED A MESSAGE FROM HEADQUARTERS. THEY'RE DISPATCHING ANOTHER TOP OFFICIAL TO GREAT BRITAIN.
WHAT!?
WHO THE HELL IS HE!?

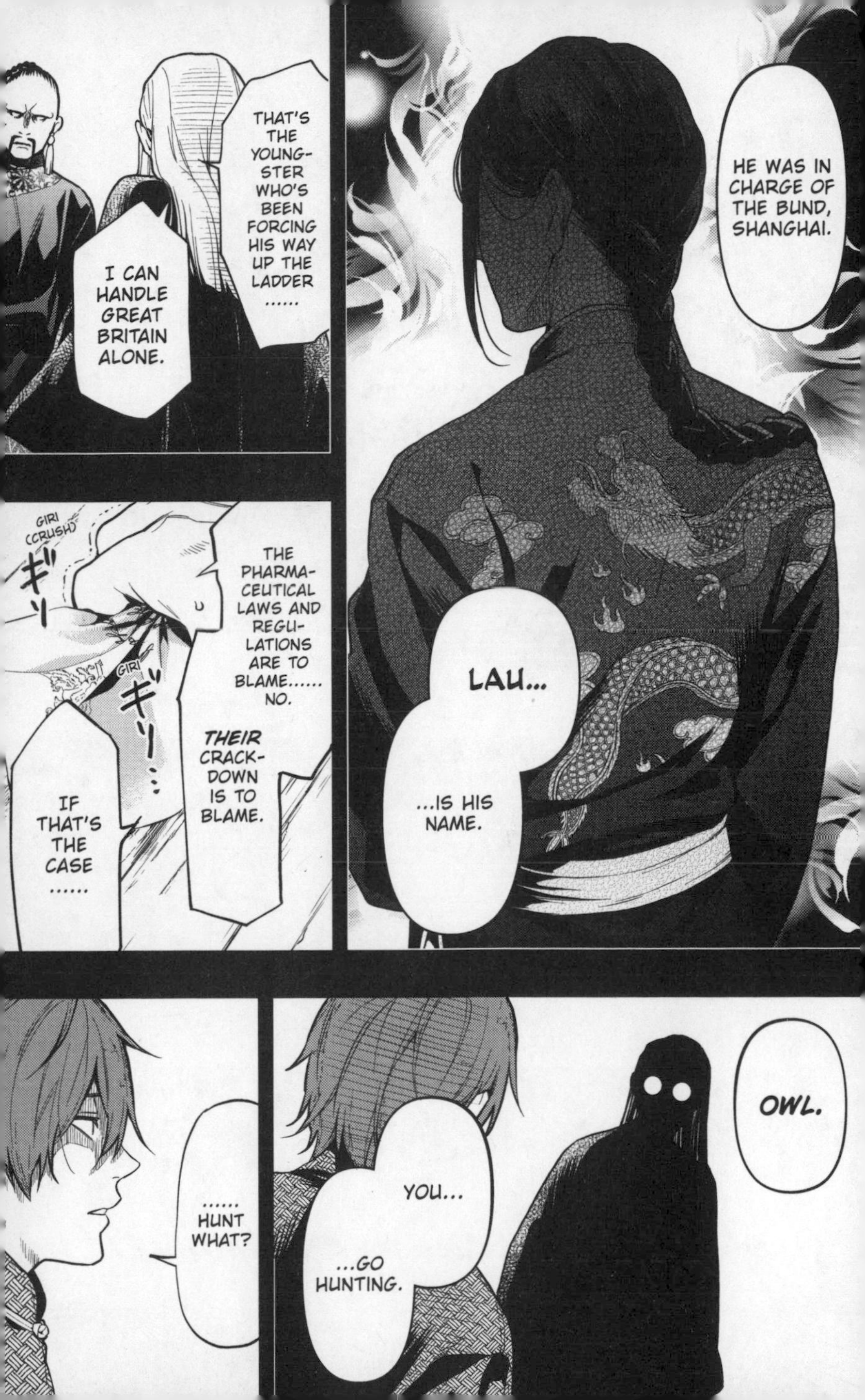
HE WAS IN CHARGE OF THE BUND, SHANGHAI.
LAU...
...IS HIS NAME.
THAT'S THE YOUNGSTER WHO'S BEEN FORCING HIS WAY UP THE LADDER......
I CAN HANDLE GREAT BRITAIN ALONE.
GIRI (CRUSH)
ギリ
GIRI
ギリ…
THE PHARMACEUTICAL LAWS AND REGULATIONS ARE TO BLAME...... NO.
THEIR CRACKDOWN IS TO BLAME.
IF THAT'S THE CASE......
OWL.
YOU...
...GO HUNTING.
......HUNT WHAT?

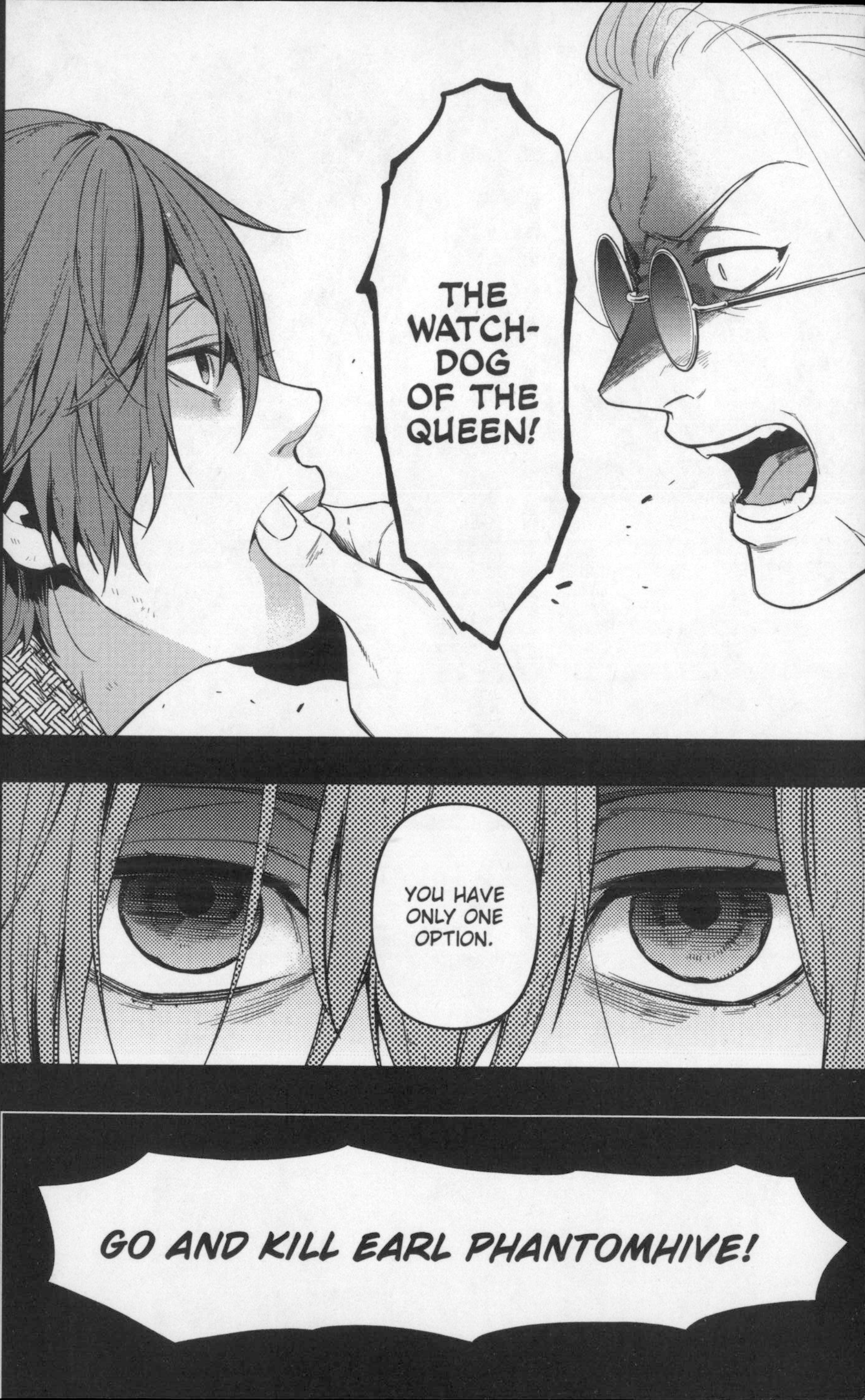
THE WATCH-DOG OF THE QUEEN!
YOU HAVE ONLY ONE OPTION.
GO AND KILL EARL PHANTOMHIVE!

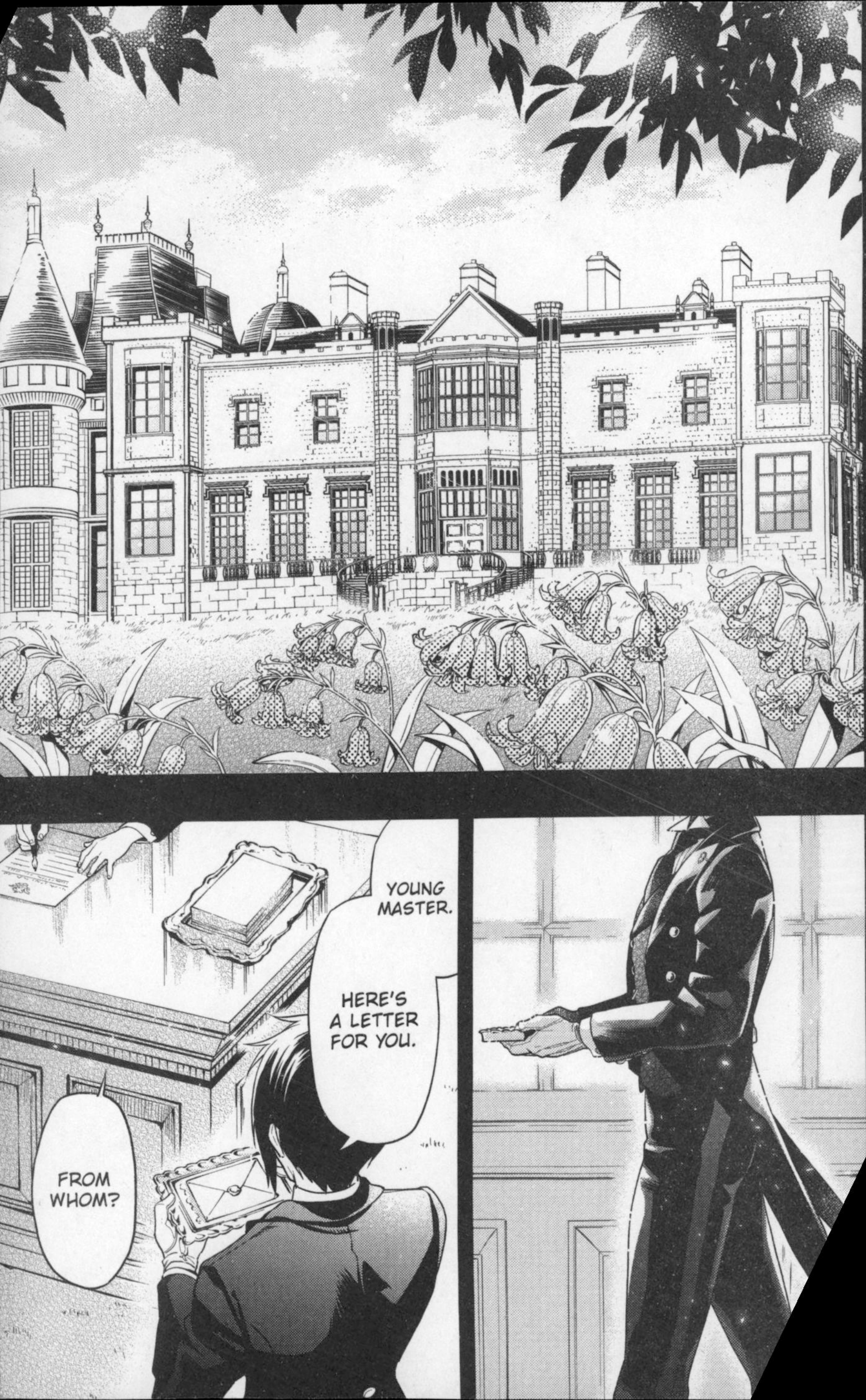
YOUNG MASTER.
HERE'S A LETTER FOR YOU.
FROM WHOM?

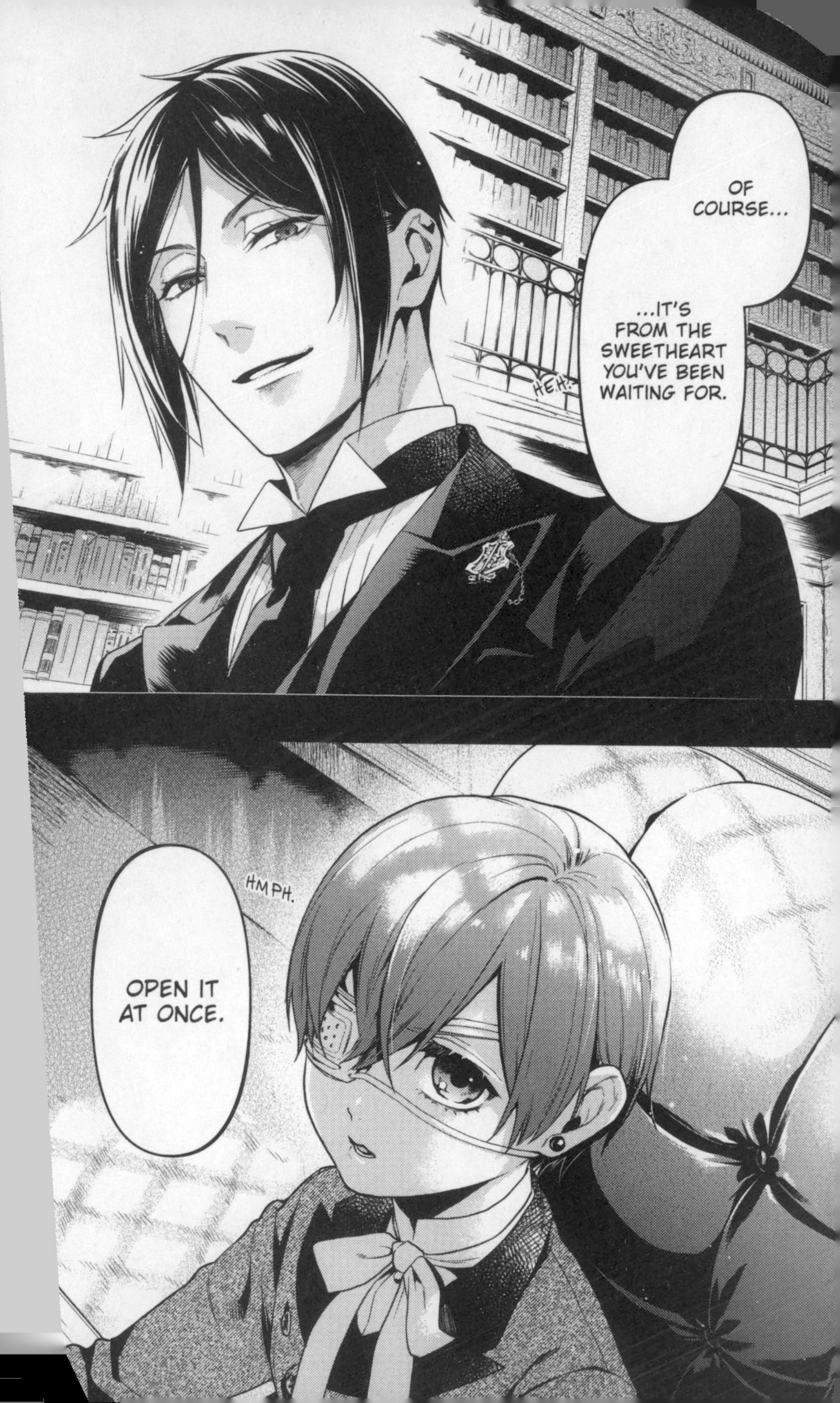
OF COURSE...
...IT'S FROM THE SWEETHEART YOU'VE BEEN WAITING FOR.
HEH.
HMPH.
OPEN IT AT ONCE.

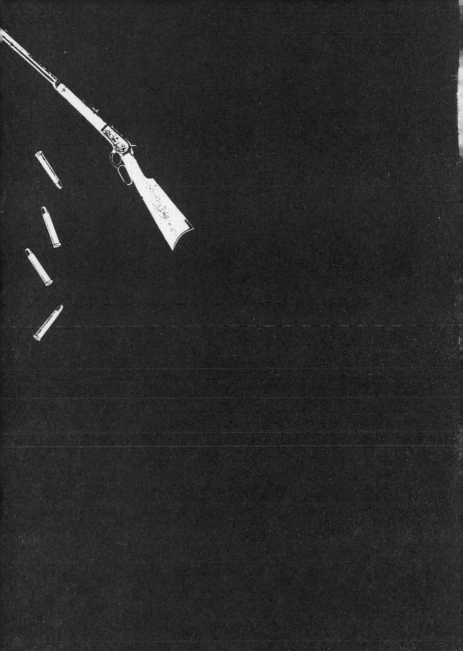

Black Butler

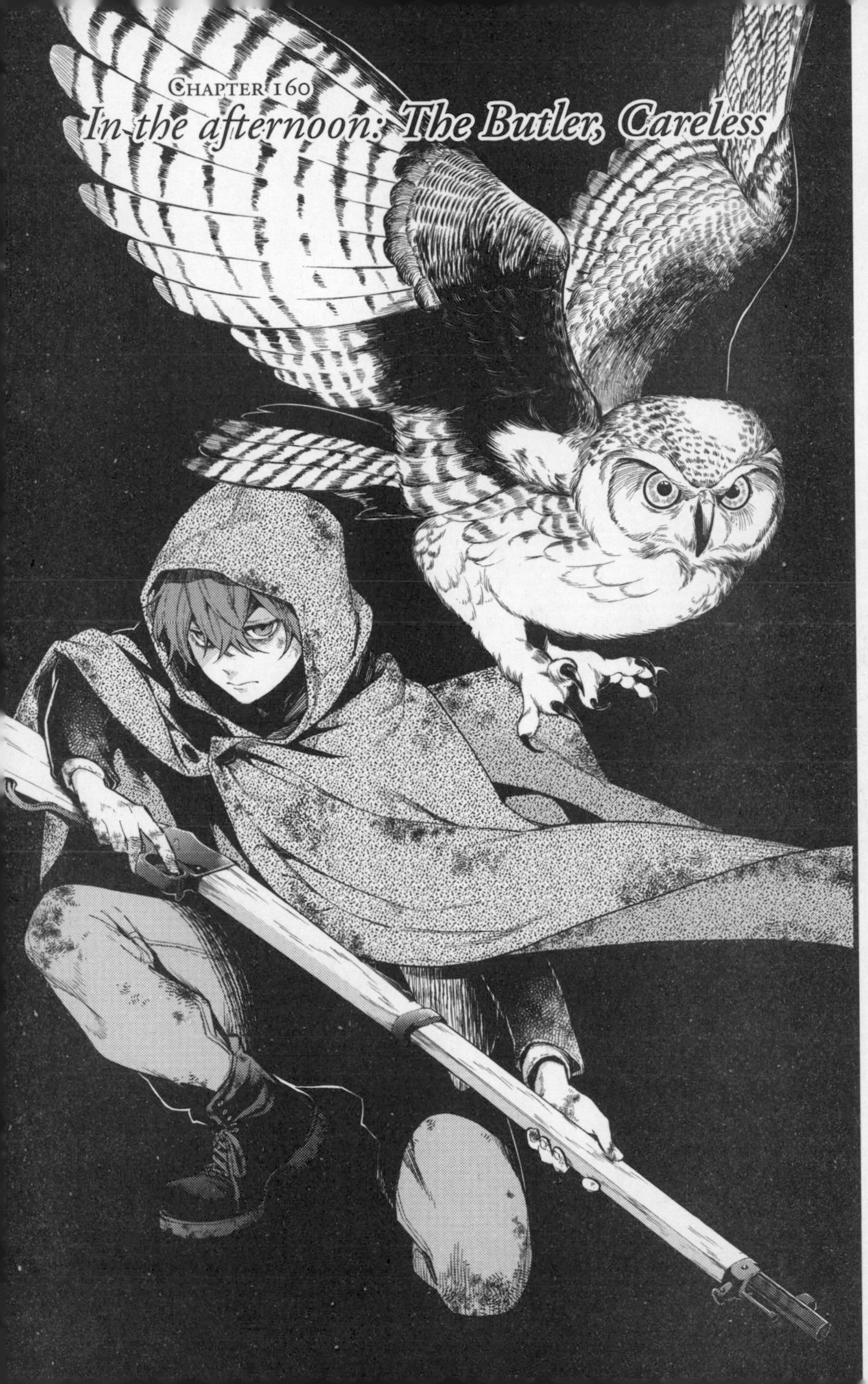
Chapter 160
In the afternoon: The Butler, Careless

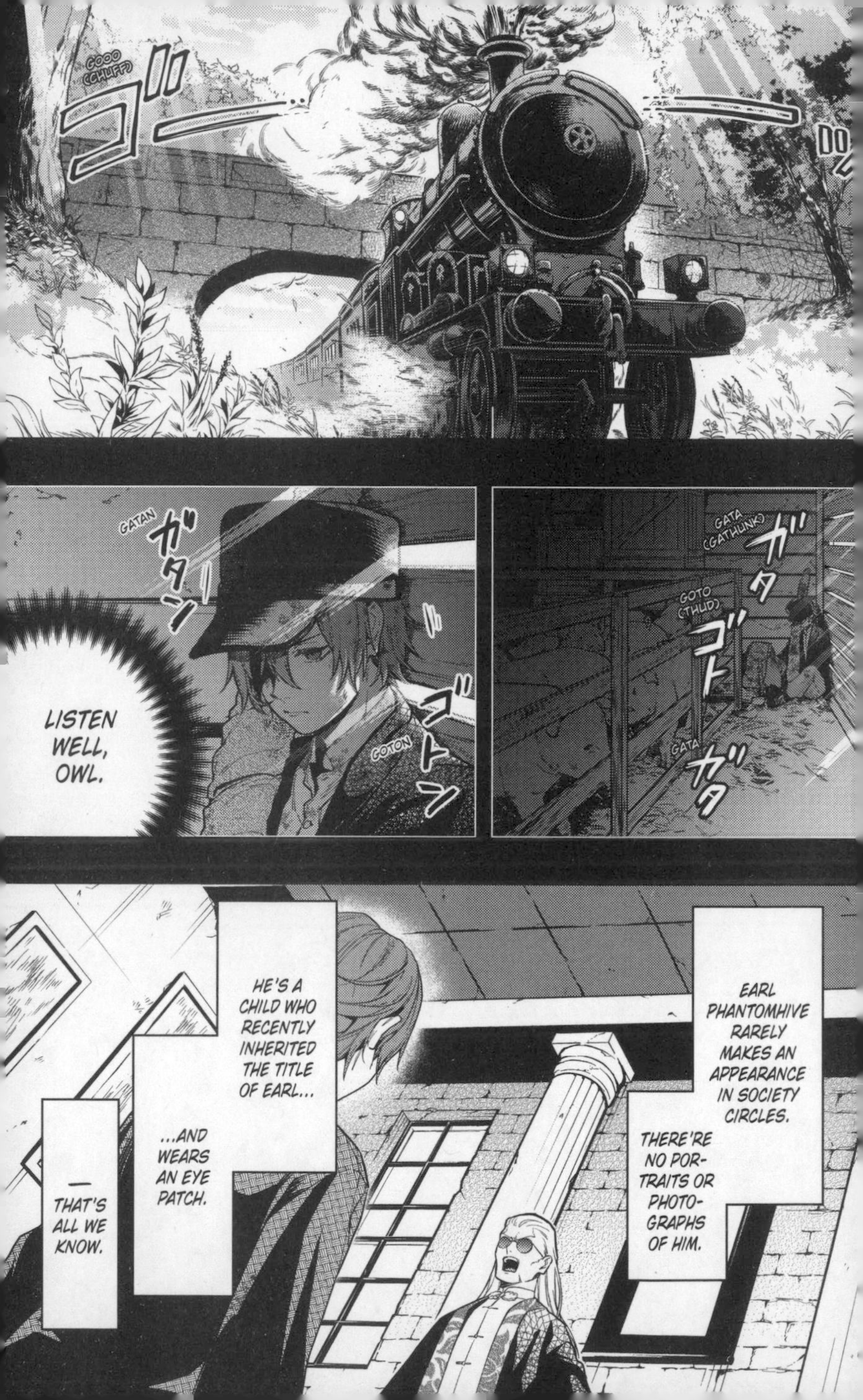
GOOO (CHUFF)
DO
GATA (GATHUNK)
GOTO (THUD)
GATA
GATAN
GOTON
LISTEN WELL, OWL.
EARL PHANTOMHIVE RARELY MAKES AN APPEARANCE IN SOCIETY CIRCLES.
THERE'RE NO POR-TRAITS OR PHOTO-GRAPHS OF HIM.
HE'S A CHILD WHO RECENTLY INHERITED THE TITLE OF EARL...
...AND WEARS AN EYE PATCH.
—THAT'S ALL WE KNOW.

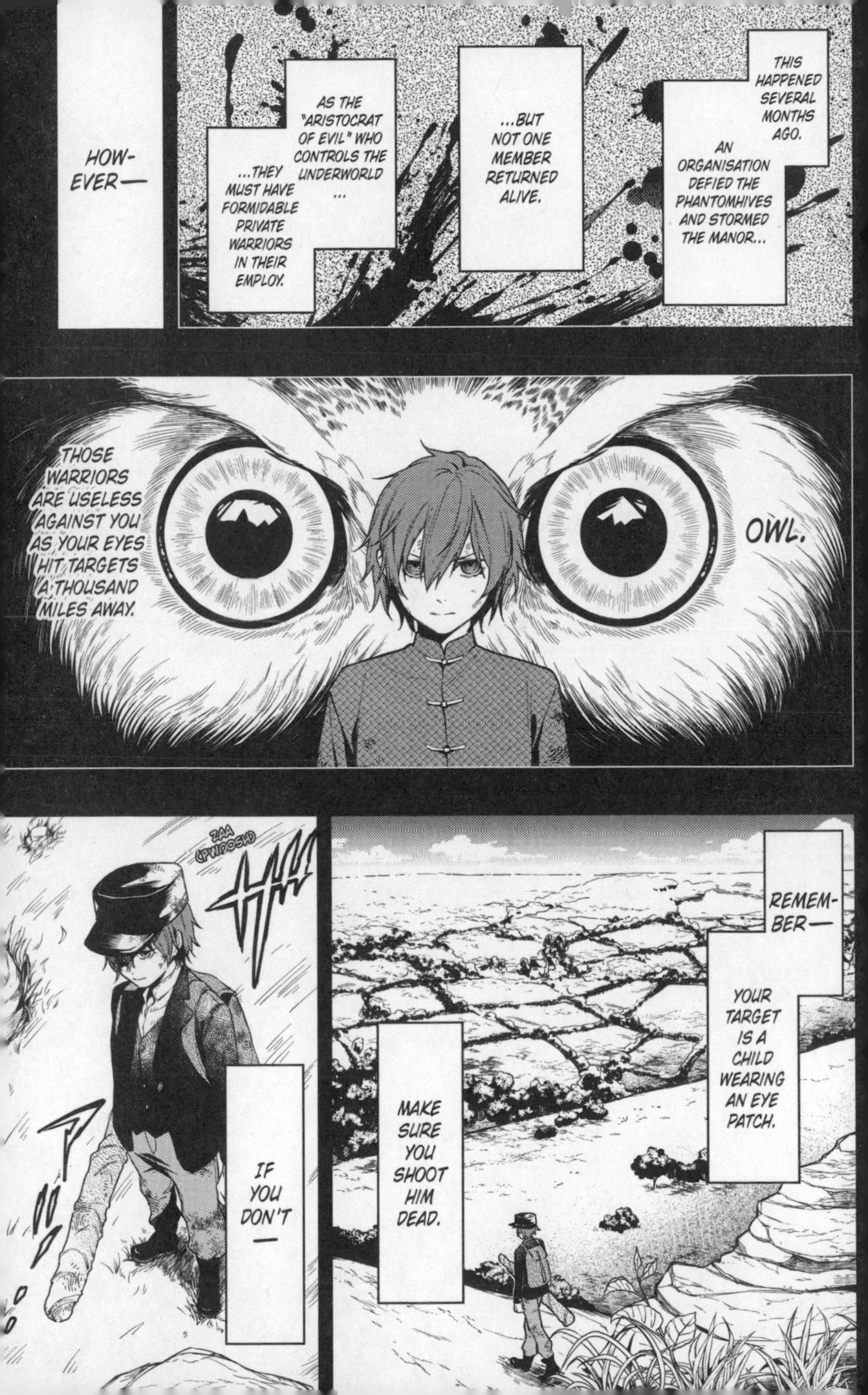
THIS HAPPENED SEVERAL MONTHS AGO.
AN ORGANISATION DEFIED THE PHANTOMHIVES AND STORMED THE MANOR...
...BUT NOT ONE MEMBER RETURNED ALIVE.
AS THE "ARISTOCRAT OF EVIL" WHO CONTROLS THE UNDERWORLD...
...THEY MUST HAVE FORMIDABLE PRIVATE WARRIORS IN THEIR EMPLOY.
HOW-EVER—
THOSE WARRIORS ARE USELESS AGAINST YOU AS YOUR EYES HIT TARGETS A THOUSAND MILES AWAY.
OWL.
REMEM-BER—
YOUR TARGET IS A CHILD WEARING AN EYE PATCH.
MAKE SURE YOU SHOOT HIM DEAD.
ZAA (PWOOSH)
IF YOU DON'T —

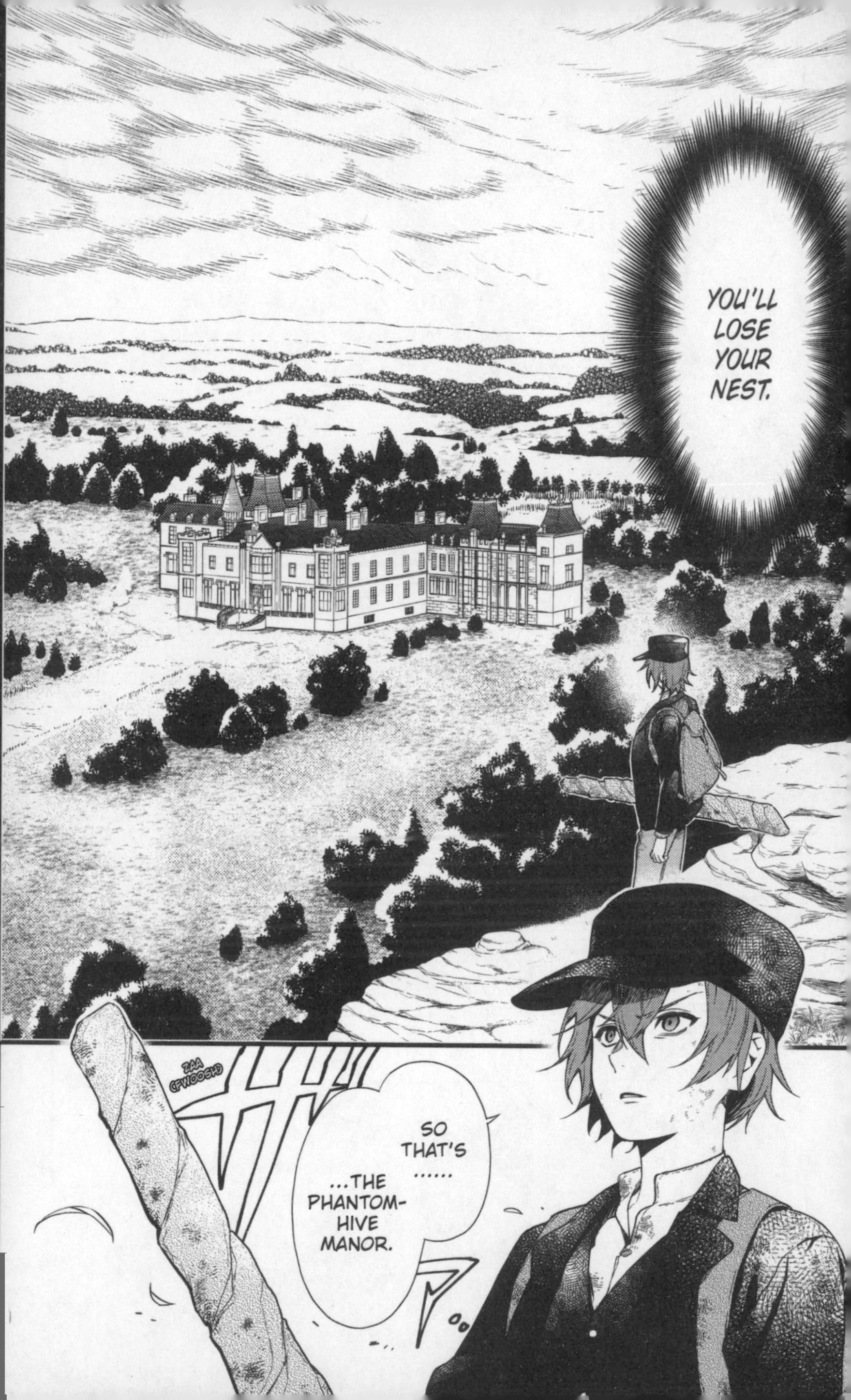
YOU'LL LOSE YOUR NEST.
ZAA (FWOOSH)
SO THAT'S ......
...THE PHANTOM-HIVE MANOR.

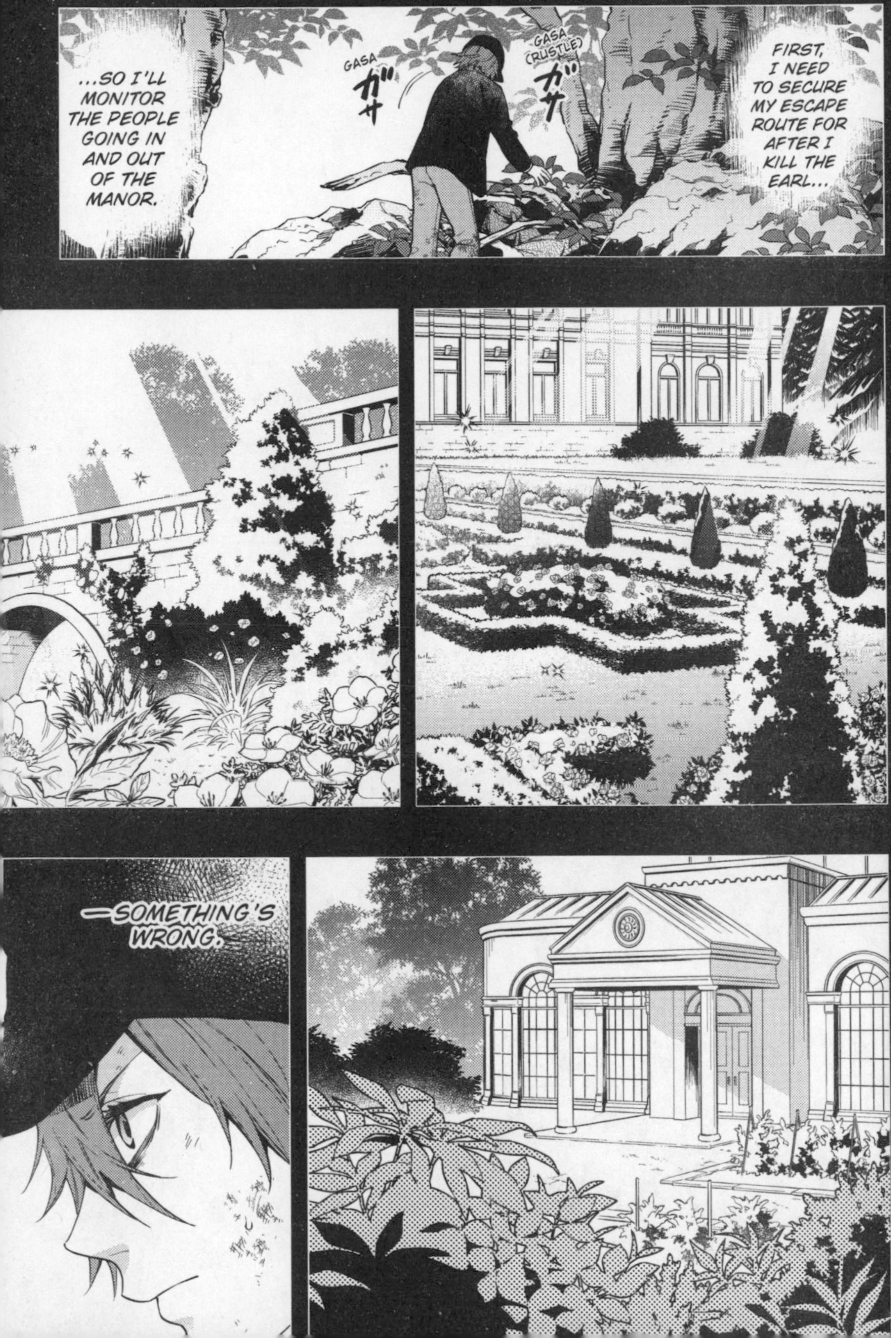
FIRST, I NEED TO SECURE MY ESCAPE ROUTE FOR AFTER I KILL THE EARL...
GASA (RUSTLE)
ガサ
GASA
ガサ
...SO I'LL MONITOR THE PEOPLE GOING IN AND OUT OF THE MANOR.
—SOMETHING'S WRONG.

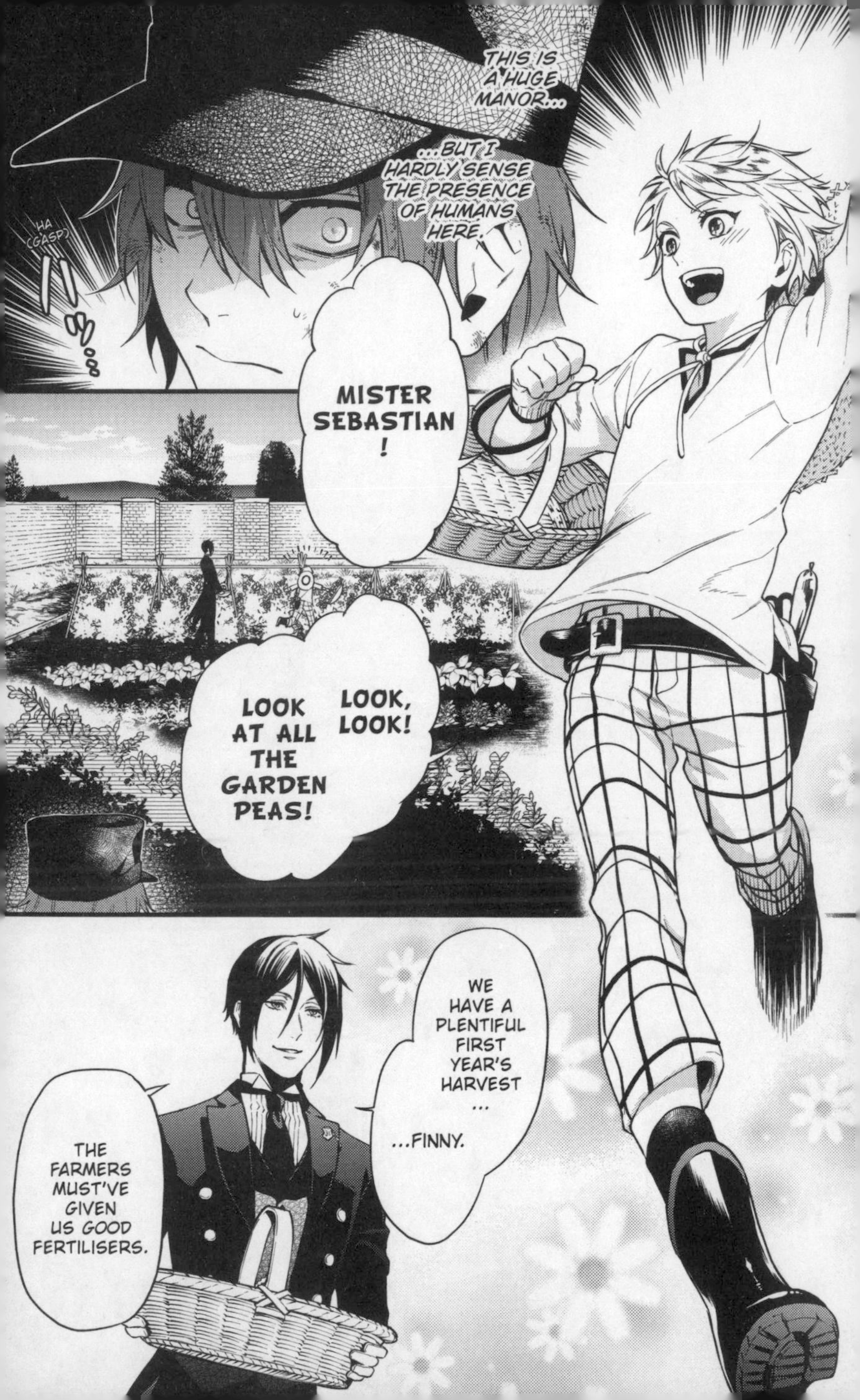
THIS IS A HUGE MANOR...
...BUT I HARDLY SENSE THE PRESENCE OF HUMANS HERE.
HA (GASP)
MISTER SEBASTIAN!
LOOK, LOOK!
LOOK AT ALL THE GARDEN PEAS!
WE HAVE A PLENTIFUL FIRST YEAR'S HARVEST ...
...FINNY.
THE FARMERS MUST'VE GIVEN US GOOD FERTILISERS.

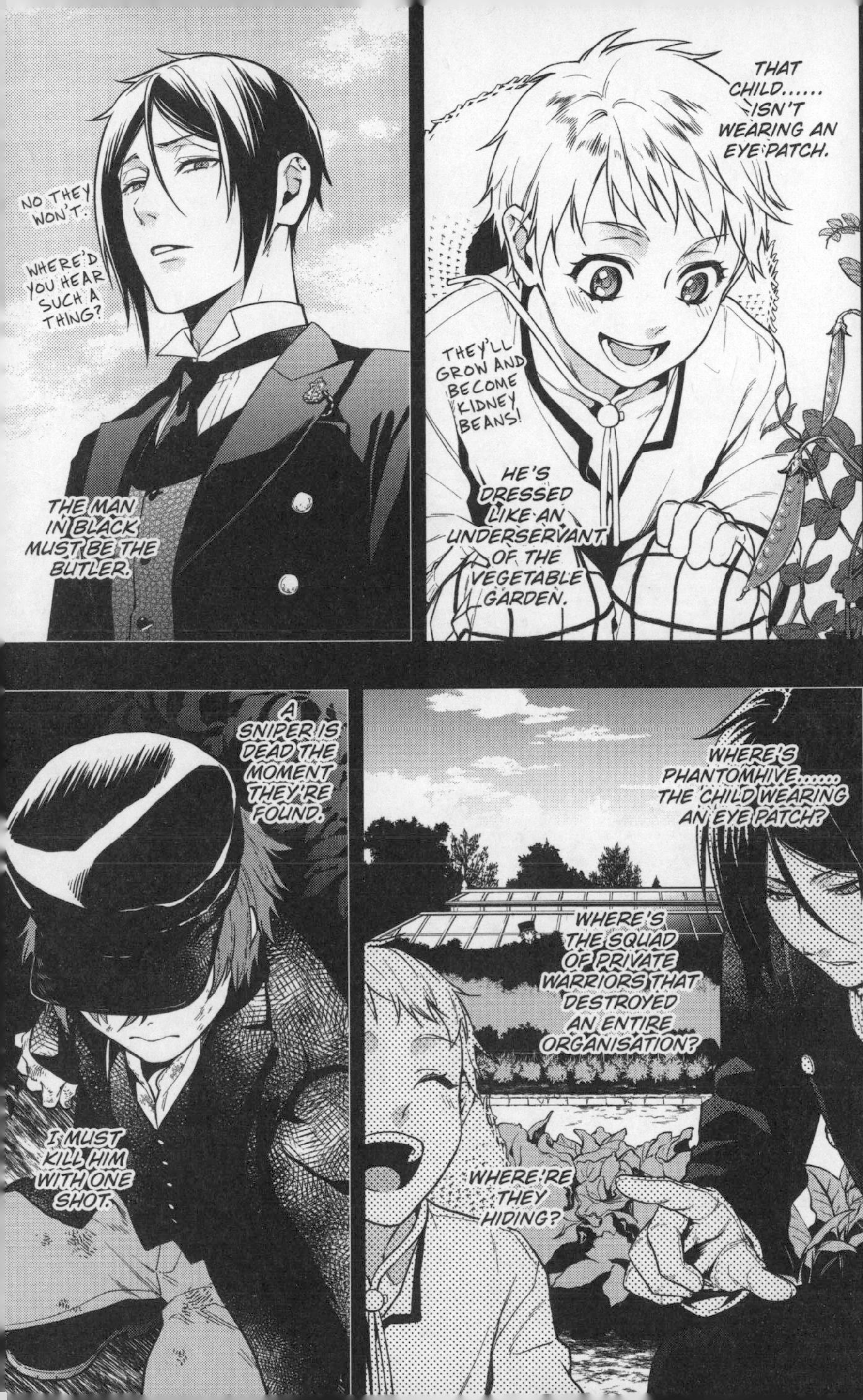
THAT CHILD...... ISN'T WEARING AN EYE PATCH.
THEY'LL GROW AND BECOME KIDNEY BEANS!
HE'S DRESSED LIKE AN UNDERSERVANT OF THE VEGETABLE GARDEN.
NO THEY WON'T.
WHERE'D YOU HEAR SUCH A THING?
THE MAN IN BLACK MUST BE THE BUTLER.
WHERE'S PHANTOMHIVE...... THE CHILD WEARING AN EYE PATCH?
WHERE'S THE SQUAD OF PRIVATE WARRIORS THAT DESTROYED AN ENTIRE ORGANISATION?
WHERE'RE THEY HIDING?
A SNIPER IS DEAD THE MOMENT THEY'RE FOUND.
I MUST KILL HIM WITH ONE SHOT.

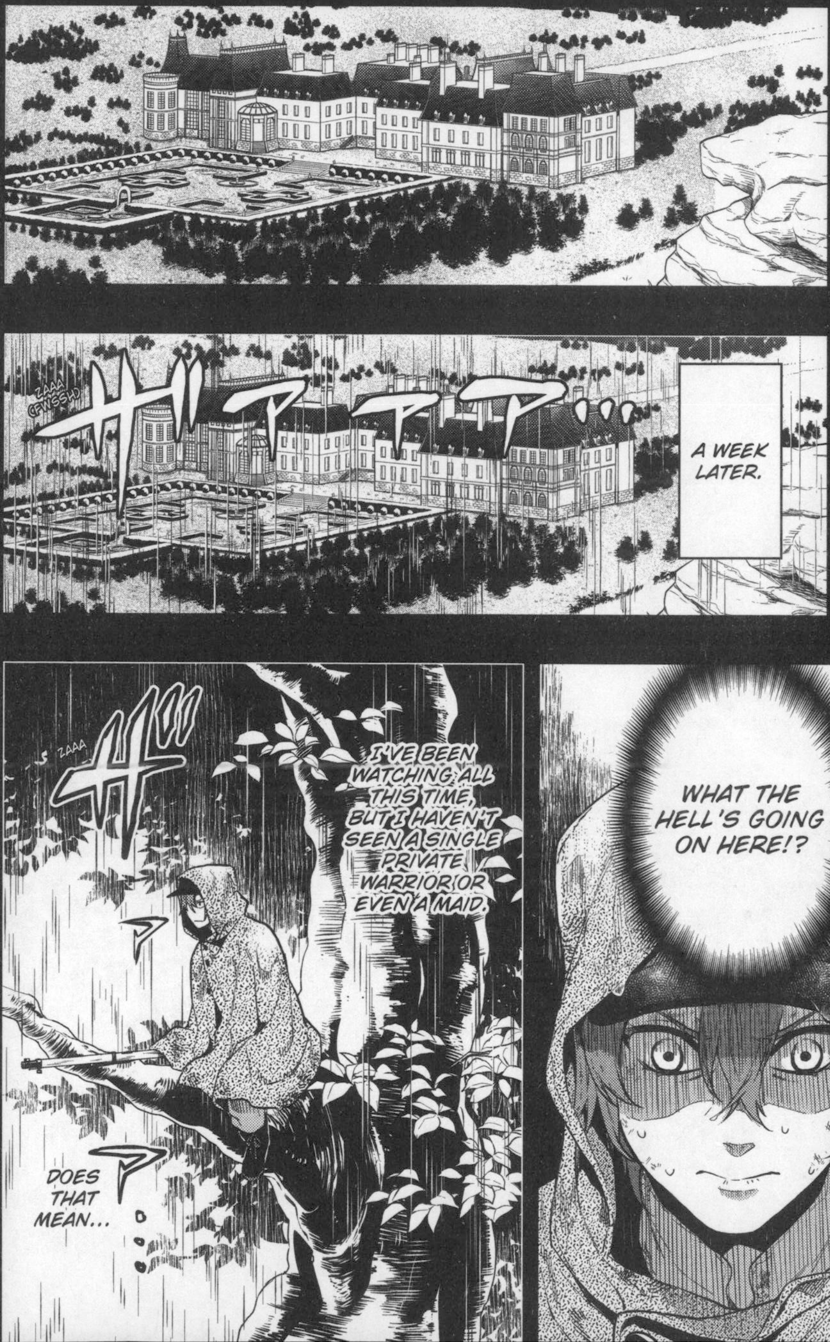
A WEEK LATER.
ZAAA (FWSSH)
WHAT THE HELL'S GOING ON HERE!?
ZAAA
I'VE BEEN WATCHING ALL THIS TIME, BUT I HAVEN'T SEEN A SINGLE PRIVATE WARRIOR OR EVEN A MAID.
DOES THAT MEAN...

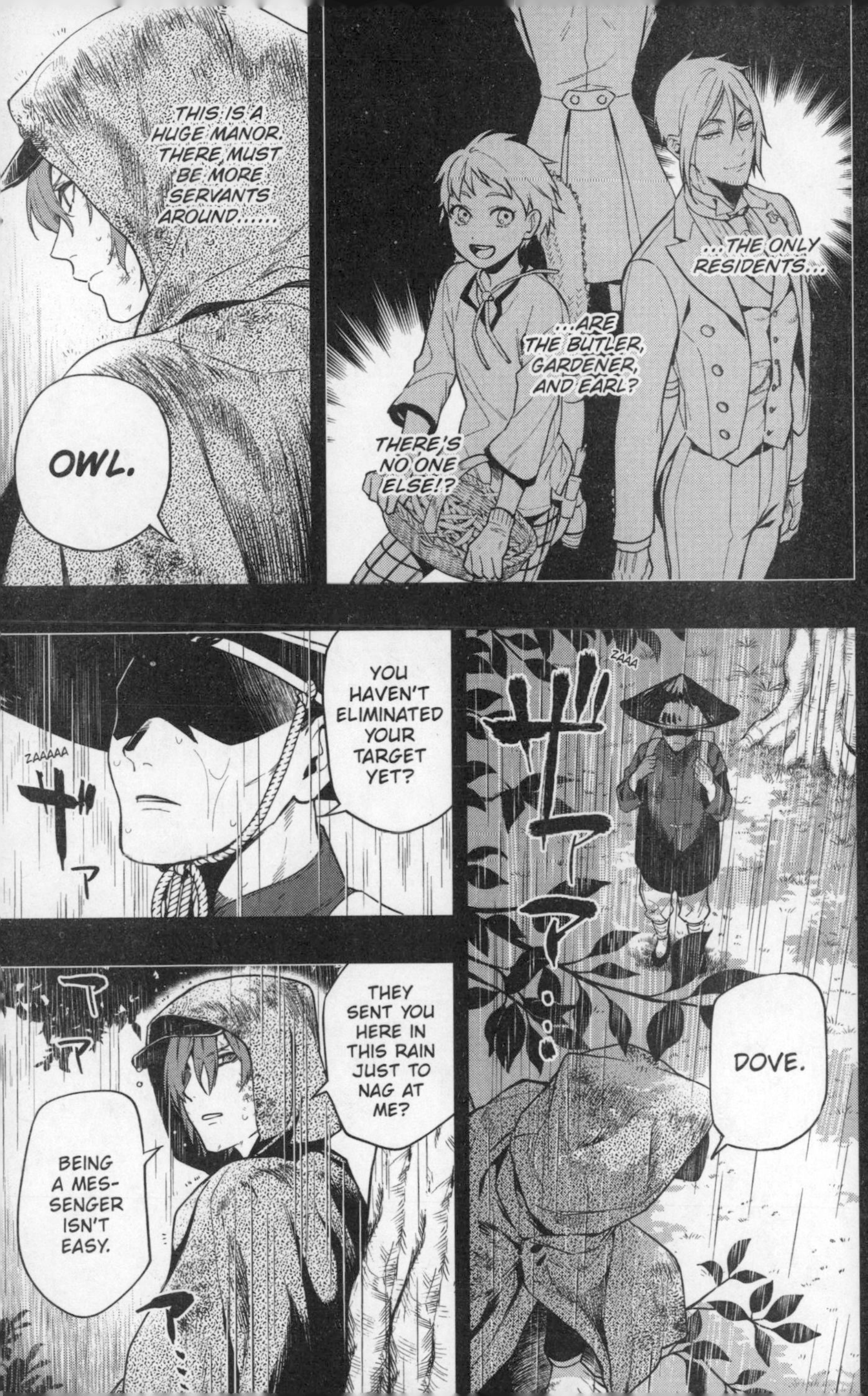
...THE ONLY RESIDENTS...
...ARE THE BUTLER, GARDENER, AND EARL?
THERE'S NO ONE ELSE!?
THIS IS A HUGE MANOR. THERE MUST BE MORE SERVANTS AROUND......
OWL.
ZAAA
...
DOVE.
YOU HAVEN'T ELIMINATED YOUR TARGET YET?
ZAAAAA
THEY SENT YOU HERE IN THIS RAIN JUST TO NAG AT ME?
BEING A MES-SENGER ISN'T EASY.

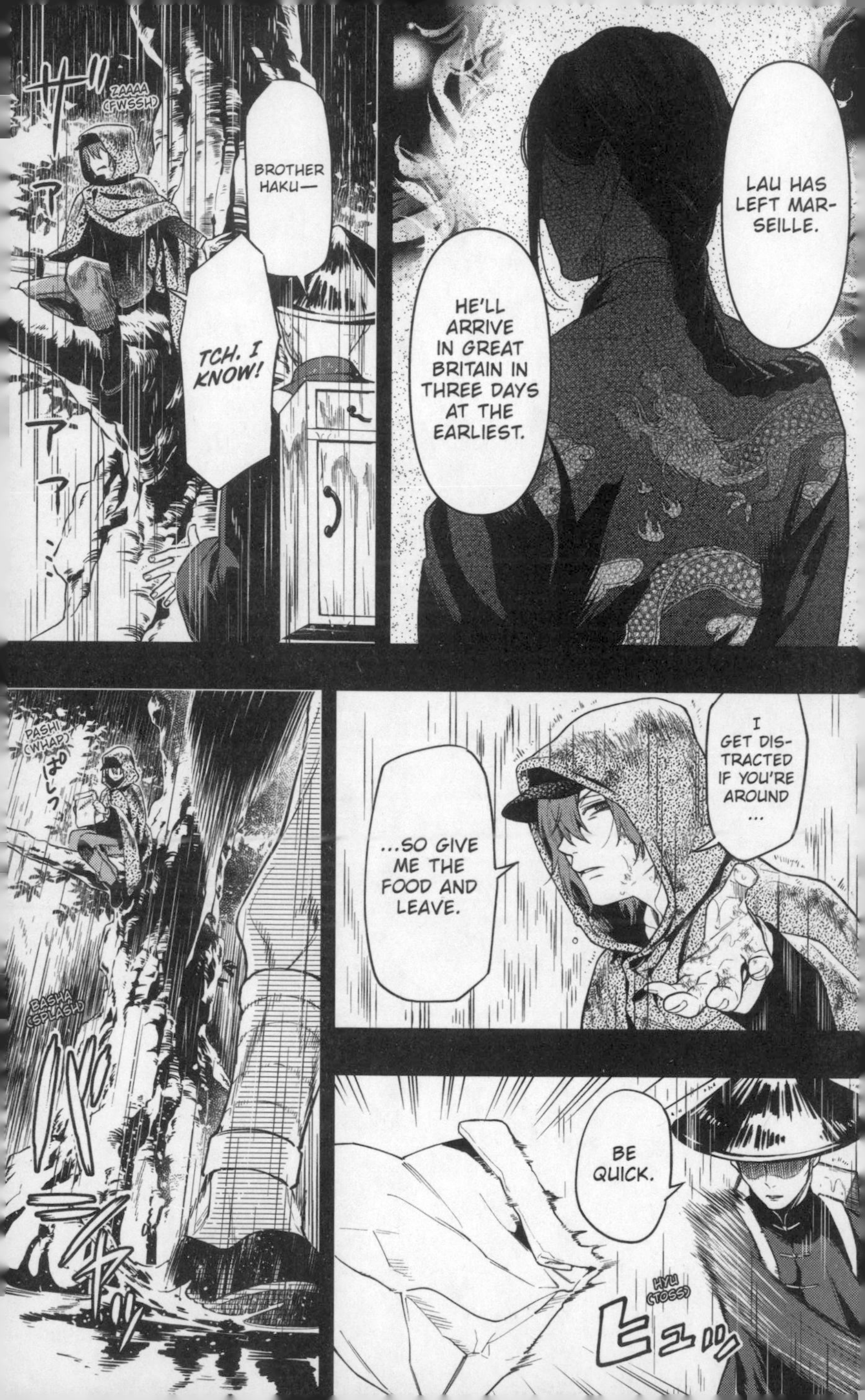
LAU HAS LEFT MAR-SEILLE.
HE'LL ARRIVE IN GREAT BRITAIN IN THREE DAYS AT THE EARLIEST.
ZAAAA (FWSSH)
BROTHER HAKU—
TCH. I KNOW!
I GET DIS-TRACTED IF YOU'RE AROUND...
...SO GIVE ME THE FOOD AND LEAVE.
BE QUICK.
HYU (TOSS)
PASHI (WHAP)
BASHA (SPLASH)

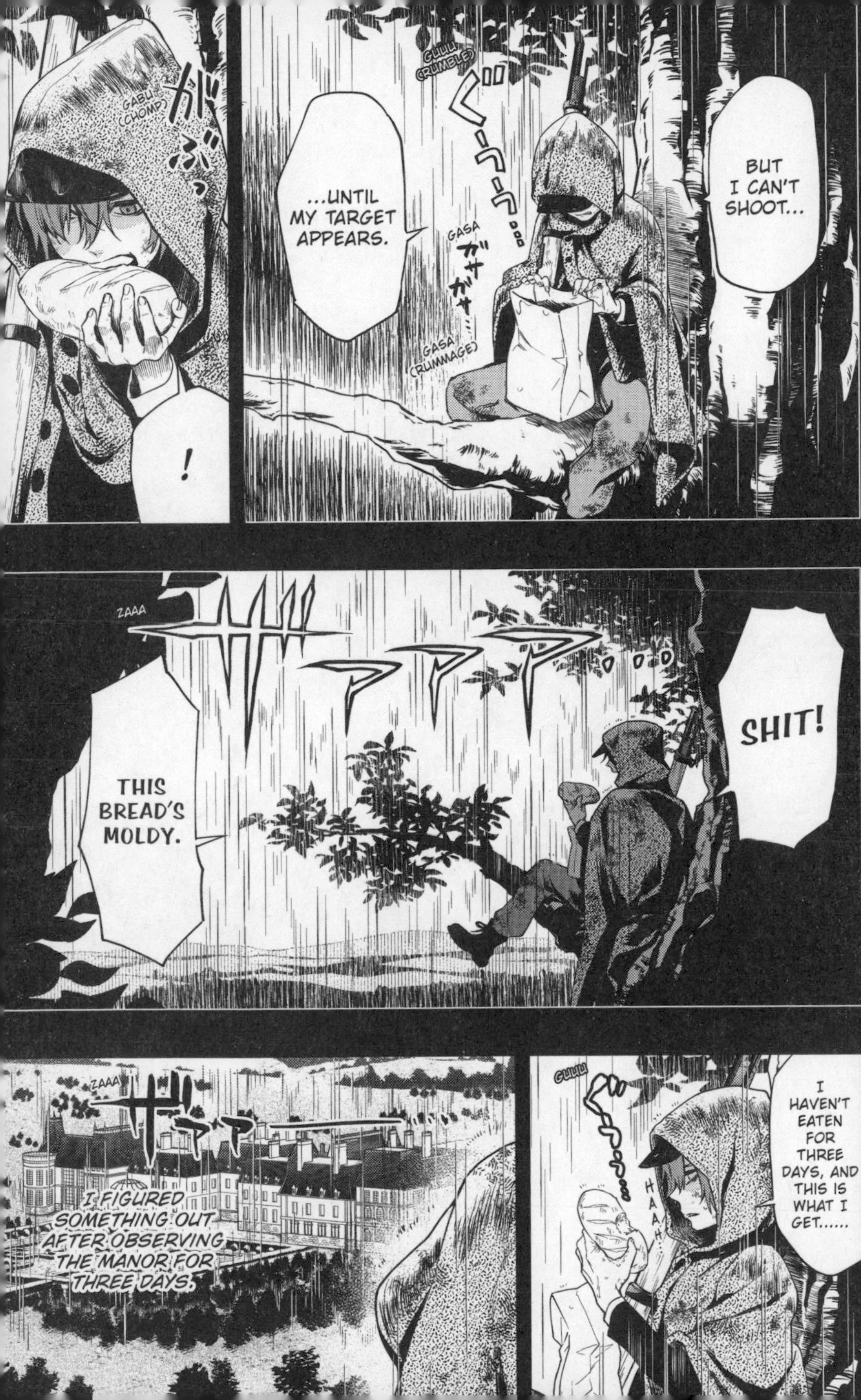
BUT I CAN'T SHOOT...
GUUU (RUMBLE)
...UNTIL MY TARGET APPEARS.
GASA
GASA (RUMMAGE)
GABU (CHOMP)
!
SHIT!
ZAAA
THIS BREAD'S MOLDY.
GUUU
I HAVEN'T EATEN FOR THREE DAYS, AND THIS IS WHAT I GET......
HAAH...
ZAAA
I FIGURED SOMETHING OUT AFTER OBSERVING THE MANOR FOR THREE DAYS.

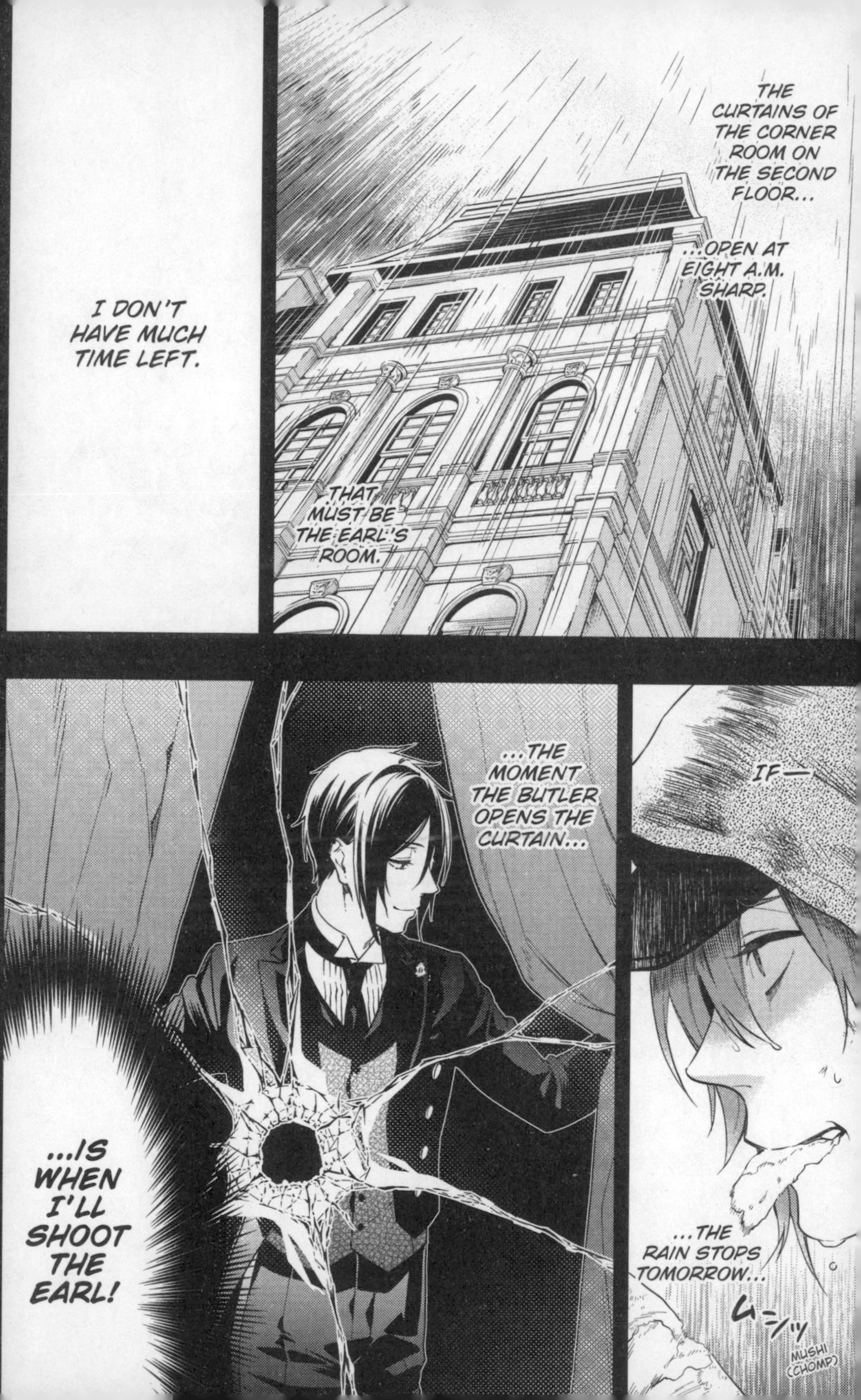
THE CURTAINS OF THE CORNER ROOM ON THE SECOND FLOOR...
...OPEN AT EIGHT A.M. SHARP.
THAT MUST BE THE EARL'S ROOM.
I DON'T HAVE MUCH TIME LEFT.
IF—
...THE RAIN STOPS TOMORROW...
ムシッ
MUSHI (CHOMP)
...THE MOMENT THE BUTLER OPENS THE CURTAIN...
...IS WHEN I'LL SHOOT THE EARL!

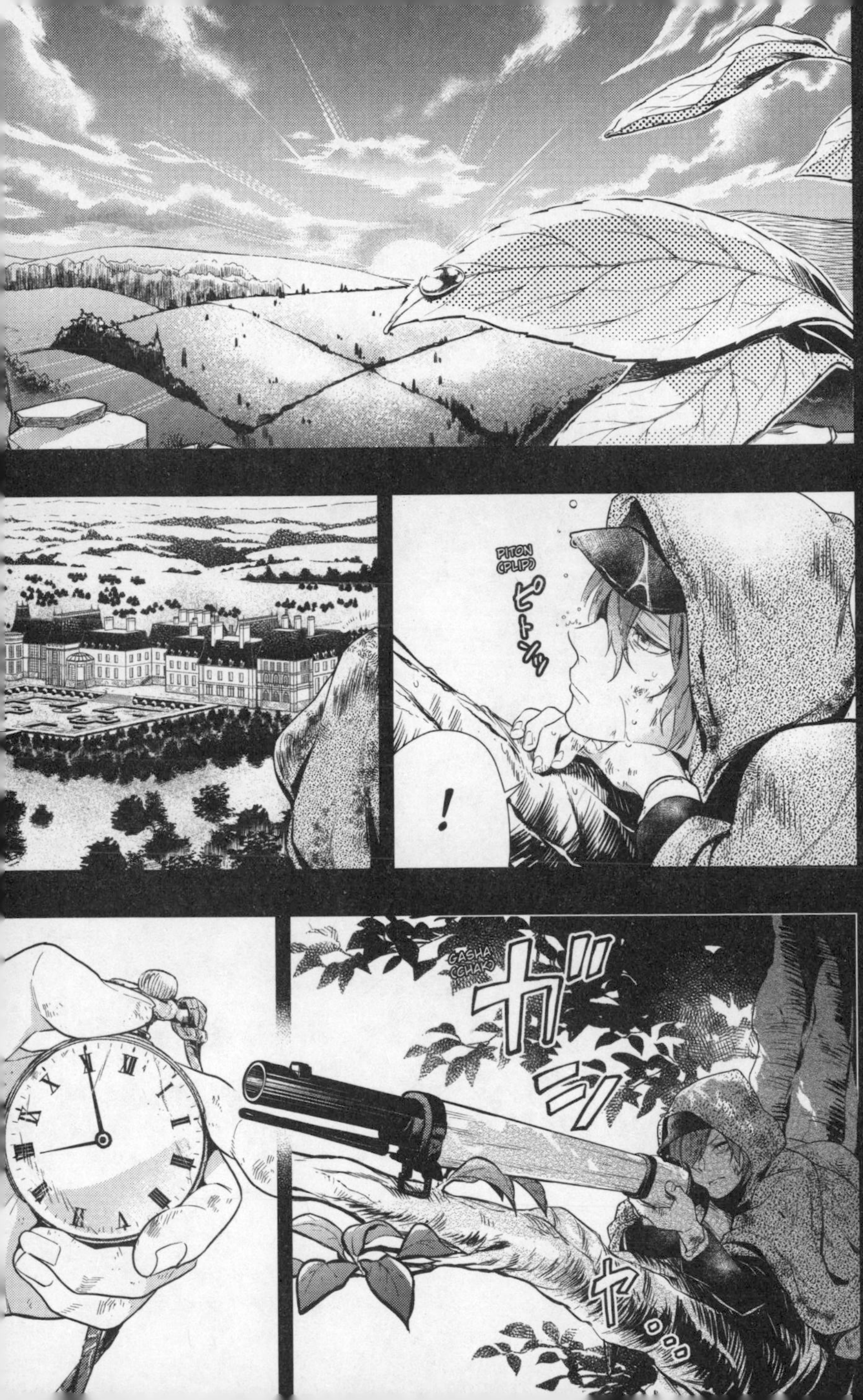
PITON (PLIP)
ピトッ
!
GASHA (CHAK)
ガシャッ
...

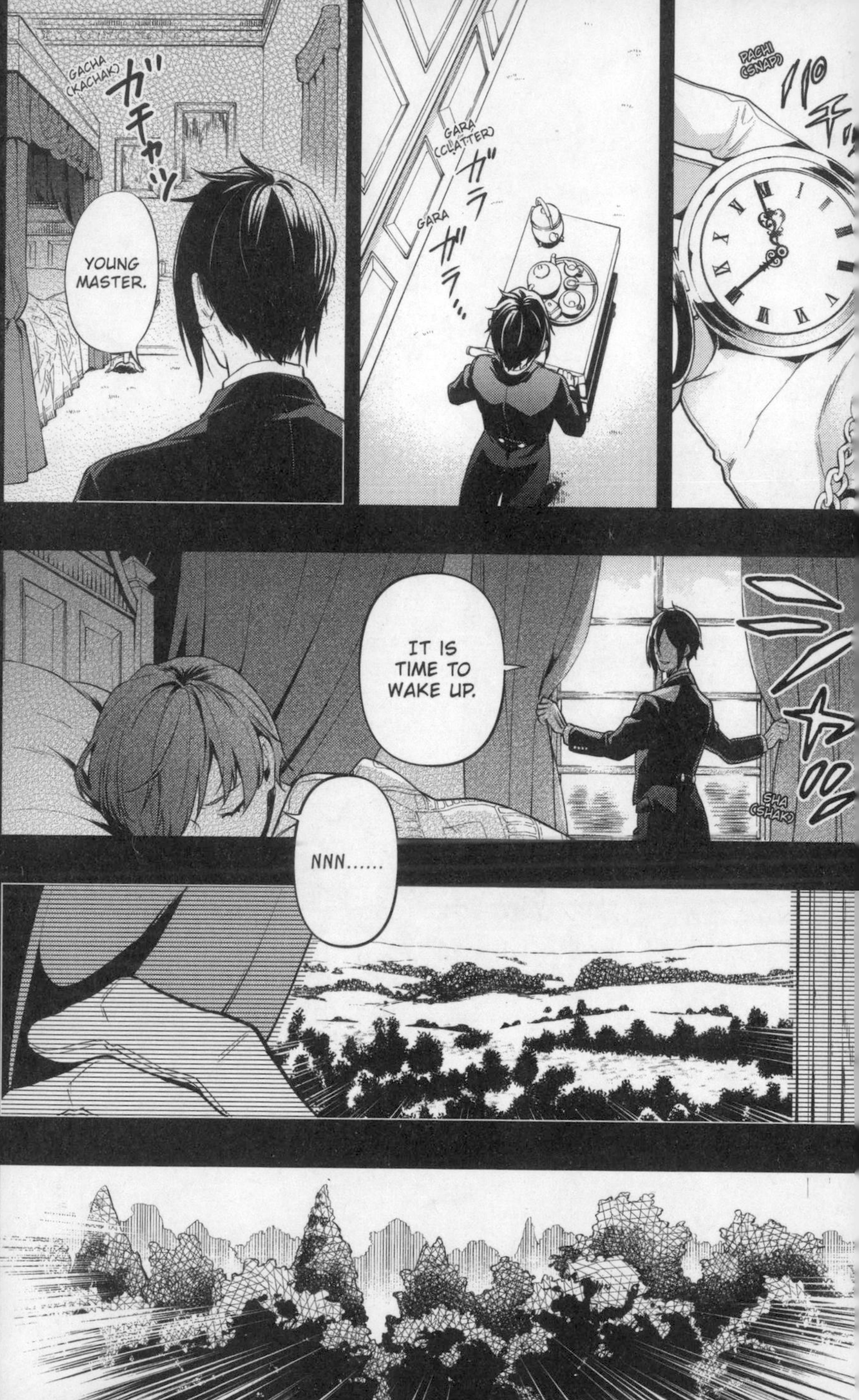
PACHI (SNAP)
パチッ
GARA (CLATTER)
ガラ
GARA
ガラ…
GACHA (KACHAK)
ガチャッ
YOUNG MASTER.
IT IS TIME TO WAKE UP.
SHA (SHAK)
シャッ
NNN......

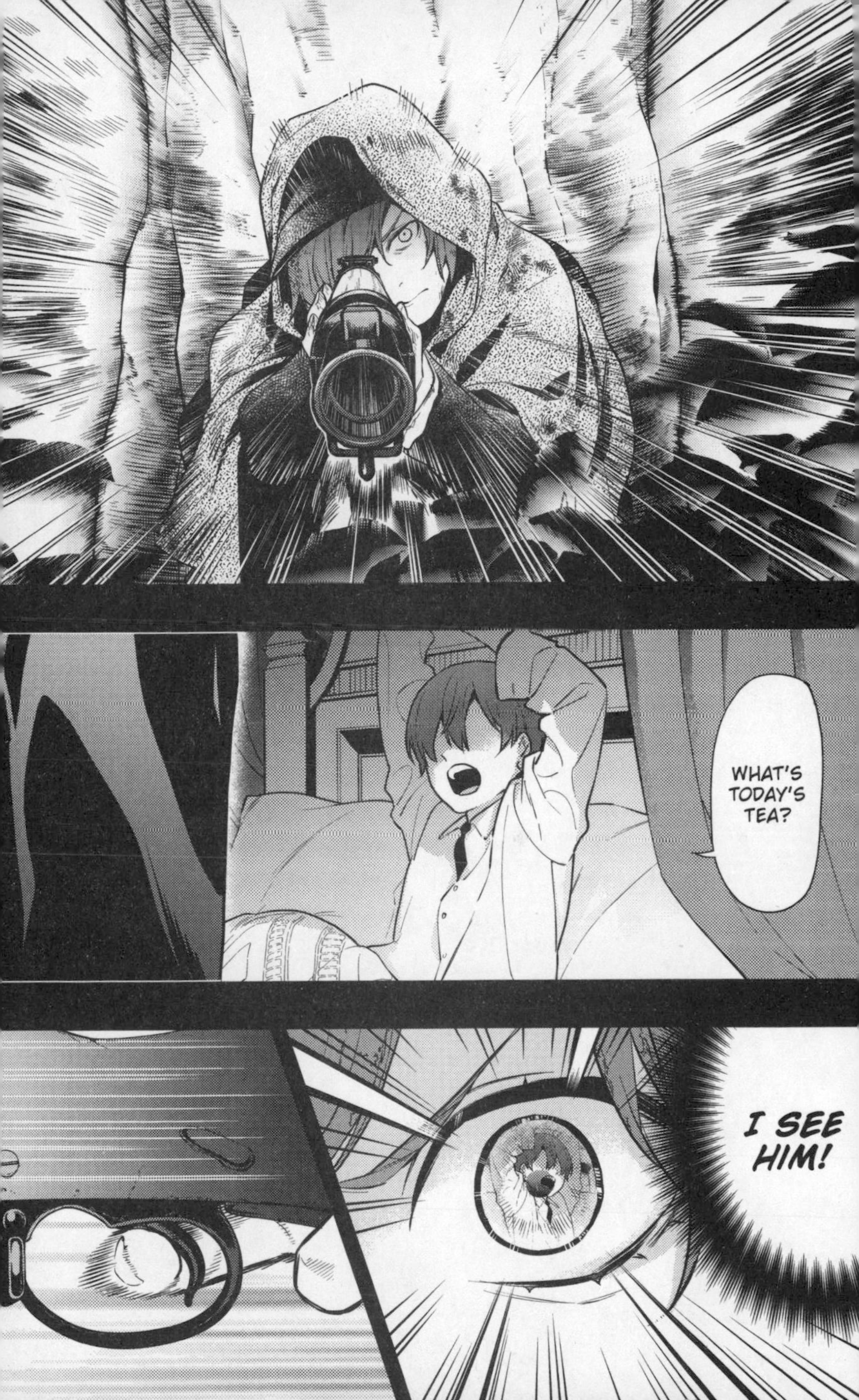
WHAT'S TODAY'S TEA?
I SEE HIM!

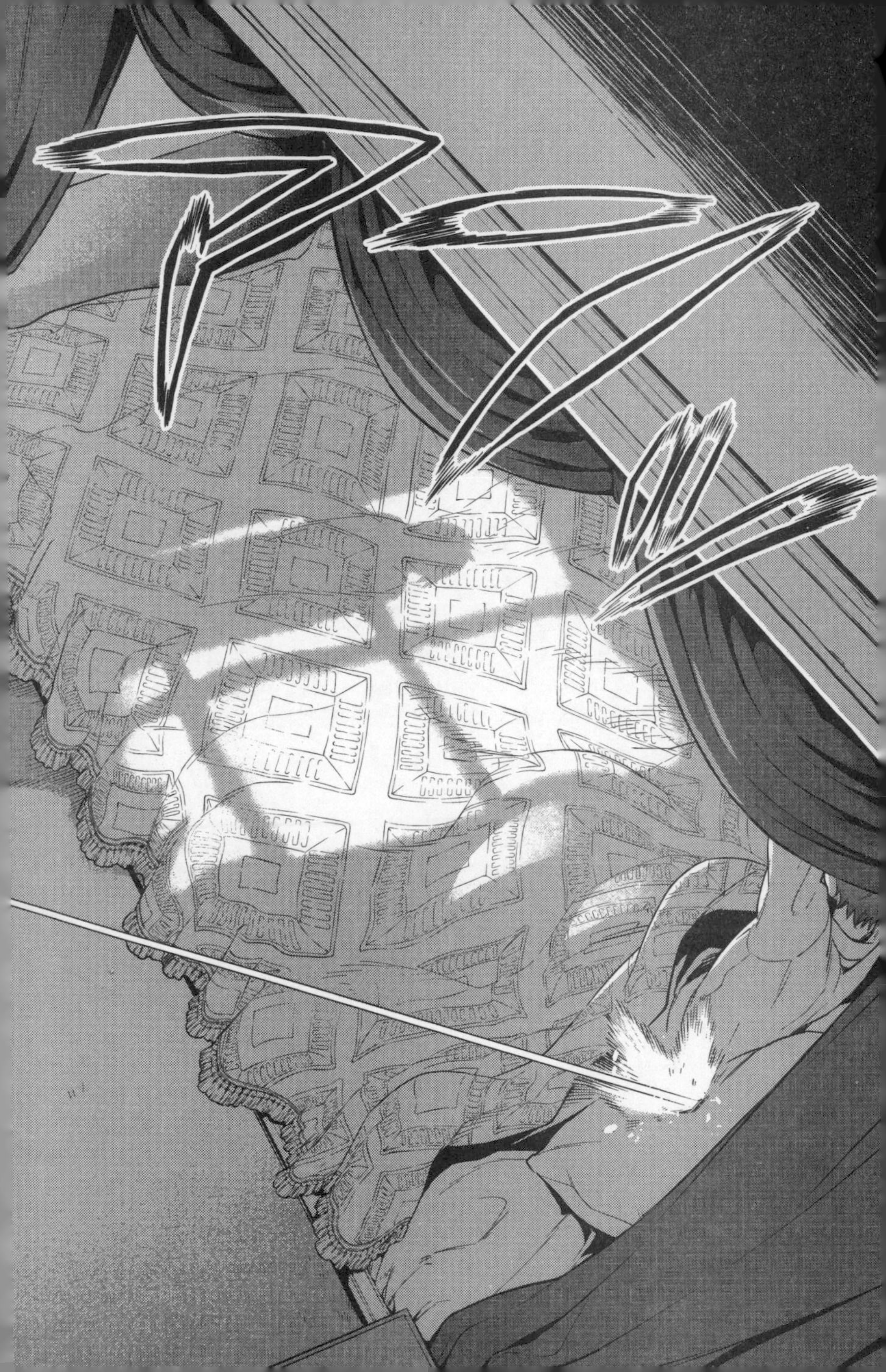

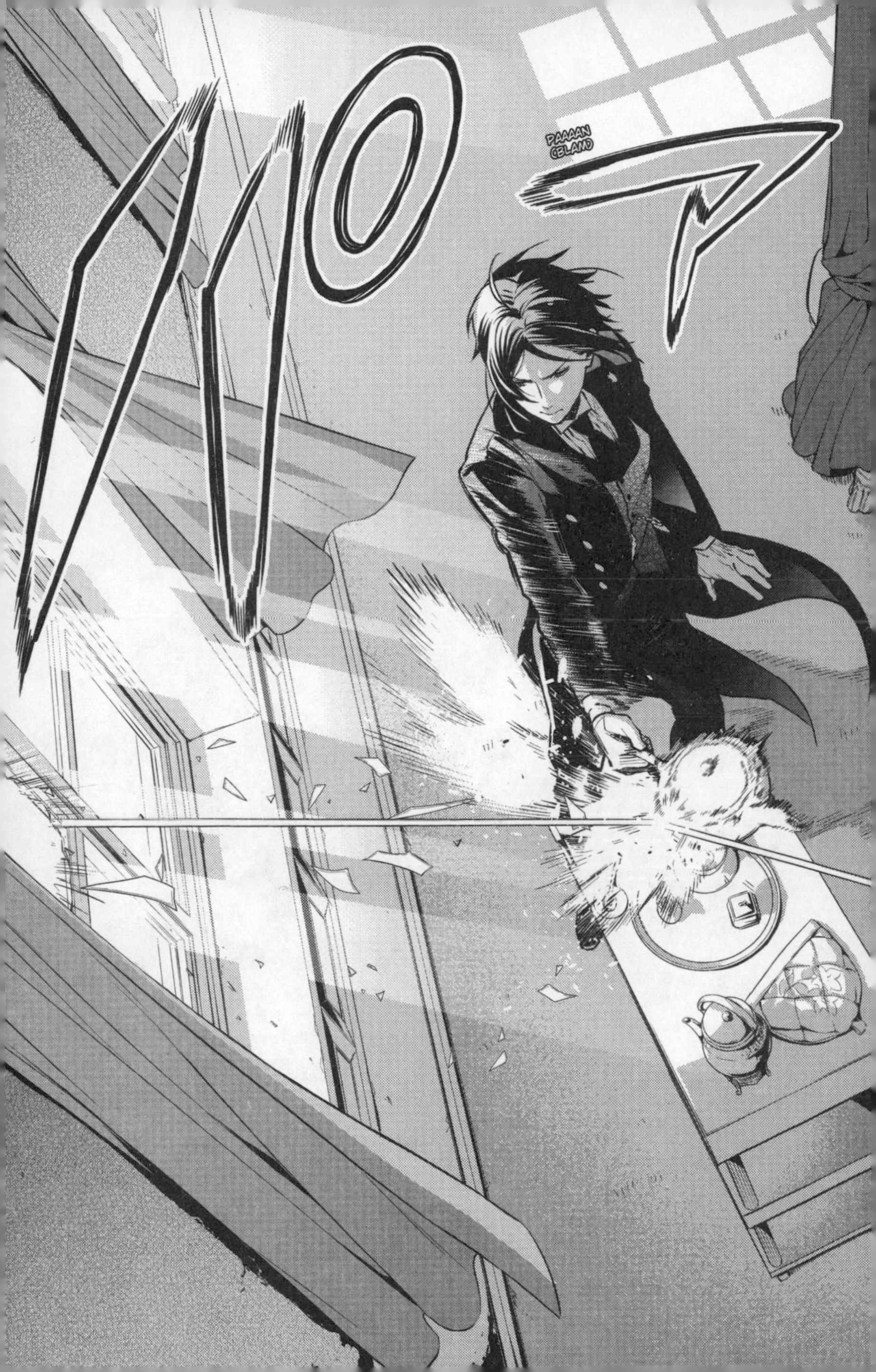
PAAAAN
(BLAM)

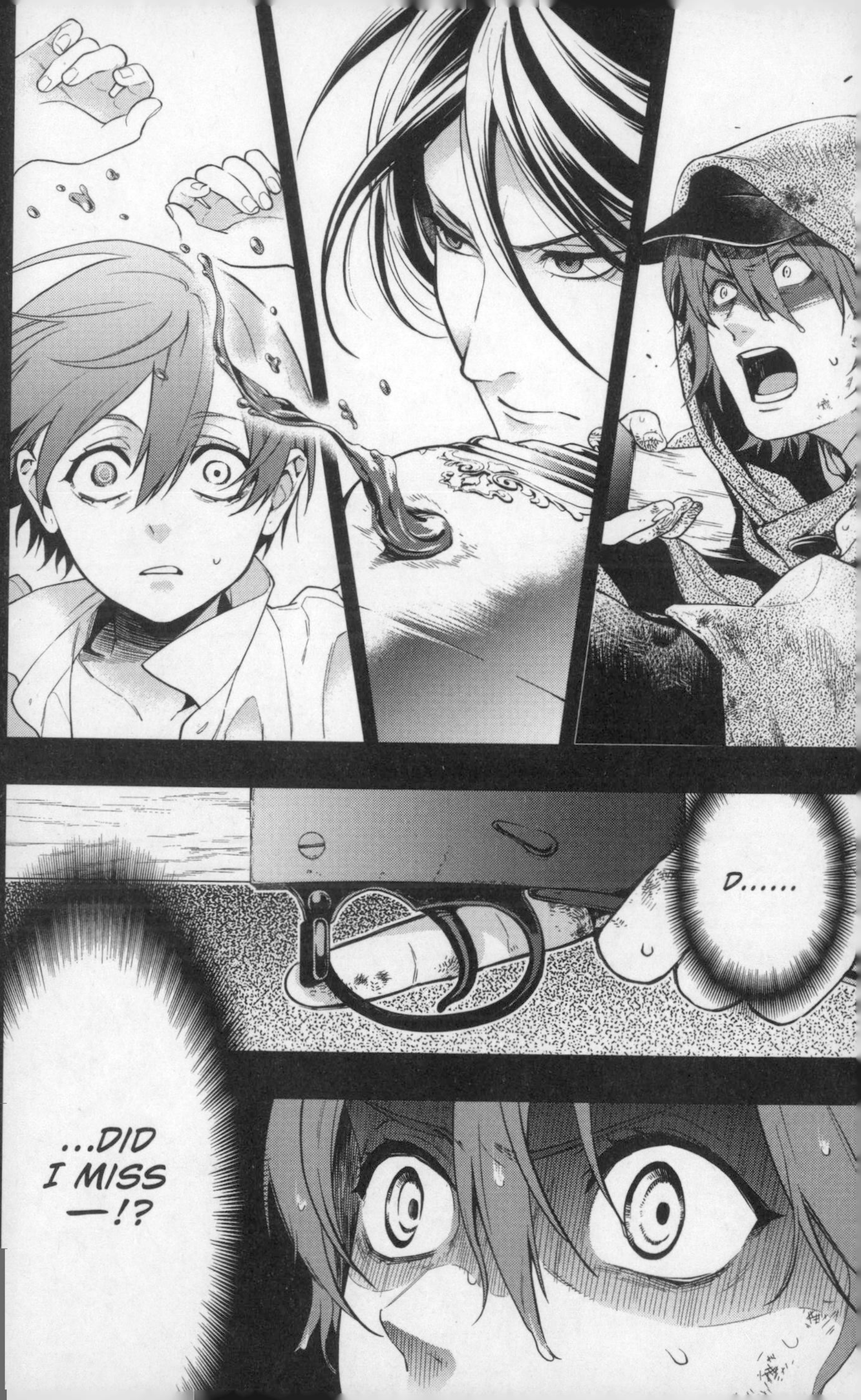
D......
...DID I MISS—!?

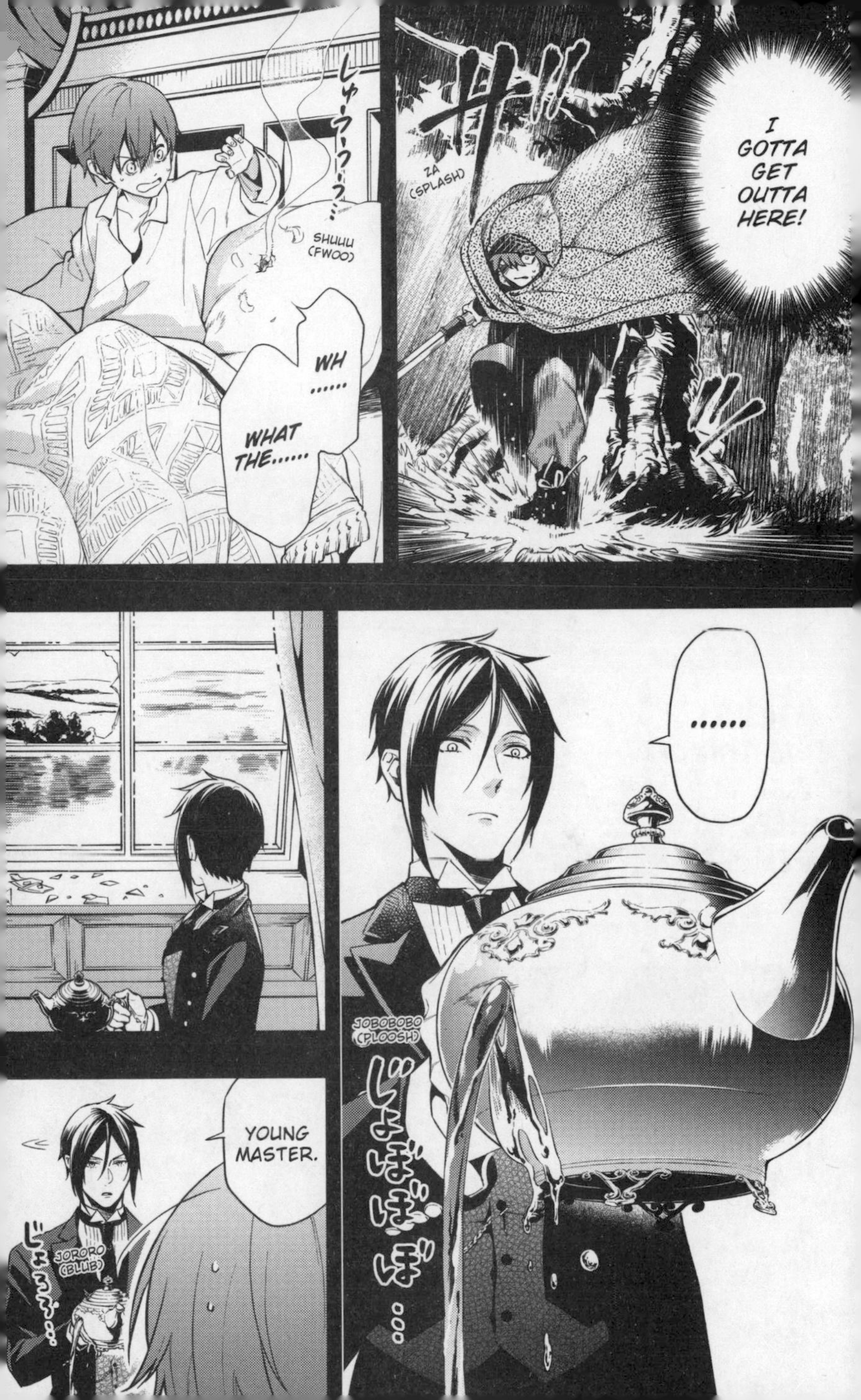
ZA (SPLASH)
I GOTTA GET OUTTA HERE!
SHUUU (FWOO)
WH......
WHAT THE......
......
JOBOBOBO (PLOOSH)
YOUNG MASTER.
JORORO (BLUB)

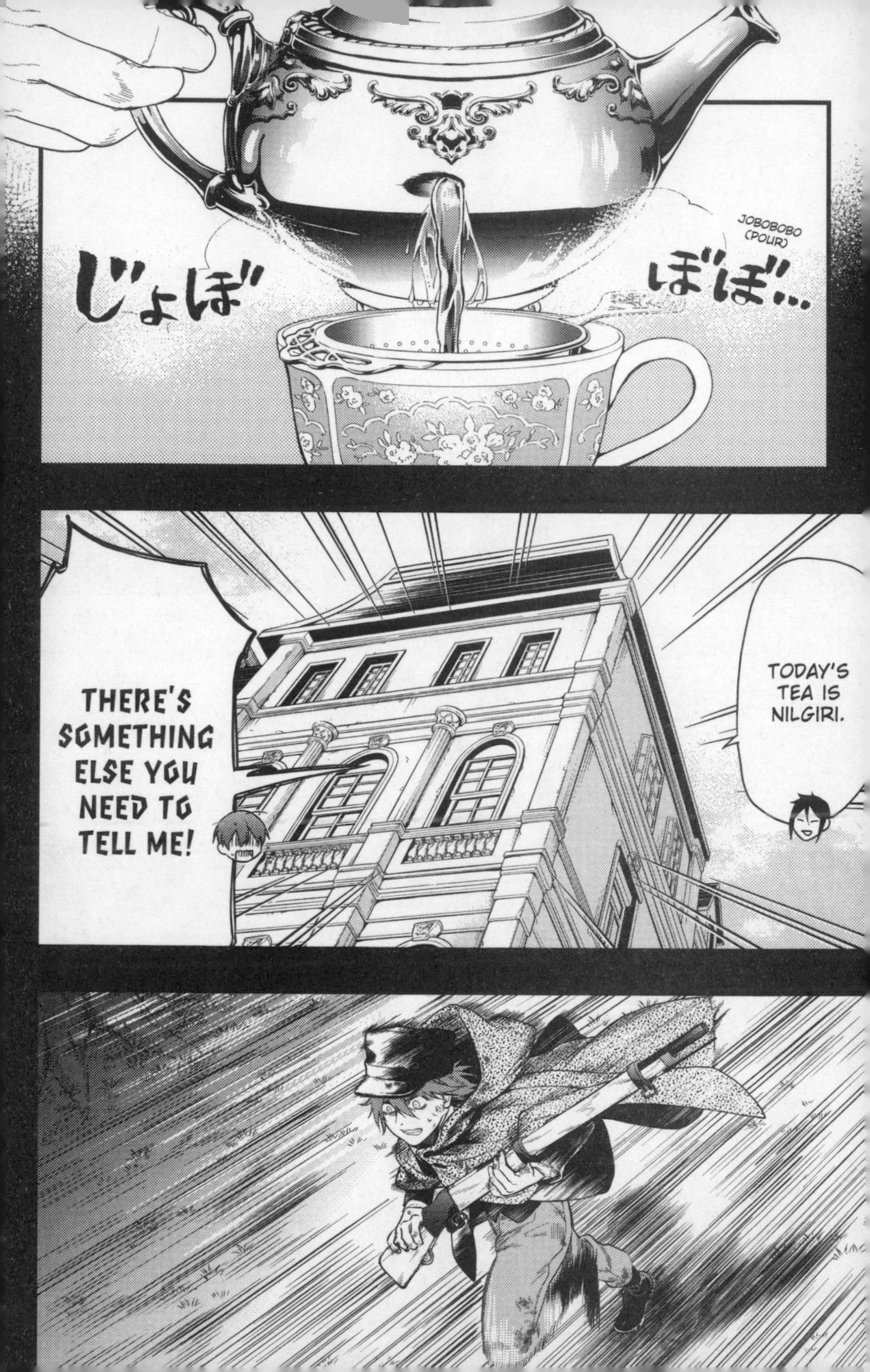
じょぼ
ぼぼ…
JOBOBOBO (POUR)
TODAY'S TEA IS NILGIRI.
THERE'S SOMETHING ELSE YOU NEED TO TELL ME!

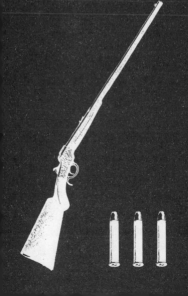

Black Butler

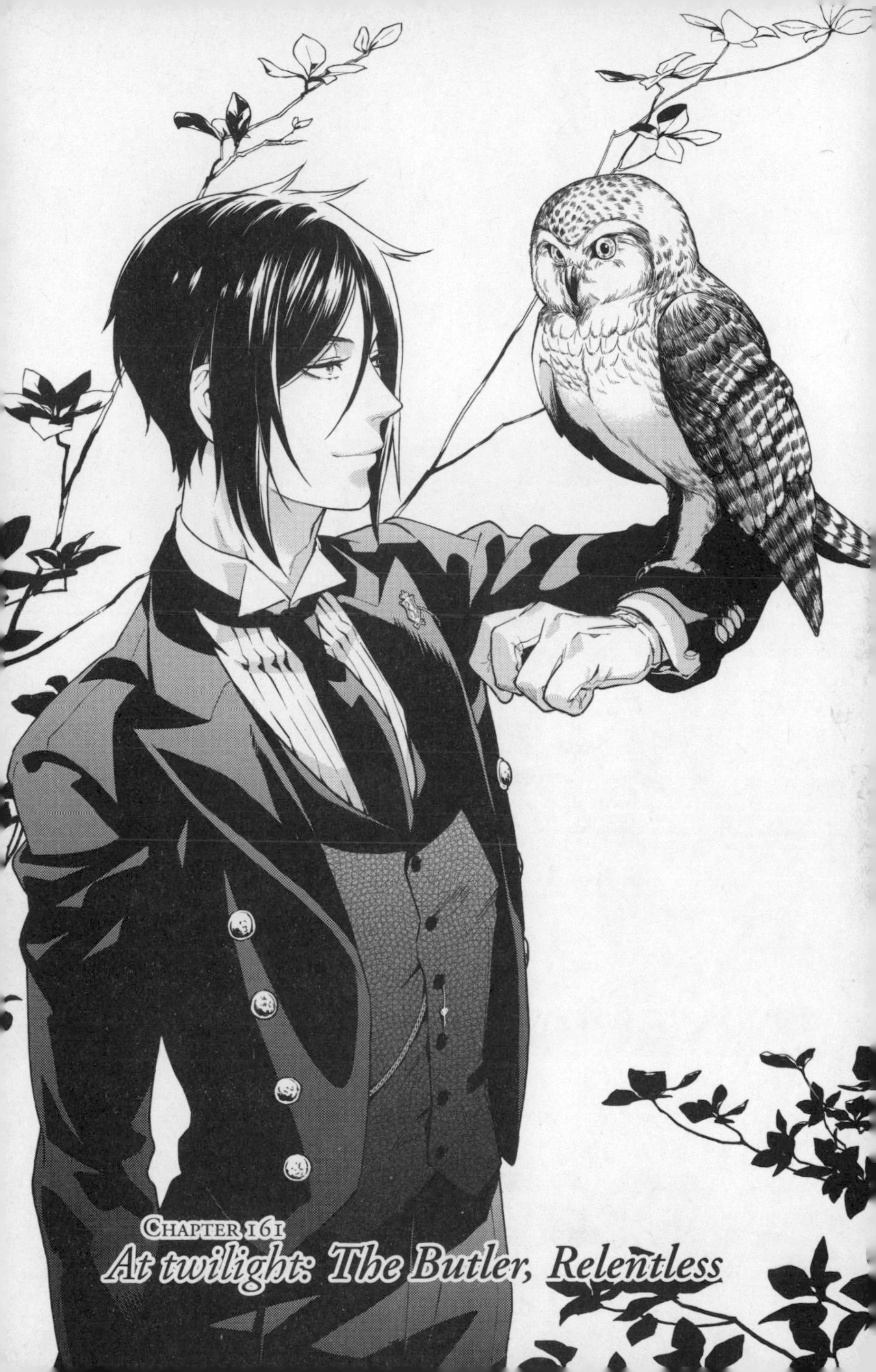
Chapter 161
At twilight: The Butler, Relentless

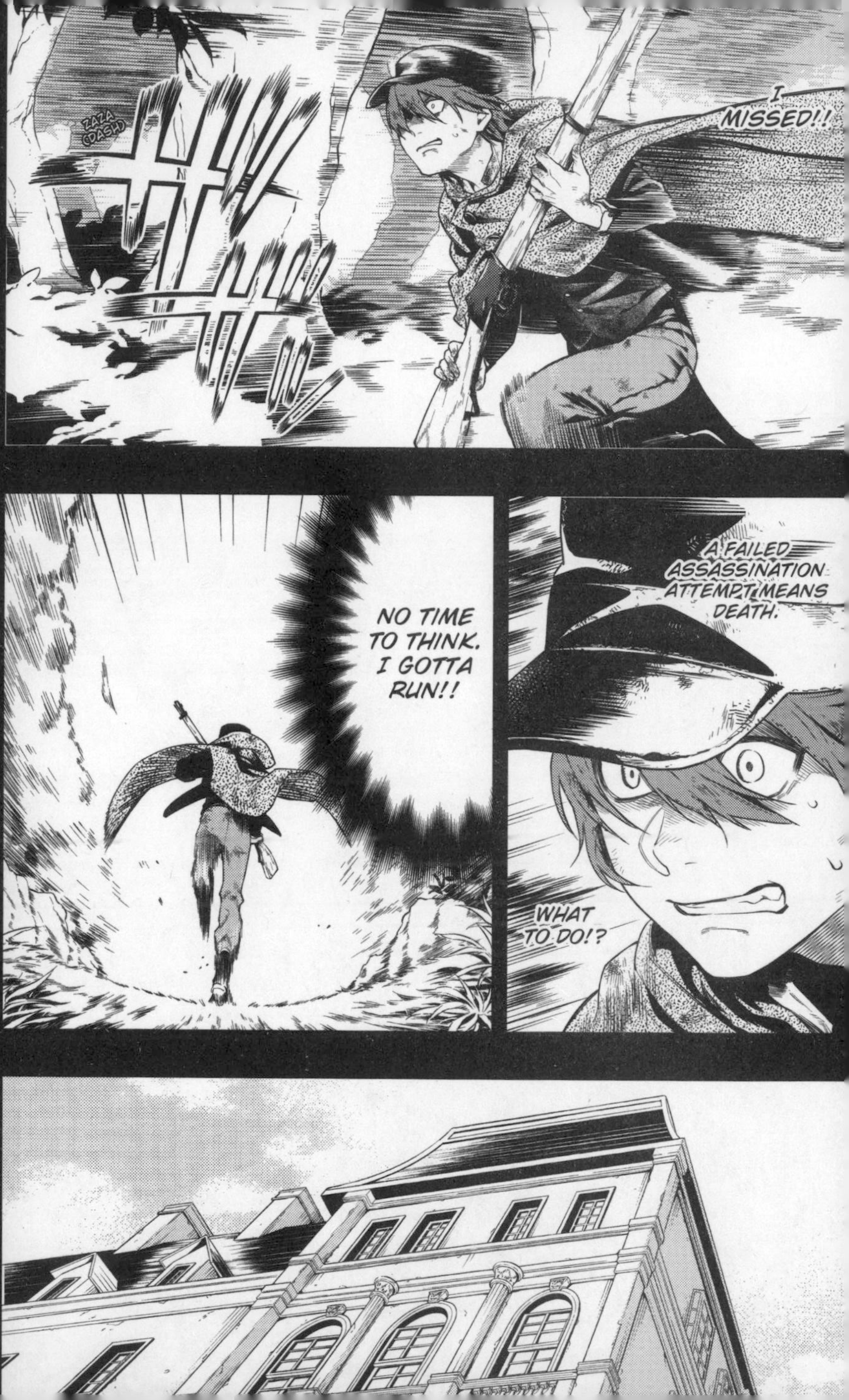
I MISSED!!
ZAZA (DASH)
A FAILED ASSASSINATION ATTEMPT MEANS DEATH.
WHAT TO DO!?
NO TIME TO THINK. I GOTTA RUN!!

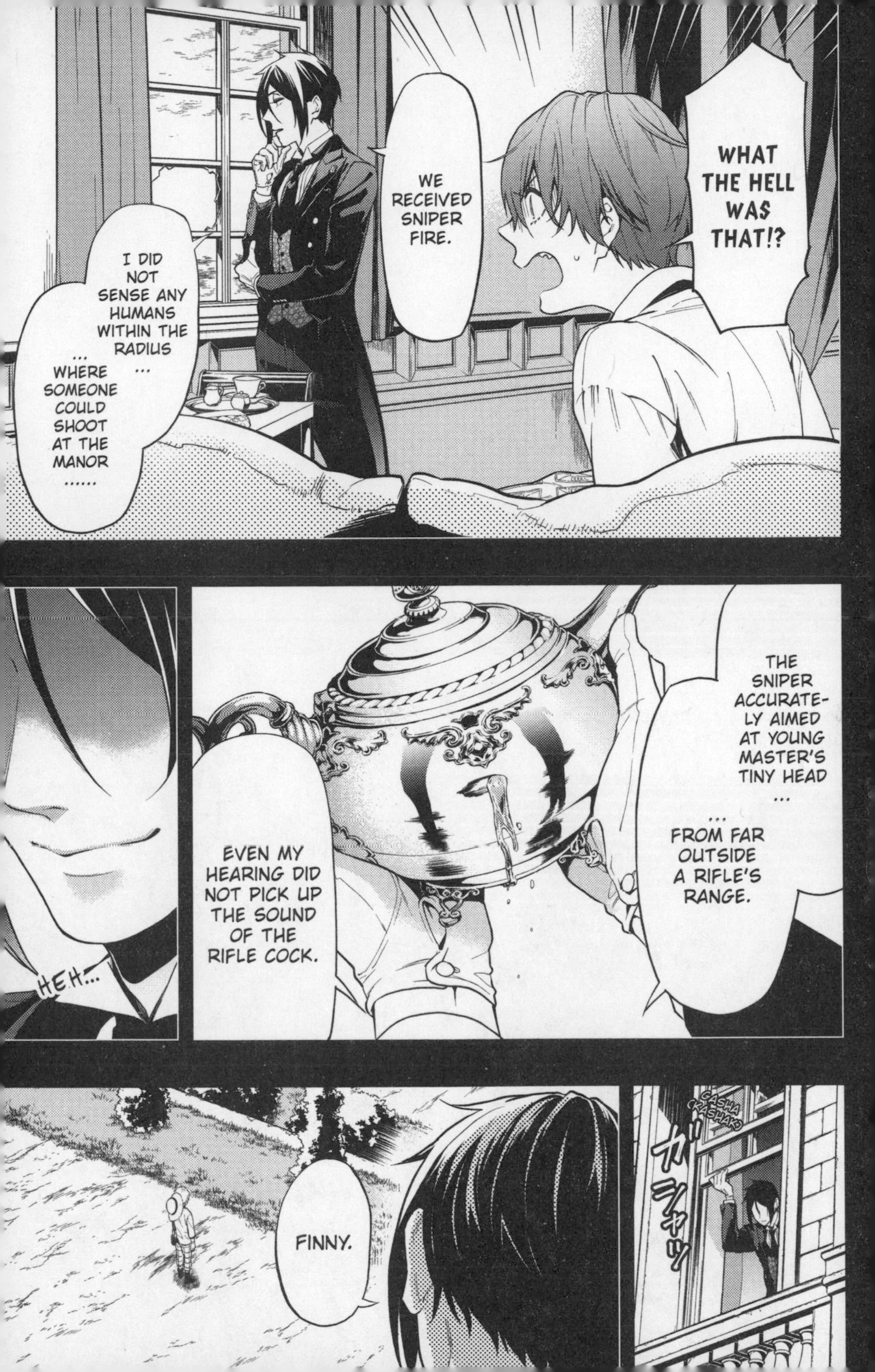
WHAT THE HELL WAS THAT!?
WE RECEIVED SNIPER FIRE.
I DID NOT SENSE ANY HUMANS WITHIN THE RADIUS ... WHERE SOMEONE COULD SHOOT AT THE MANOR ......
THE SNIPER ACCURATELY AIMED AT YOUNG MASTER'S TINY HEAD ... FROM FAR OUTSIDE A RIFLE'S RANGE.
EVEN MY HEARING DID NOT PICK UP THE SOUND OF THE RIFLE COCK.
HEH...
GASHA KASHAN
ガシャッ
FINNY.

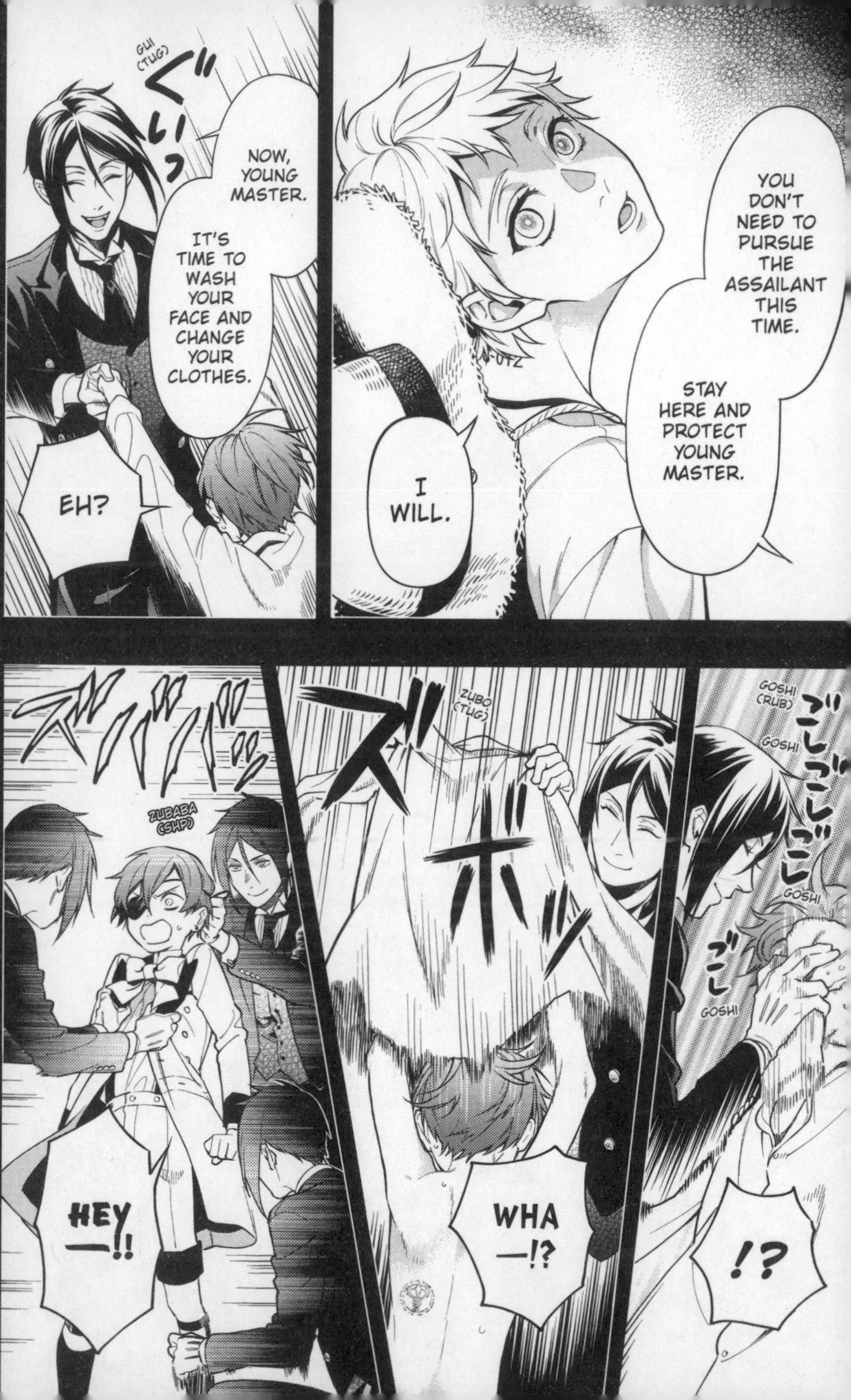
YOU DON'T NEED TO PURSUE THE ASSAILANT THIS TIME.
STAY HERE AND PROTECT YOUNG MASTER.
I WILL.
GUI (TUG)
NOW, YOUNG MASTER.
IT'S TIME TO WASH YOUR FACE AND CHANGE YOUR CLOTHES.
EH?
GOSHI (RUB)
GOSHI
GOSHI
GOSHI
!?
ZUBO (TUG)
WHA—!?
ZUBABA (SHP)
HEY—!!

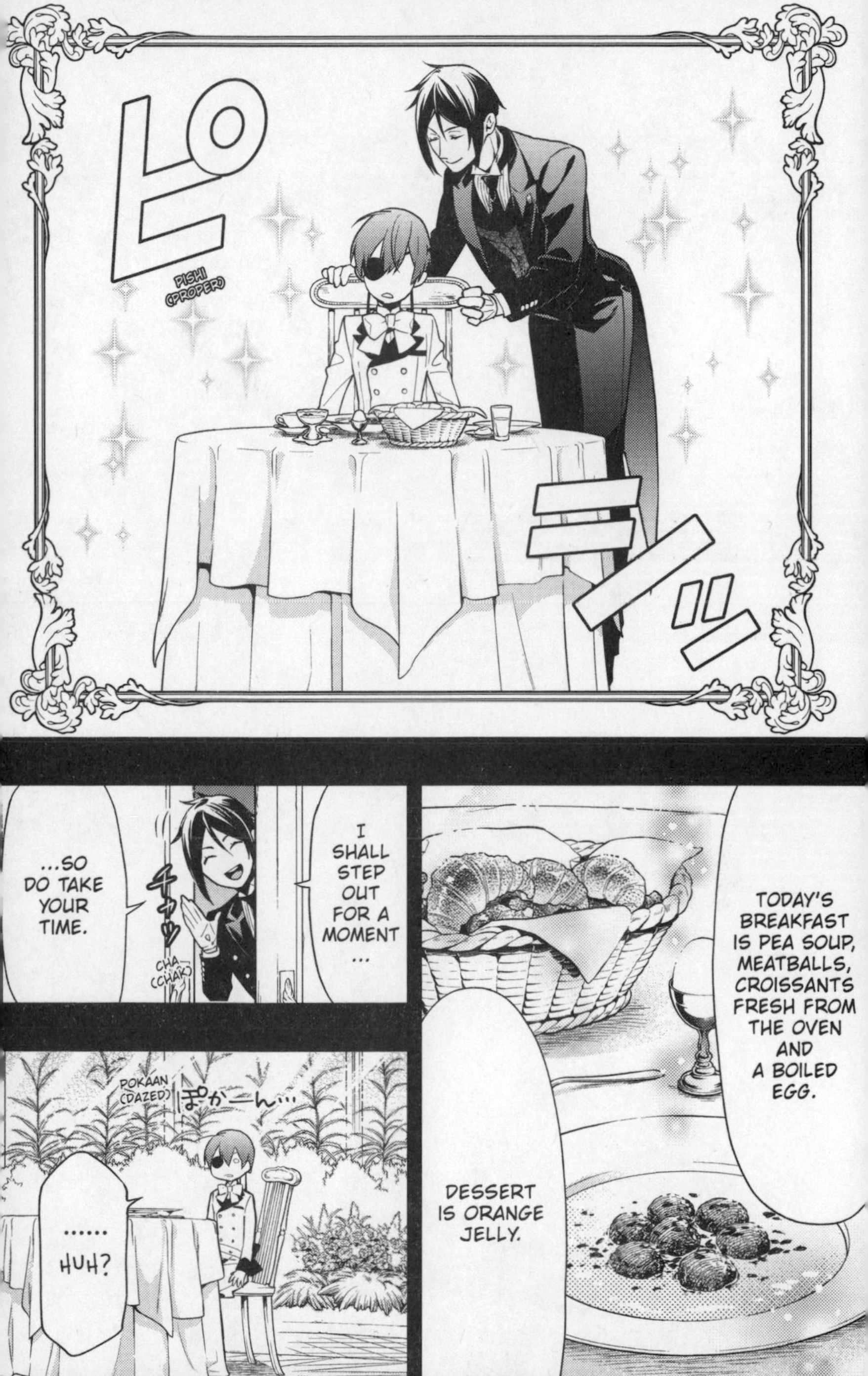
PISHI (PROPER)
TODAY'S BREAKFAST IS PEA SOUP, MEATBALLS, CROISSANTS FRESH FROM THE OVEN AND A BOILED EGG.
DESSERT IS ORANGE JELLY.
I SHALL STEP OUT FOR A MOMENT...
...SO DO TAKE YOUR TIME.
CHA (CHAK)
POKAAN (DAZED)
ぽかーん…
......HUH?

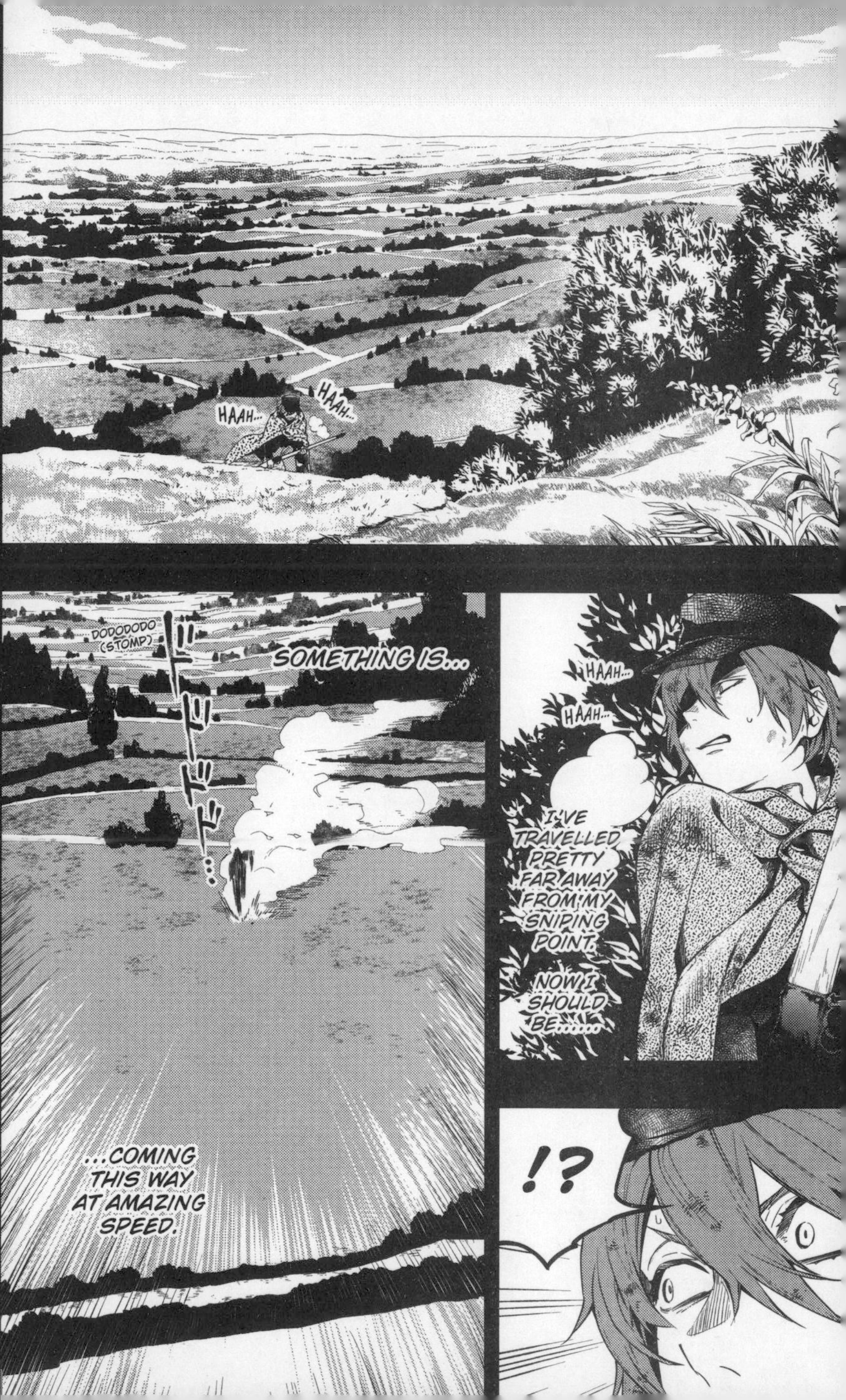
HAAH...
HAAH...
HAAH...
HAAH...
I'VE TRAVELLED PRETTY FAR AWAY FROM MY SNIPING POINT.
NOW I SHOULD BE......
!?
DODODODO (STOMP)
SOMETHING IS...
...COMING THIS WAY AT AMAZING SPEED.

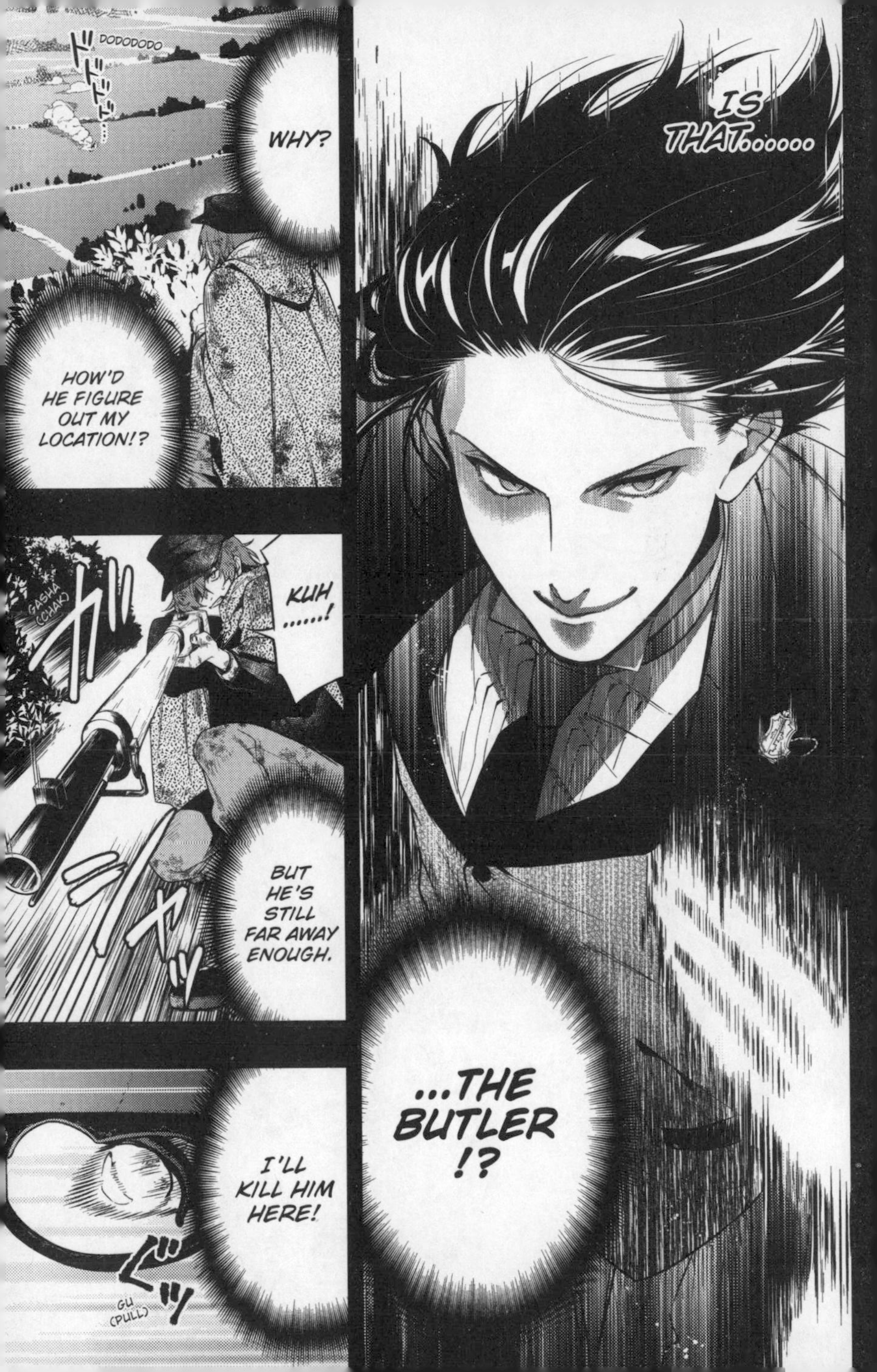

IS THAT......
...THE BUTLER!?
DODODODO
WHY?
HOW'D HE FIGURE OUT MY LOCATION!?
KUH ......!
GASHA (CHAK)
BUT HE'S STILL FAR AWAY ENOUGH.
I'LL KILL HIM HERE!
GU (PULL)

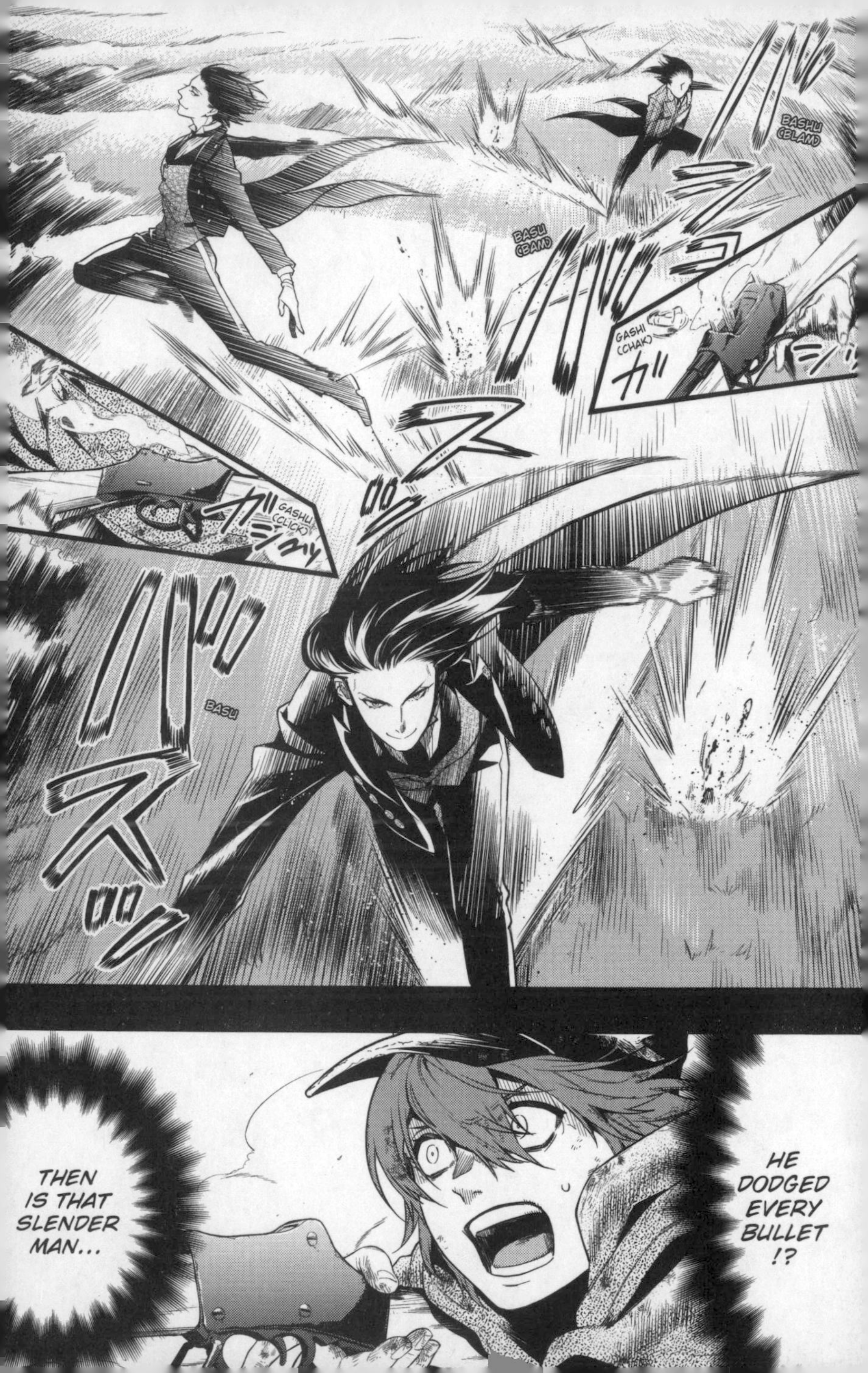
BASHU (BLAM)
BASU (BAM)
GASHI (CHAK)
GASHU (CLICK)
BASU
HE DODGED EVERY BULLET !?
THEN IS THAT SLENDER MAN...

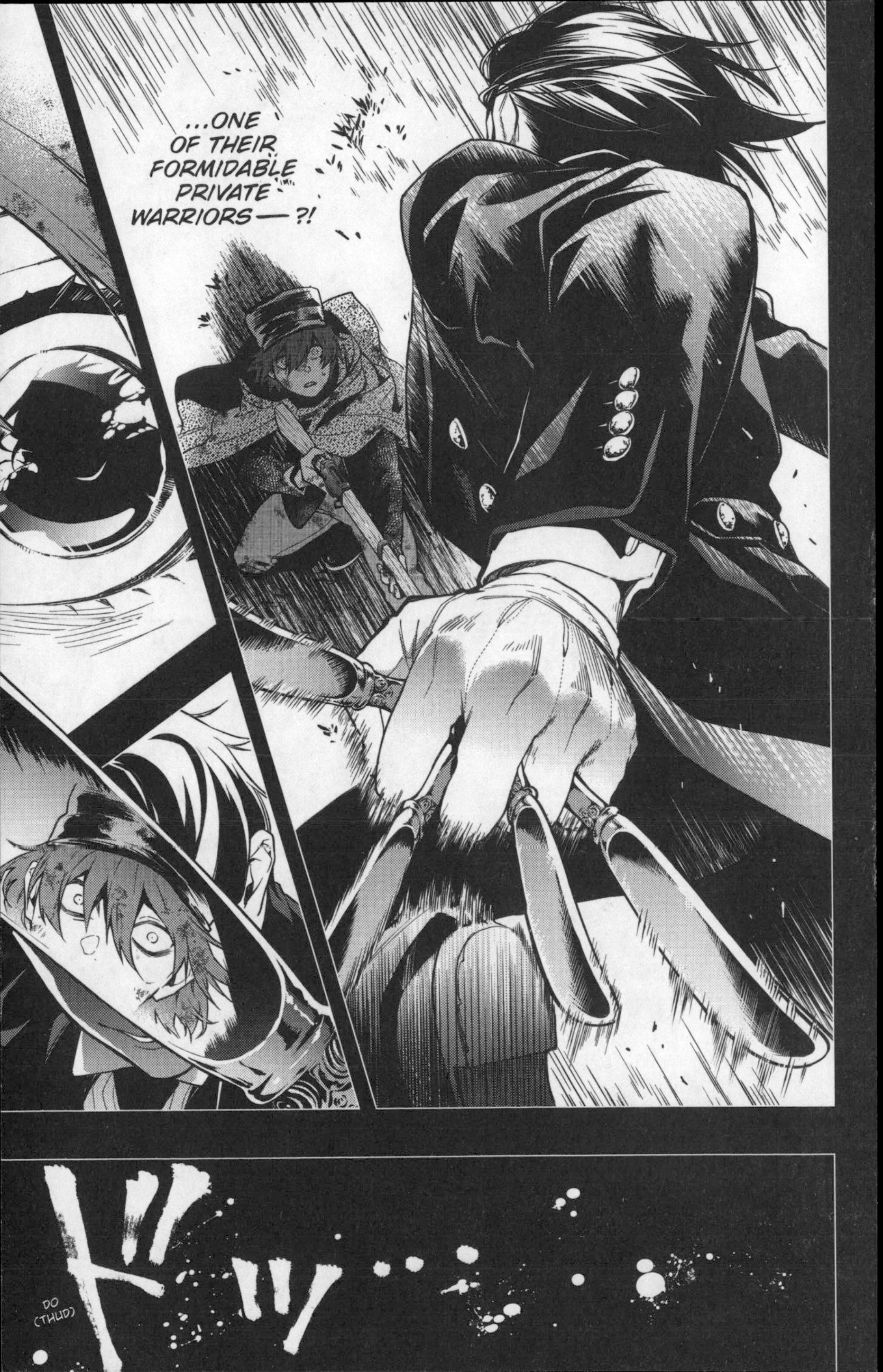
...ONE OF THEIR FORMIDABLE PRIVATE WARRIORS—?!
DO (THUD)

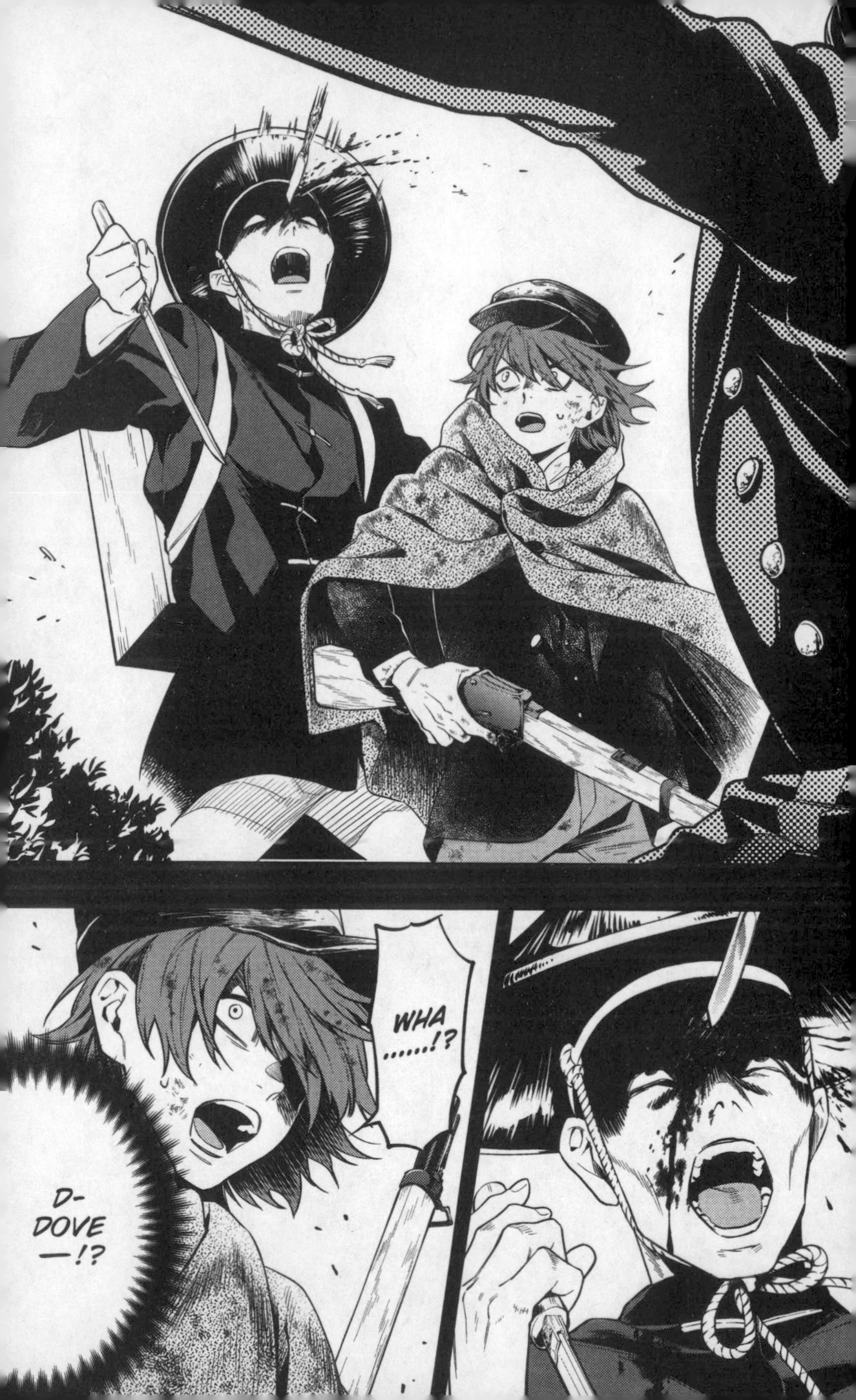
WHA ......!?
D-DOVE —!?

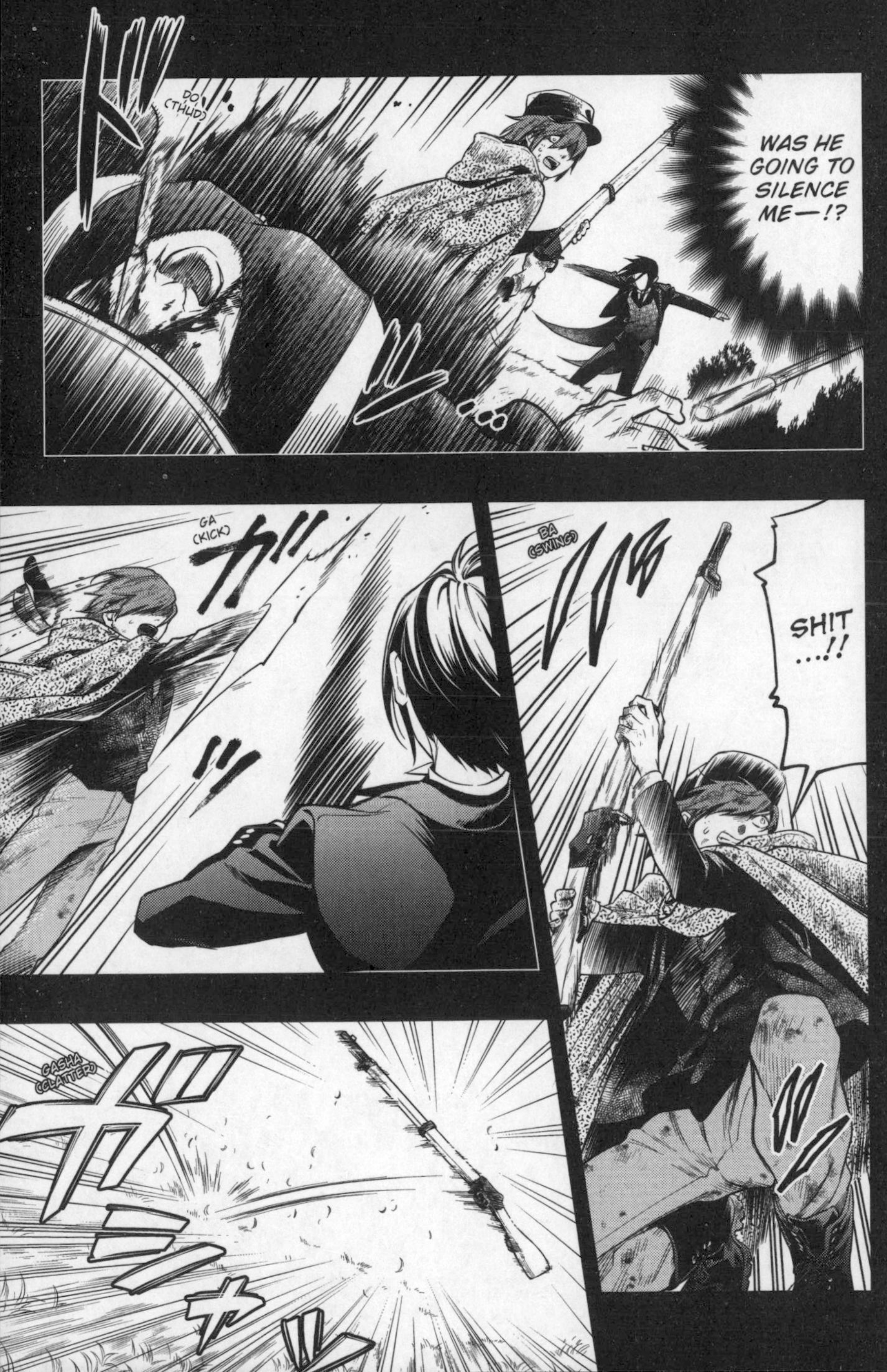
DO (THUD)
WAS HE GOING TO SILENCE ME—!?
BA (SWING)
SHIT ...!!
GA (KICK)
GASHA (CLATTER)

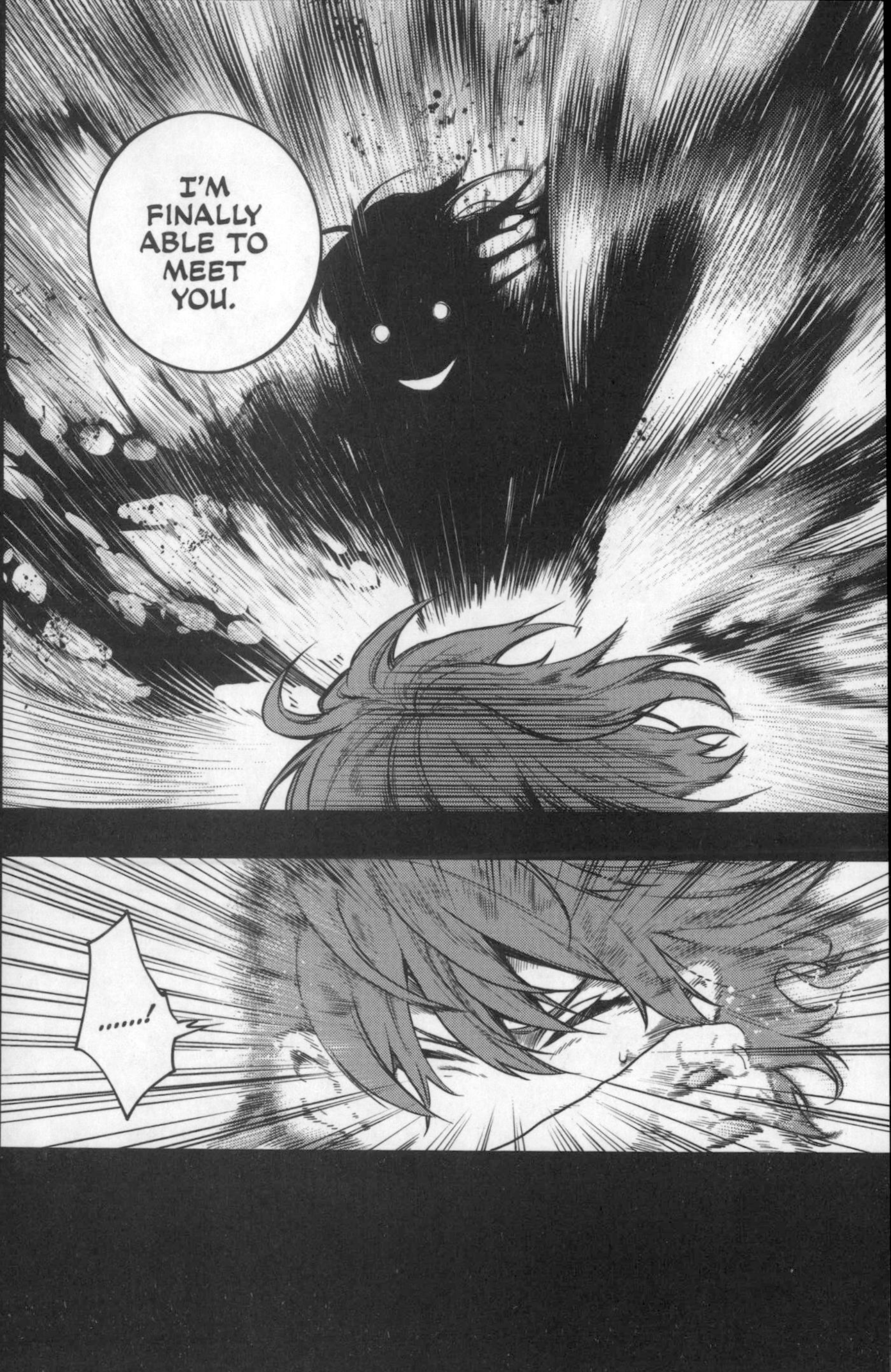
I'M FINALLY ABLE TO MEET YOU.
......!

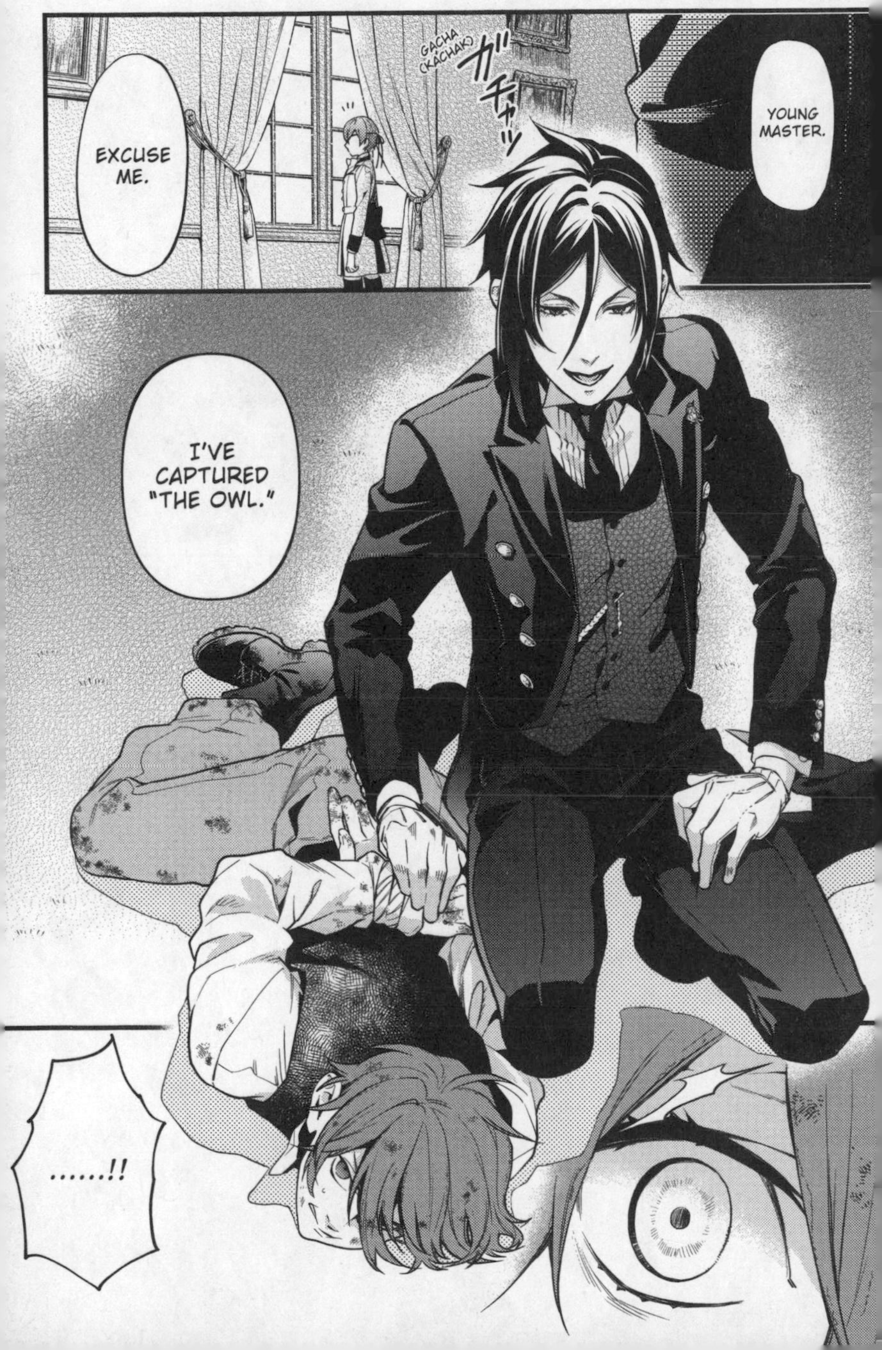
YOUNG MASTER.
GACHA (KACHAK)
ガチャッ
EXCUSE ME.
I'VE CAPTURED "THE OWL."
......!!

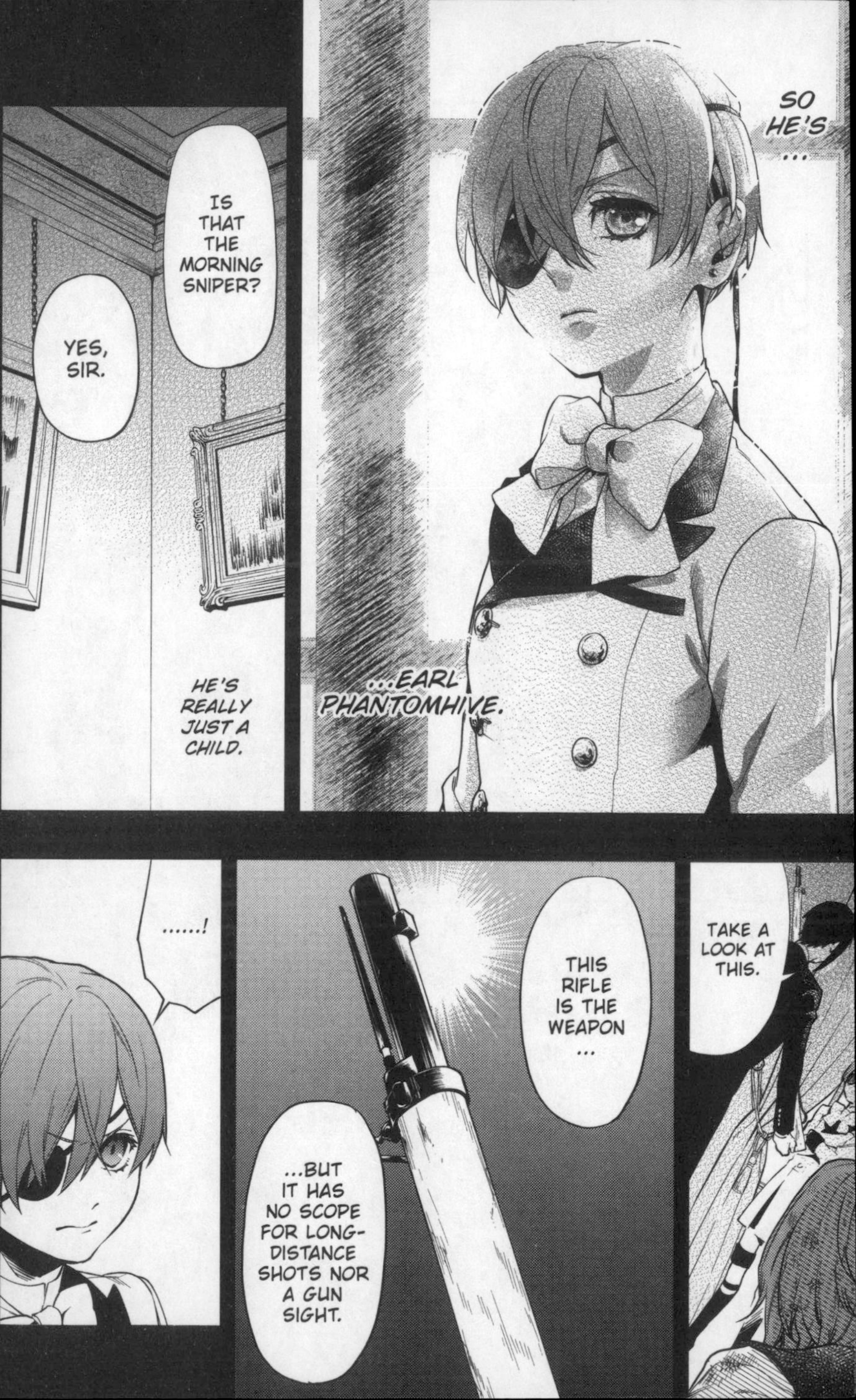

SO HE'S ...
...EARL PHANTOMHIVE.
IS THAT THE MORNING SNIPER?
YES, SIR.
HE'S REALLY JUST A CHILD.
TAKE A LOOK AT THIS.
THIS RIFLE IS THE WEAPON ...
...BUT IT HAS NO SCOPE FOR LONG-DISTANCE SHOTS NOR A GUN SIGHT.
......!

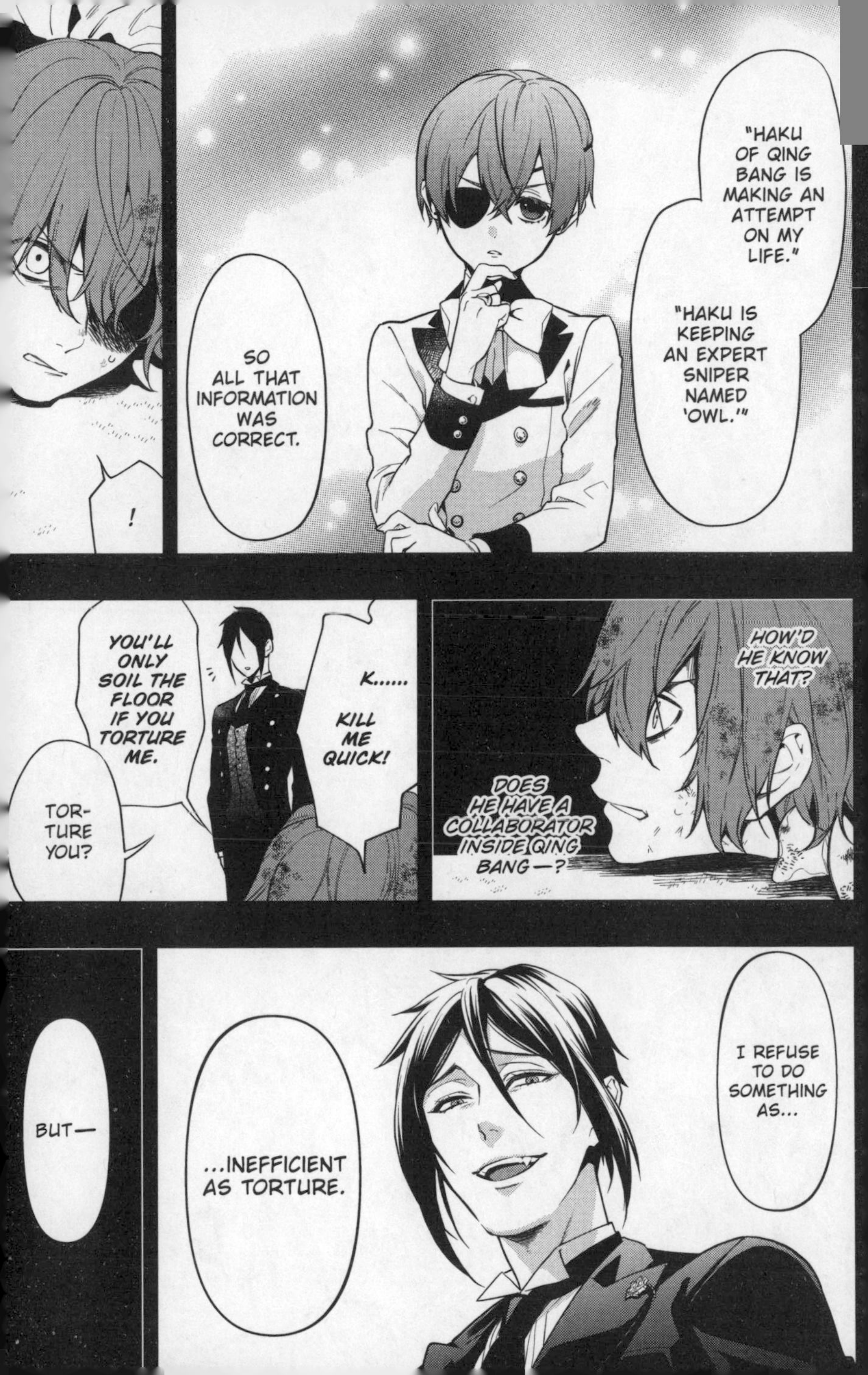
"HAKU OF QING BANG IS MAKING AN ATTEMPT ON MY LIFE."
"HAKU IS KEEPING AN EXPERT SNIPER NAMED 'OWL.'"
SO ALL THAT INFORMATION WAS CORRECT.
!
HOW'D HE KNOW THAT?
DOES HE HAVE A COLLABORATOR INSIDE QING BANG—?
K......
KILL ME QUICK!
YOU'LL ONLY SOIL THE FLOOR IF YOU TORTURE ME.
TOR-TURE YOU?
I REFUSE TO DO SOMETHING AS...
...INEFFICIENT AS TORTURE.
BUT—

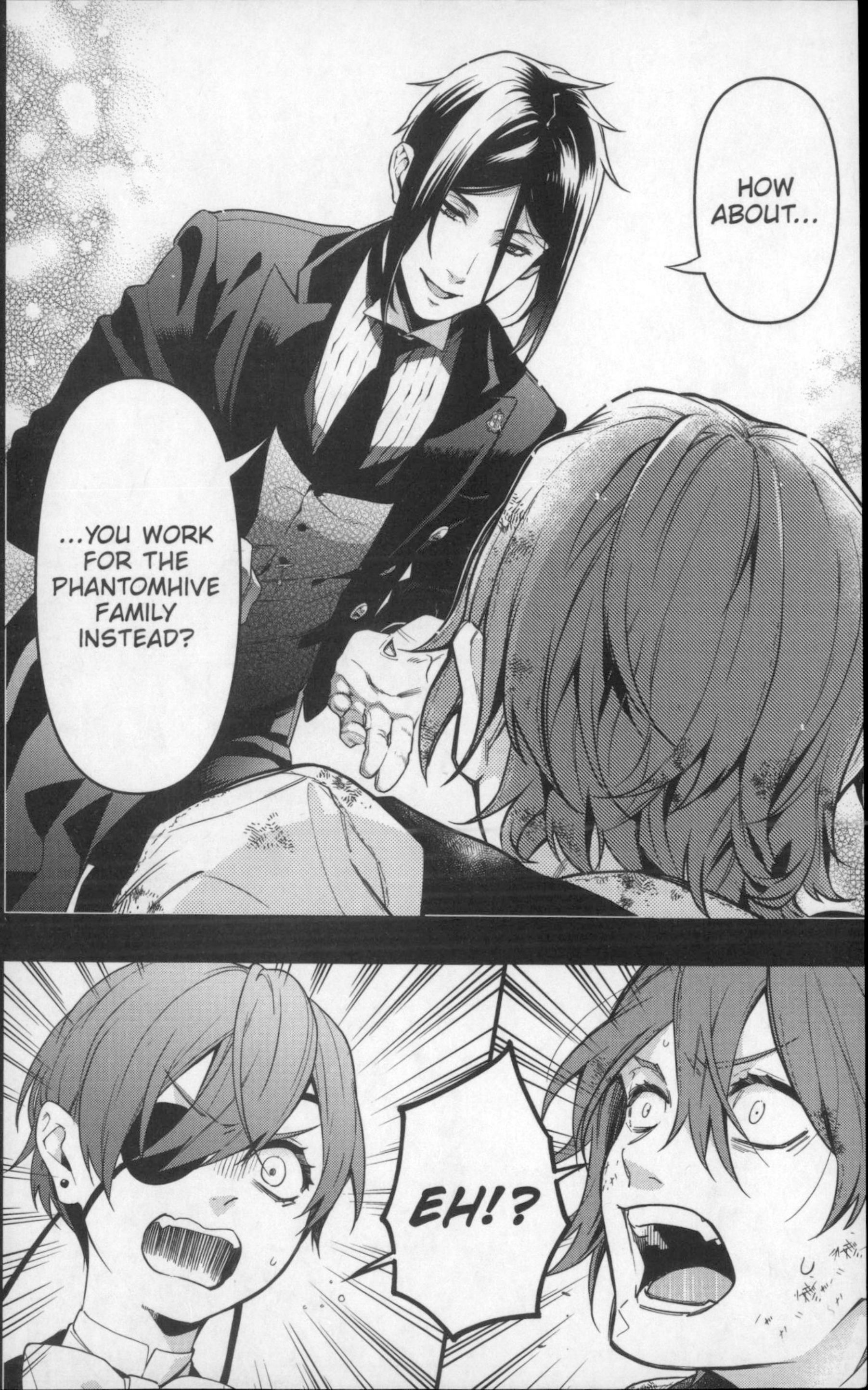
HOW ABOUT...
...YOU WORK FOR THE PHANTOMHIVE FAMILY INSTEAD?
EH!?

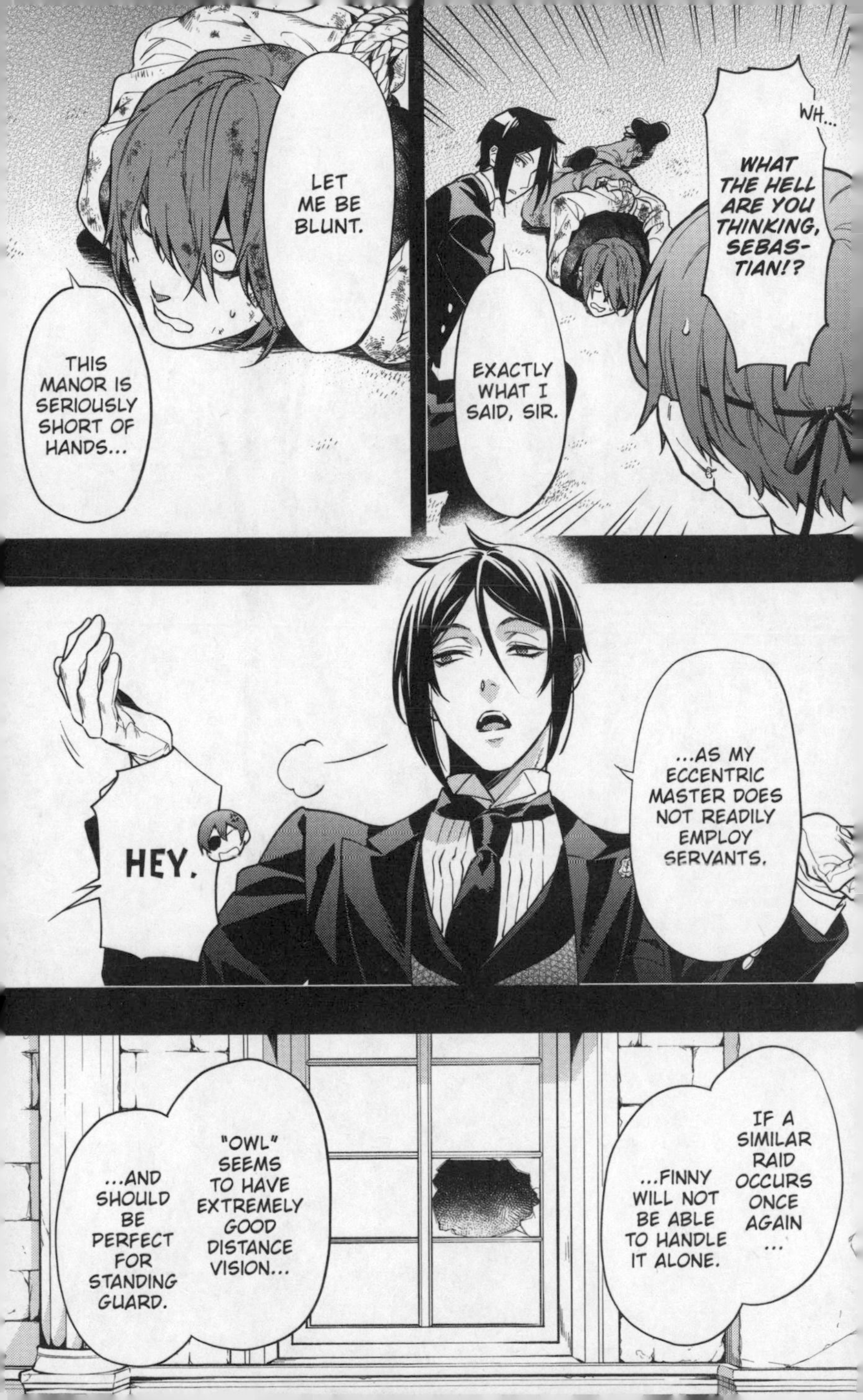
WH...
WHAT THE HELL ARE YOU THINKING, SEBASTIAN!?
EXACTLY WHAT I SAID, SIR.
LET ME BE BLUNT.
THIS MANOR IS SERIOUSLY SHORT OF HANDS...
...AS MY ECCENTRIC MASTER DOES NOT READILY EMPLOY SERVANTS.
HEY.
IF A SIMILAR RAID OCCURS ONCE AGAIN ...
...FINNY WILL NOT BE ABLE TO HANDLE IT ALONE.
"OWL" SEEMS TO HAVE EXTREMELY GOOD DISTANCE VISION...
...AND SHOULD BE PERFECT FOR STANDING GUARD.

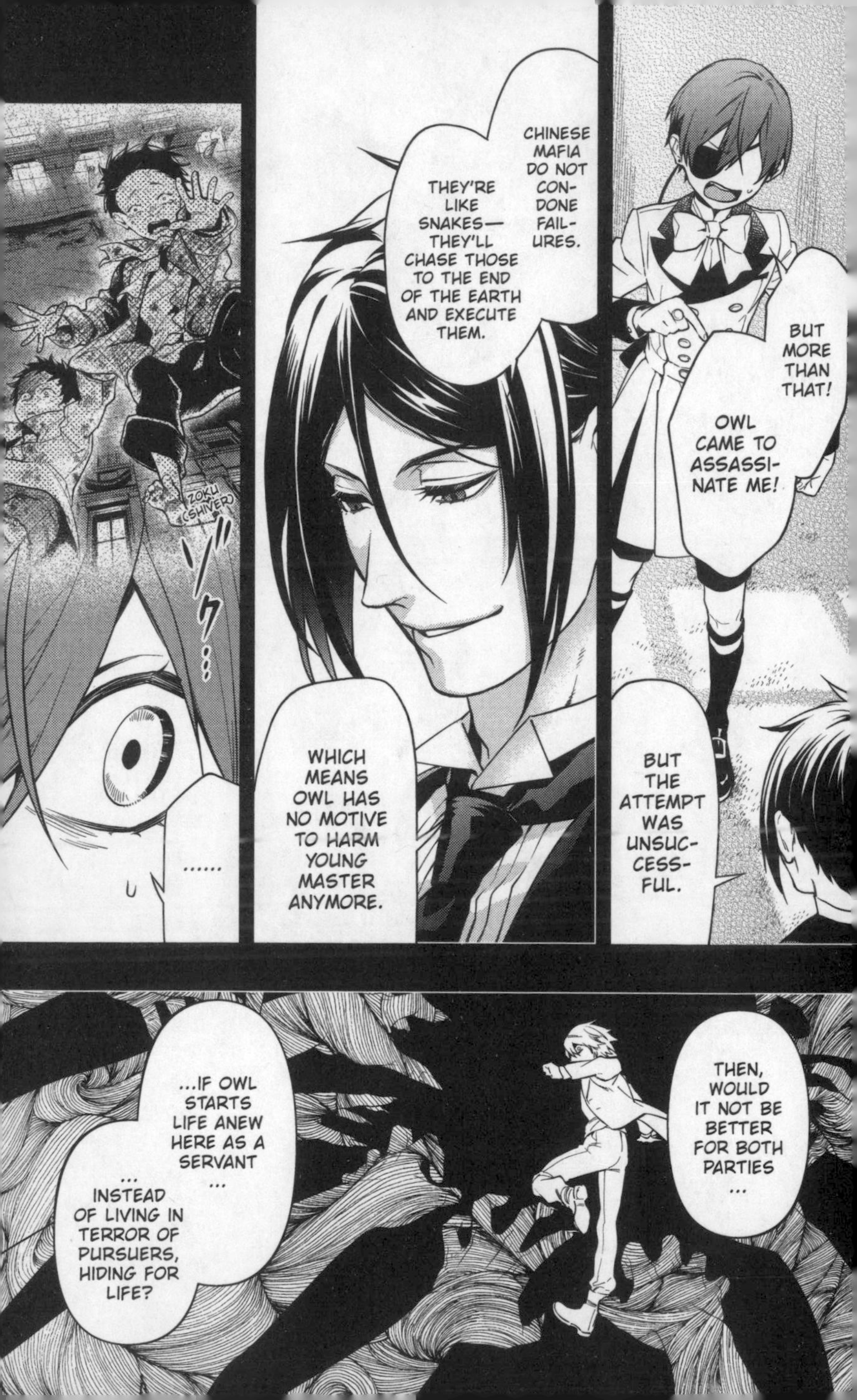
BUT MORE THAN THAT!
OWL CAME TO ASSASSINATE ME!
BUT THE ATTEMPT WAS UNSUCCESSFUL.
CHINESE MAFIA DO NOT CONDONE FAILURES.
THEY'RE LIKE SNAKES—THEY'LL CHASE THOSE TO THE END OF THE EARTH AND EXECUTE THEM.
WHICH MEANS OWL HAS NO MOTIVE TO HARM YOUNG MASTER ANYMORE.
ZOKU (SHIVER)
......
THEN, WOULD IT NOT BE BETTER FOR BOTH PARTIES ...
...IF OWL STARTS LIFE ANEW HERE AS A SERVANT ...
... INSTEAD OF LIVING IN TERROR OF PURSUERS, HIDING FOR LIFE?

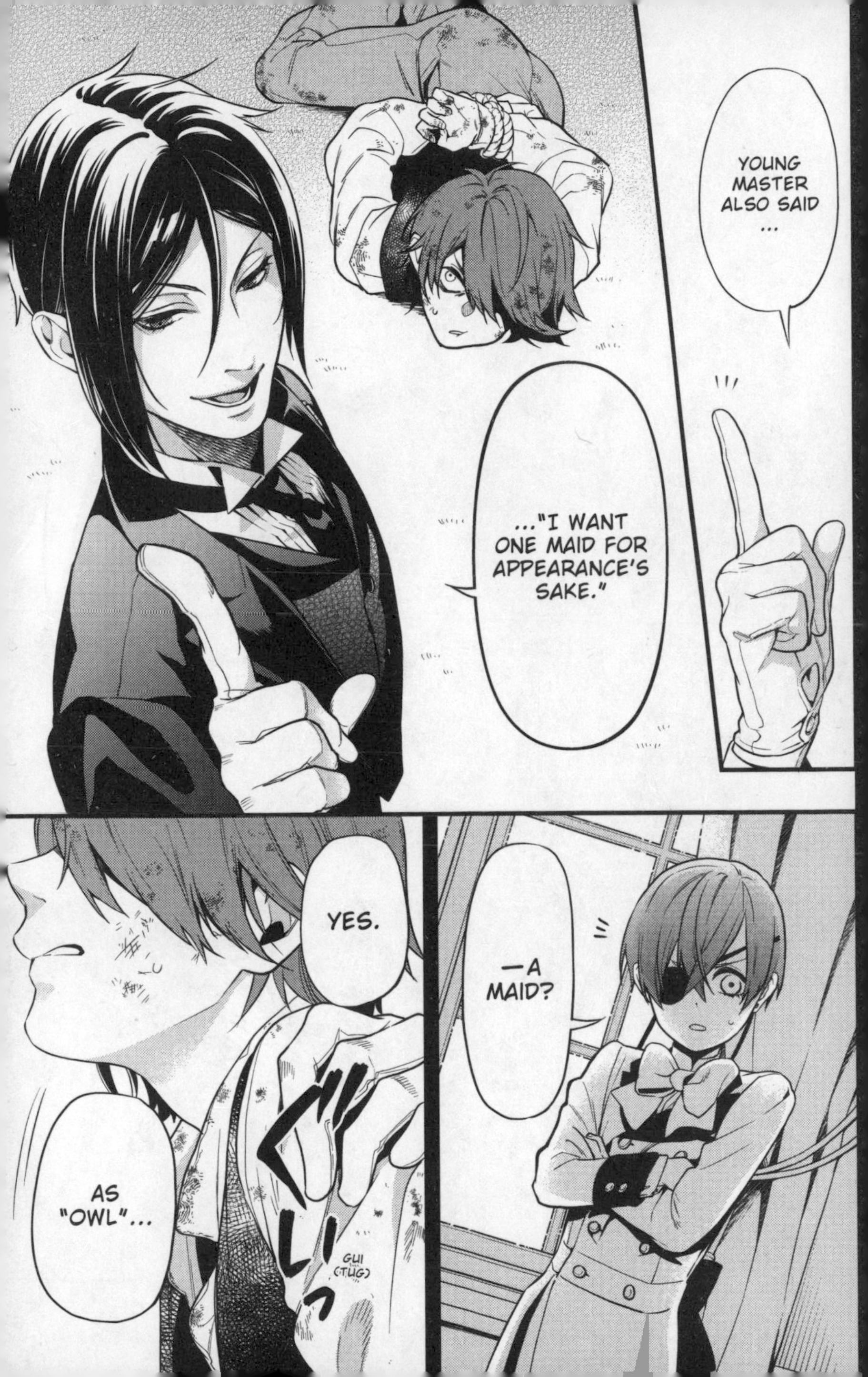
YOUNG MASTER ALSO SAID ...
..."I WANT ONE MAID FOR APPEARANCE'S SAKE."
—A MAID?
YES.
AS "OWL"...
GUI (TUG)

Black Butler

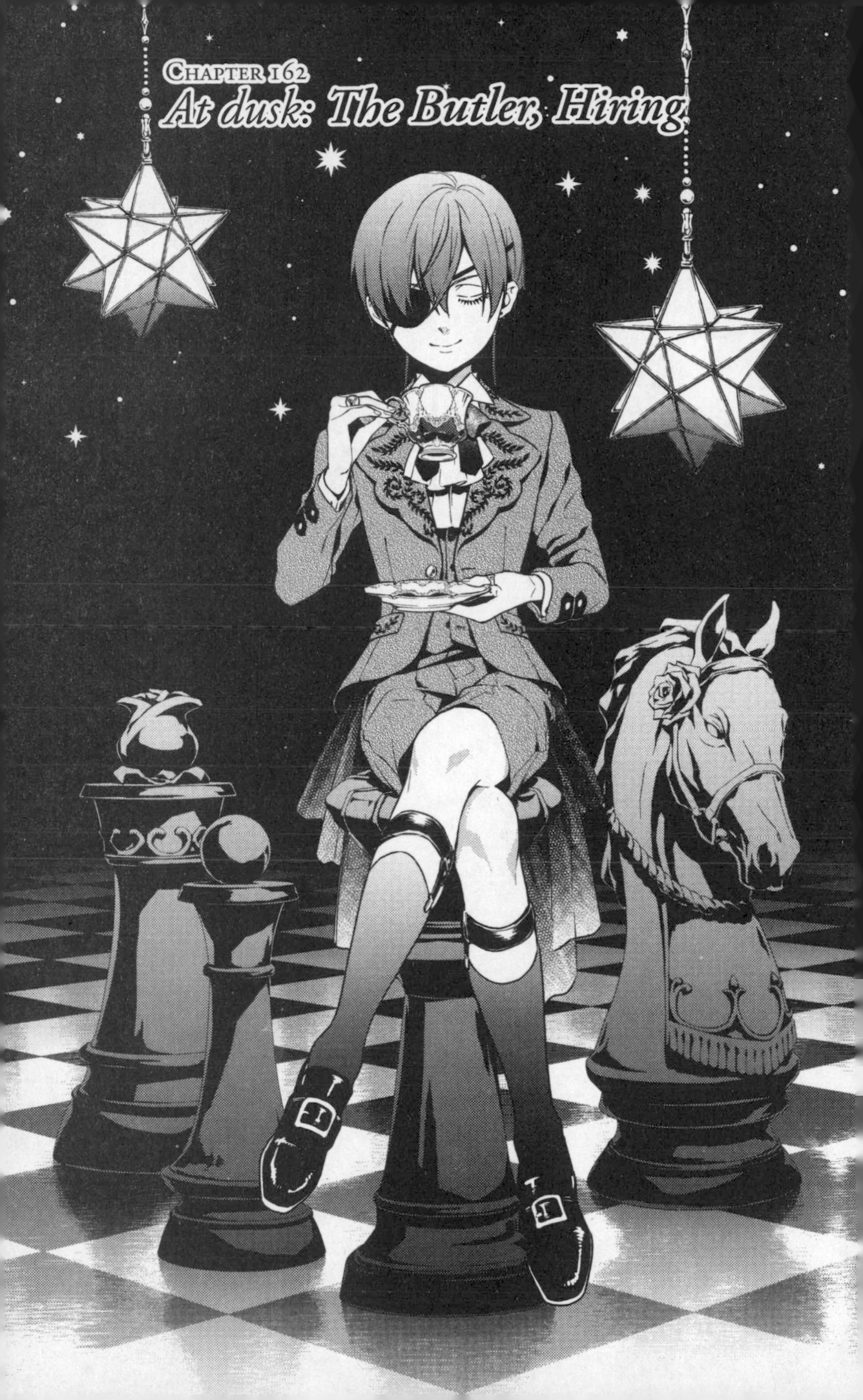
Chapter 162
At dusk: The Butler, Hiring

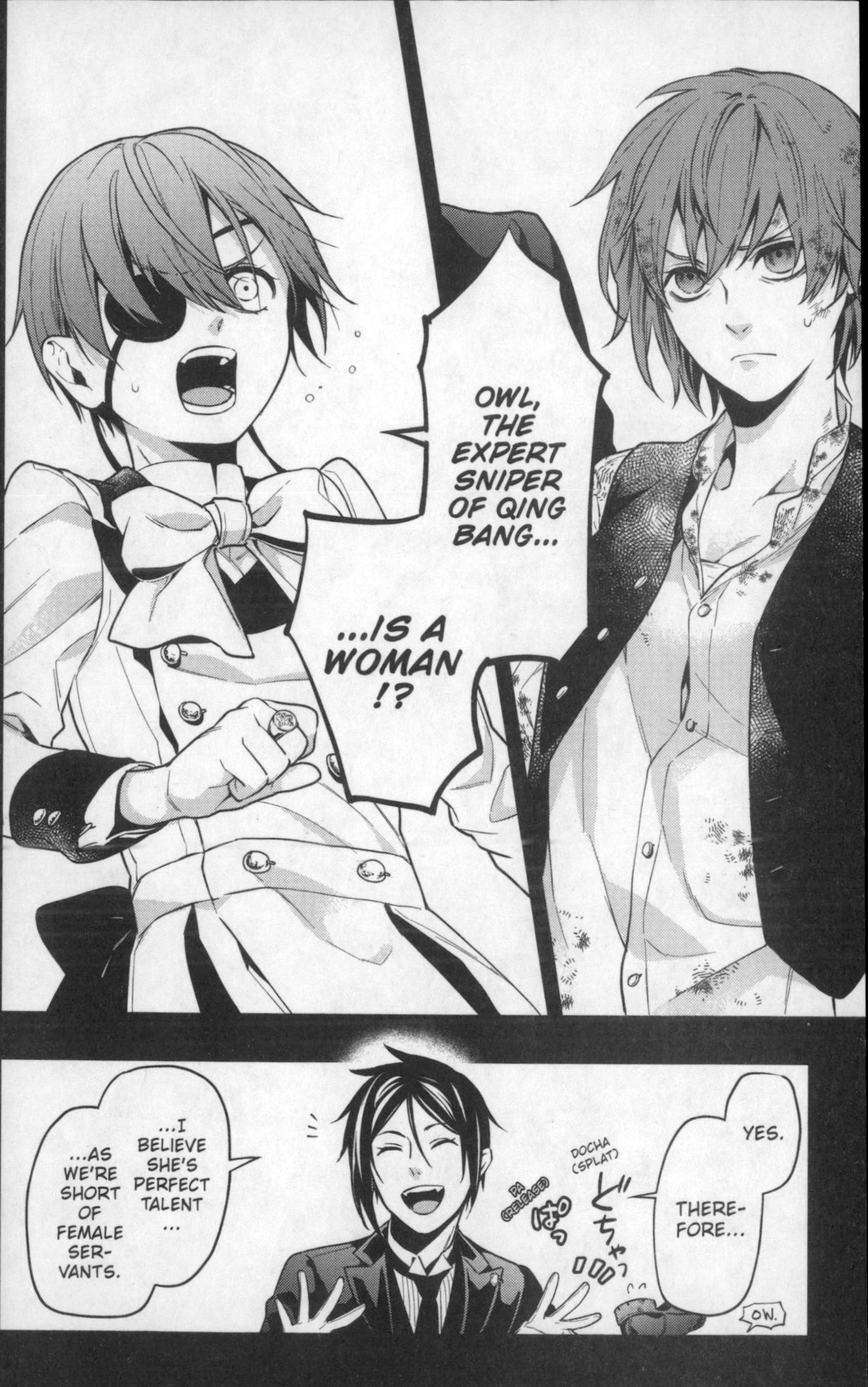
OWL, THE EXPERT SNIPER OF QING BANG...
...IS A WOMAN!?
YES.
THEREFORE...
DOCHA (SPLAT)
どちゃっ
PA (RELEASE)
ぱっ
OW.
...I BELIEVE SHE'S PERFECT TALENT...
...AS WE'RE SHORT OF FEMALE SER-VANTS.

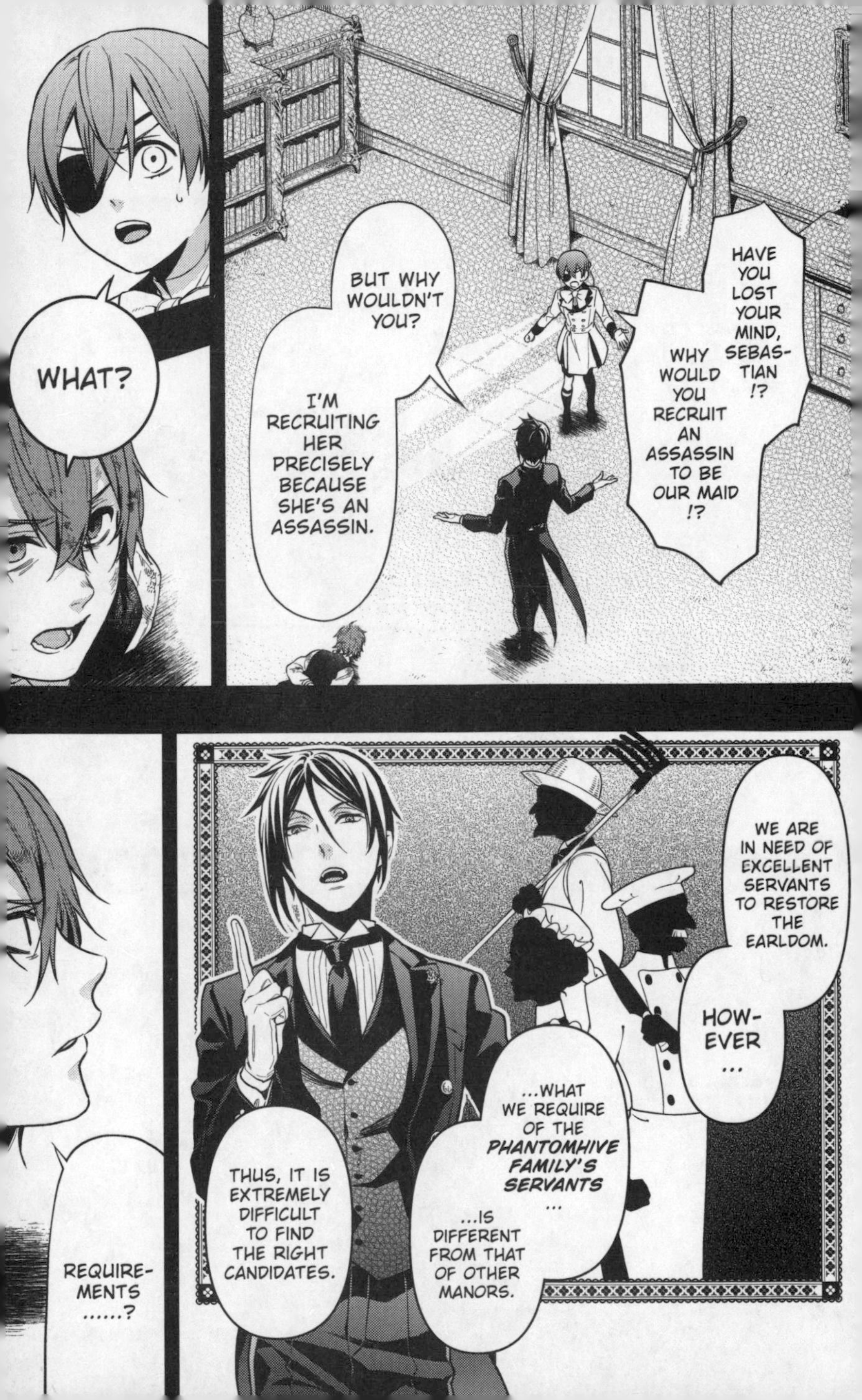
HAVE YOU LOST YOUR MIND, SEBASTIAN!?
WHY WOULD YOU RECRUIT AN ASSASSIN TO BE OUR MAID!?
BUT WHY WOULDN'T YOU?
I'M RECRUITING HER PRECISELY BECAUSE SHE'S AN ASSASSIN.
WHAT?
WE ARE IN NEED OF EXCELLENT SERVANTS TO RESTORE THE EARLDOM.
HOWEVER...
...WHAT WE REQUIRE OF THE *PHANTOMHIVE FAMILY'S SERVANTS*...
...IS DIFFERENT FROM THAT OF OTHER MANORS.
THUS, IT IS EXTREMELY DIFFICULT TO FIND THE RIGHT CANDIDATES.
REQUIREMENTS......?

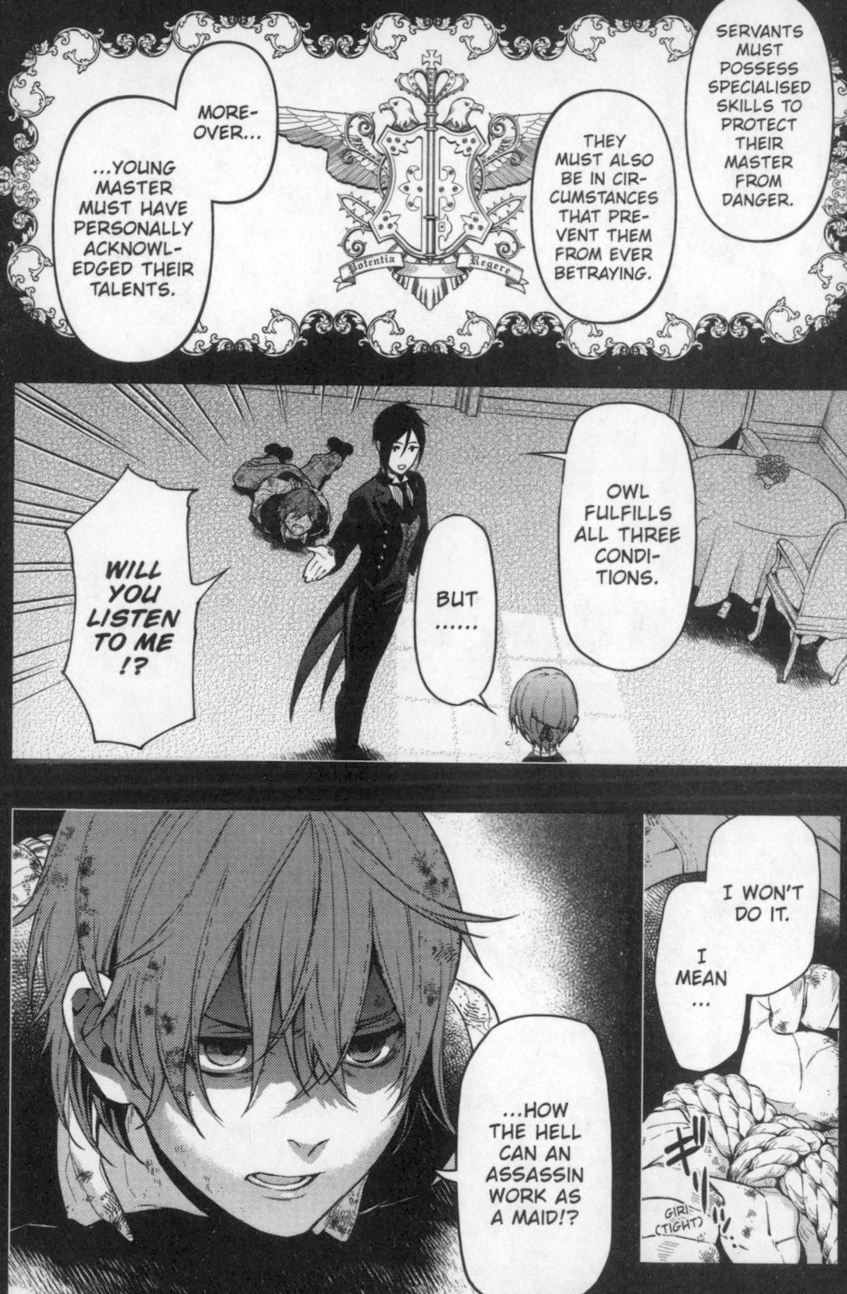
SERVANTS MUST POSSESS SPECIALISED SKILLS TO PROTECT THEIR MASTER FROM DANGER.
THEY MUST ALSO BE IN CIRCUMSTANCES THAT PREVENT THEM FROM EVER BETRAYING.
Potentia Regere
MOREOVER...
...YOUNG MASTER MUST HAVE PERSONALLY ACKNOWLEDGED THEIR TALENTS.
OWL FULFILLS ALL THREE CONDITIONS.
BUT ......
WILL YOU LISTEN TO ME !?
I WON'T DO IT.
I MEAN ...
ギリ
GIRI (TIGHT)
...HOW THE HELL CAN AN ASSASSIN WORK AS A MAID!?

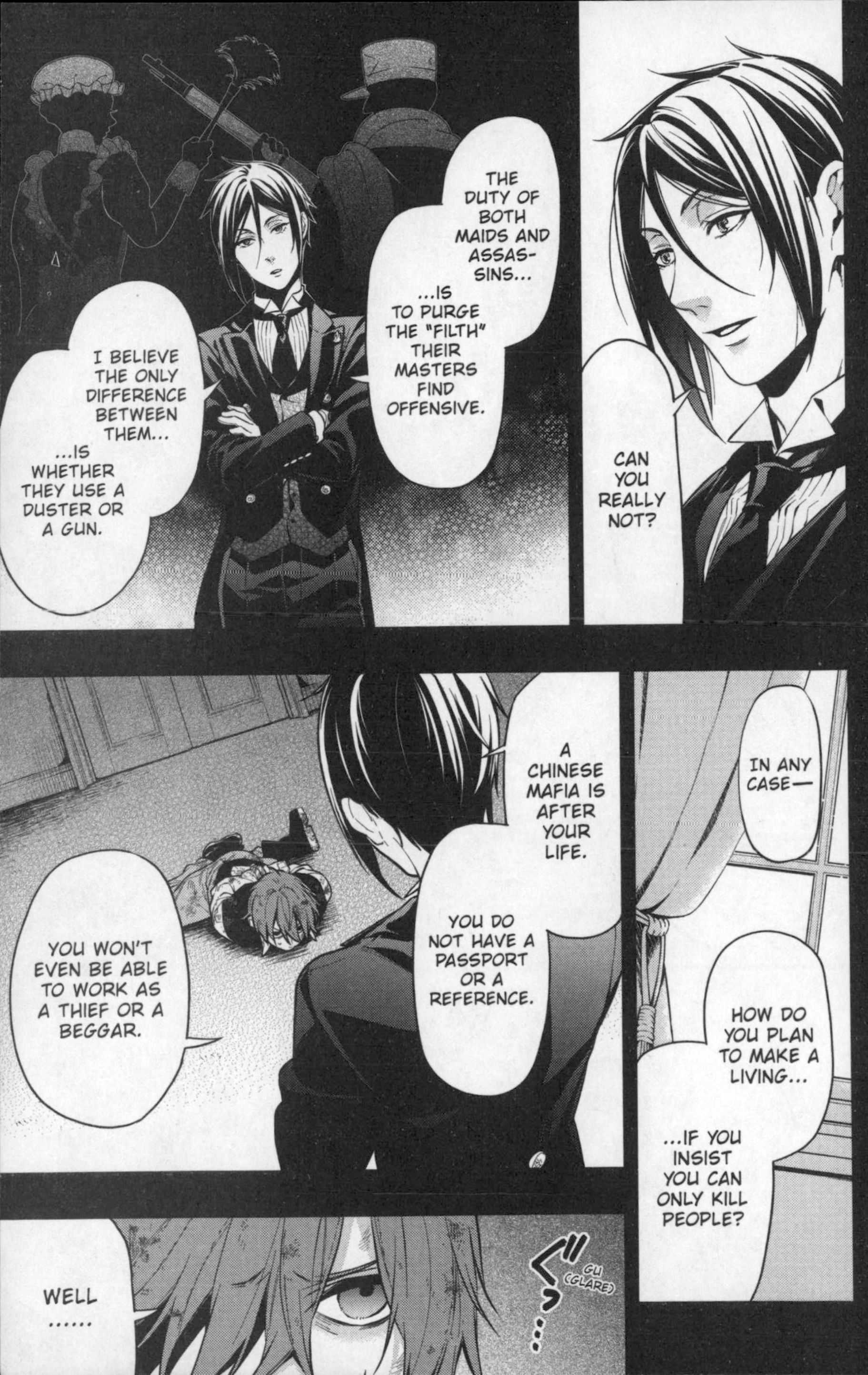
CAN YOU REALLY NOT?
THE DUTY OF BOTH MAIDS AND ASSAS-SINS...
...IS TO PURGE THE "FILTH" THEIR MASTERS FIND OFFENSIVE.
I BELIEVE THE ONLY DIFFERENCE BETWEEN THEM...
...IS WHETHER THEY USE A DUSTER OR A GUN.
IN ANY CASE—
HOW DO YOU PLAN TO MAKE A LIVING...
...IF YOU INSIST YOU CAN ONLY KILL PEOPLE?
A CHINESE MAFIA IS AFTER YOUR LIFE.
YOU DO NOT HAVE A PASSPORT OR A REFERENCE.
YOU WON'T EVEN BE ABLE TO WORK AS A THIEF OR A BEGGAR.
ぐっ…
GU (GLARE)
WELL ......

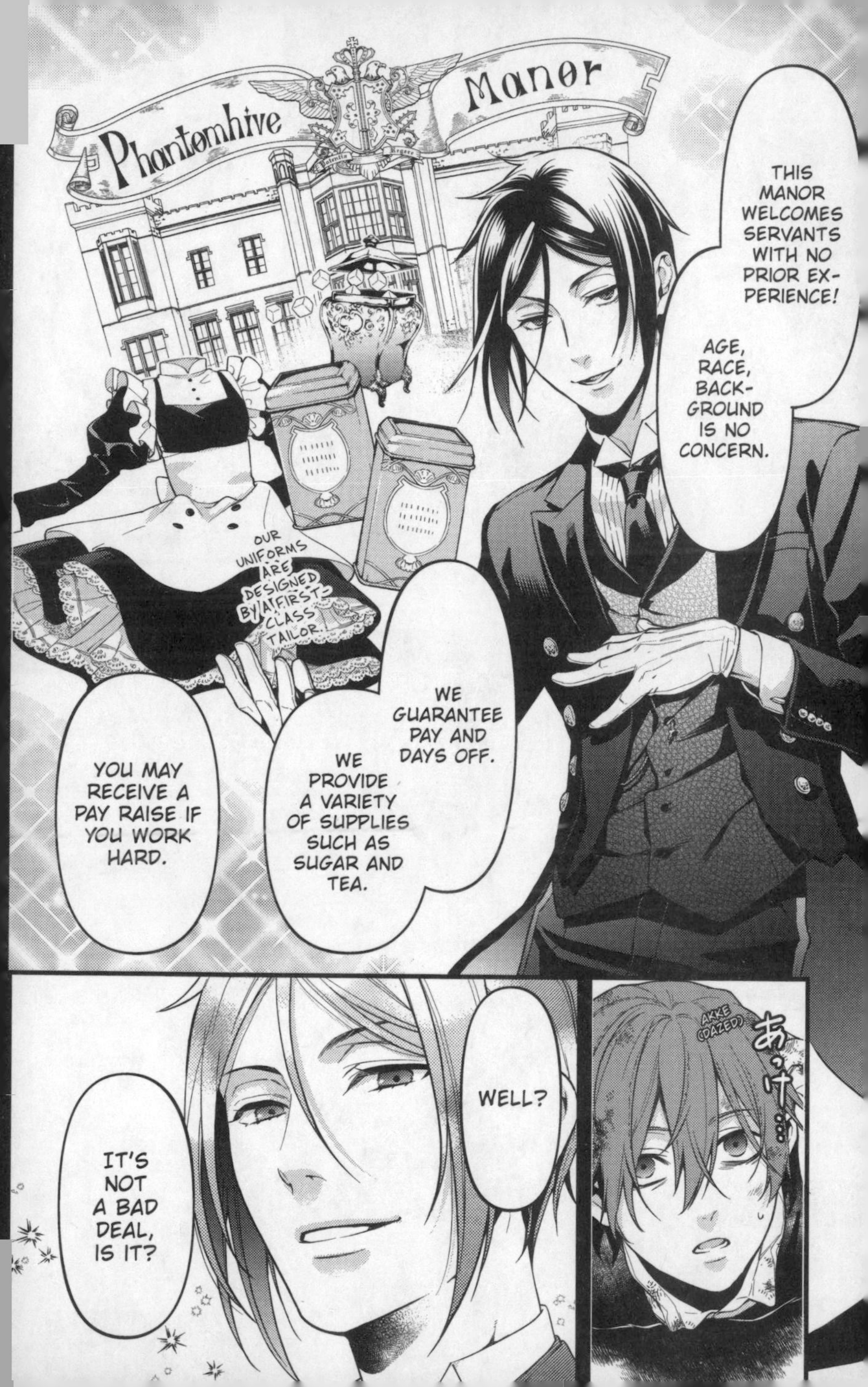
Phantomhive Manor
THIS MANOR WELCOMES SERVANTS WITH NO PRIOR EXPERIENCE!
AGE, RACE, BACKGROUND IS NO CONCERN.
OUR UNIFORMS ARE DESIGNED BY A FIRST-CLASS TAILOR.
WE GUARANTEE PAY AND DAYS OFF.
WE PROVIDE A VARIETY OF SUPPLIES SUCH AS SUGAR AND TEA.
YOU MAY RECEIVE A PAY RAISE IF YOU WORK HARD.
あっけ…
AKKE (DAZED)
WELL?
IT'S NOT A BAD DEAL, IS IT?

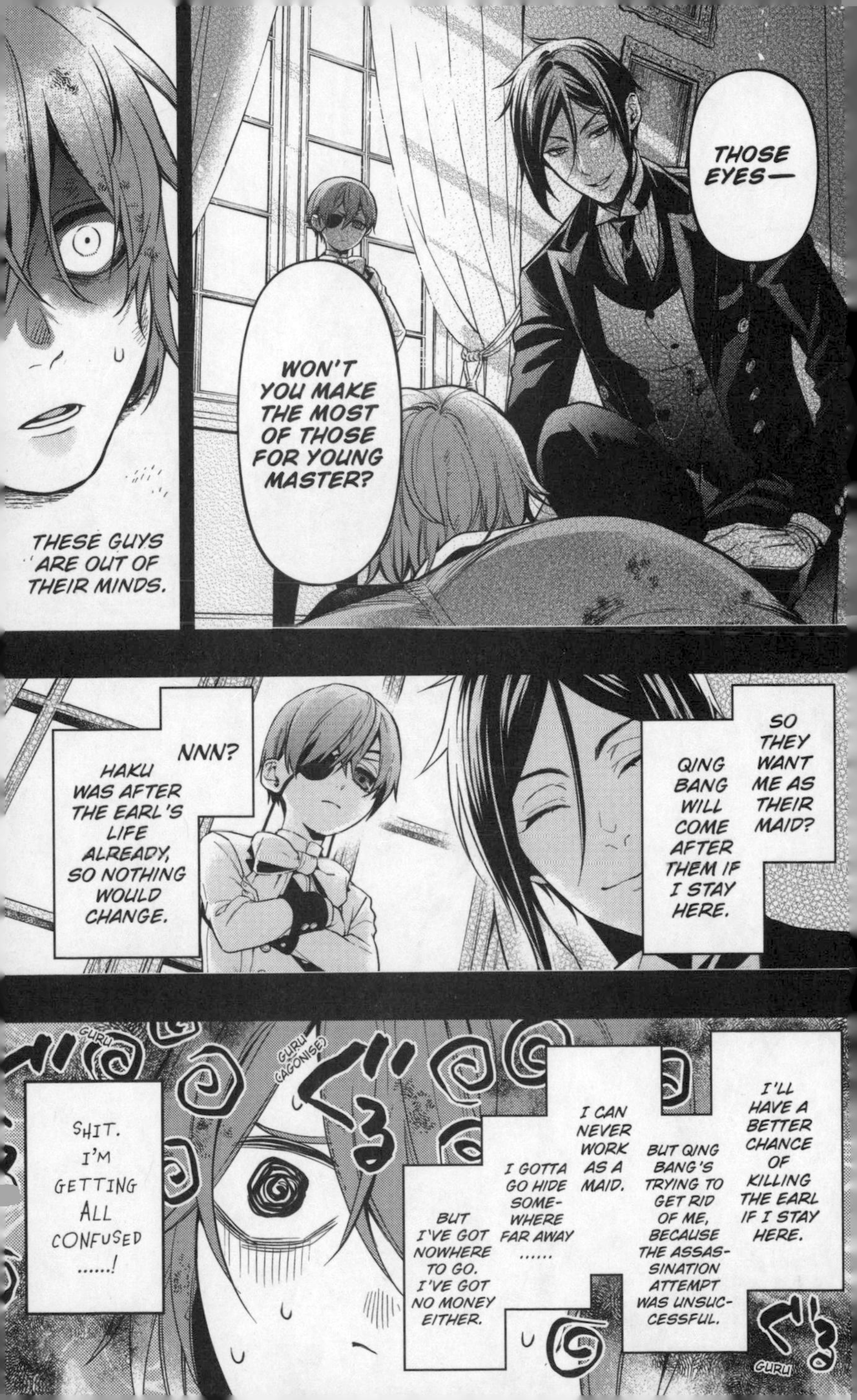
THOSE EYES—
WON'T YOU MAKE THE MOST OF THOSE FOR YOUNG MASTER?
THESE GUYS ARE OUT OF THEIR MINDS.
SO THEY WANT ME AS THEIR MAID?
QING BANG WILL COME AFTER THEM IF I STAY HERE.
NNN?
HAKU WAS AFTER THE EARL'S LIFE ALREADY, SO NOTHING WOULD CHANGE.
GURU
I'LL HAVE A BETTER CHANCE OF KILLING THE EARL IF I STAY HERE.
BUT QING BANG'S TRYING TO GET RID OF ME, BECAUSE THE ASSAS-SINATION ATTEMPT WAS UNSUC-CESSFUL.
I CAN NEVER WORK AS A MAID.
I GOTTA GO HIDE SOME-WHERE FAR AWAY ......
BUT I'VE GOT NOWHERE TO GO. I'VE GOT NO MONEY EITHER.
GURU (AGONISE)
GURU
SHIT. I'M GETTING ALL CONFUSED ......!

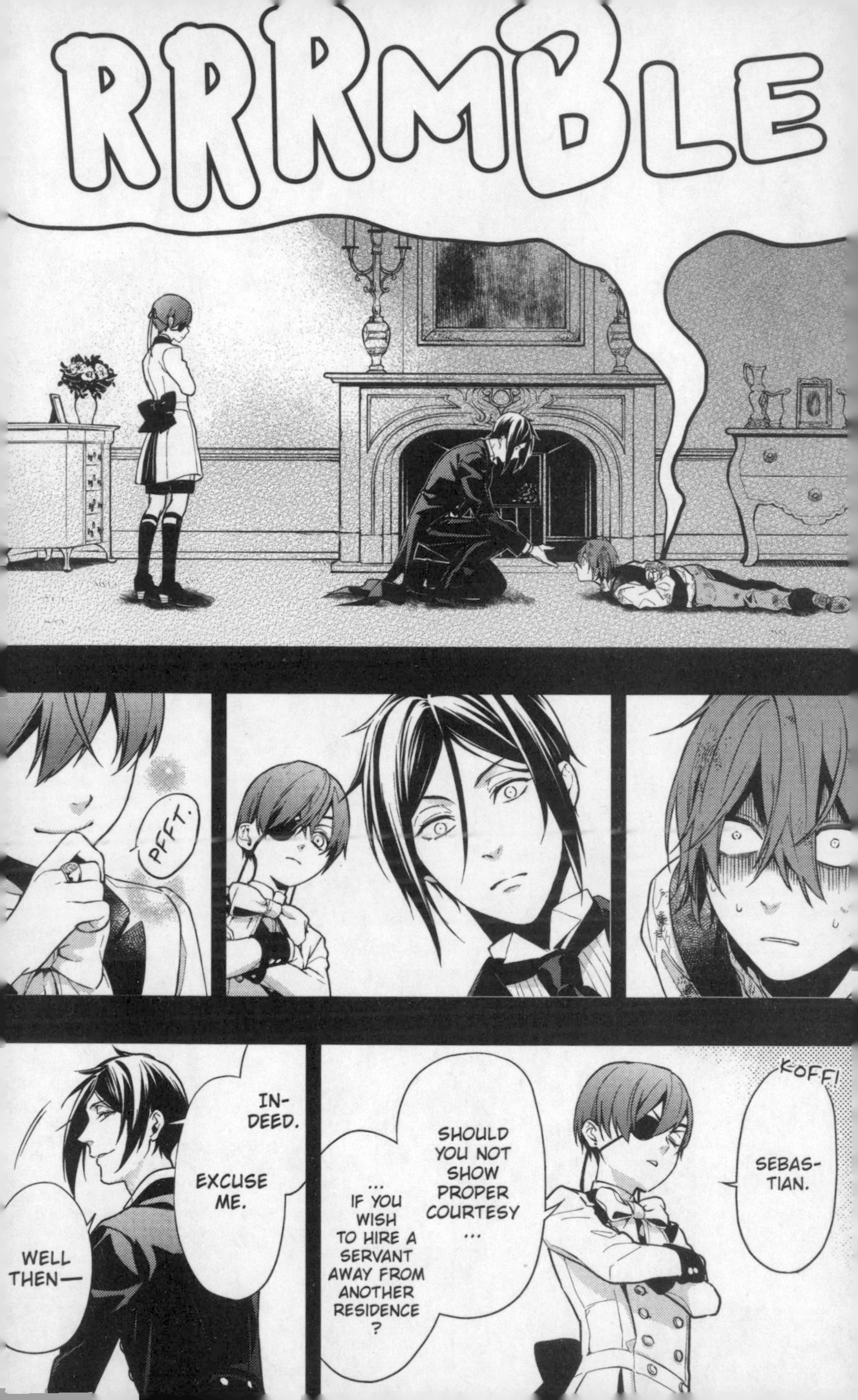
RRRMBLE
PFFT.
KOFF!
SEBAS-TIAN.
SHOULD YOU NOT SHOW PROPER COURTESY...
...IF YOU WISH TO HIRE A SERVANT AWAY FROM ANOTHER RESIDENCE?
IN-DEED.
EXCUSE ME.
WELL THEN—

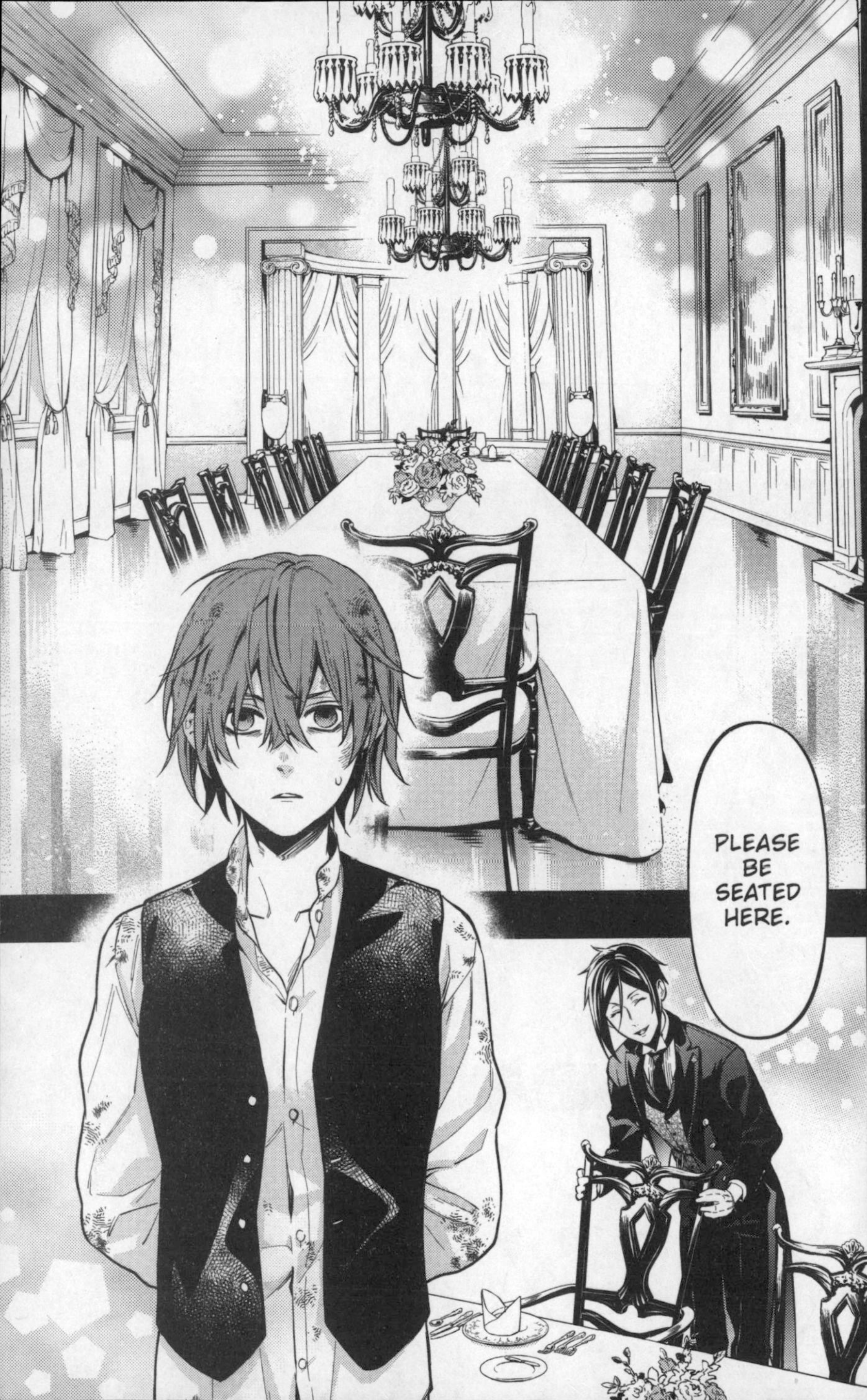
PLEASE BE SEATED HERE.

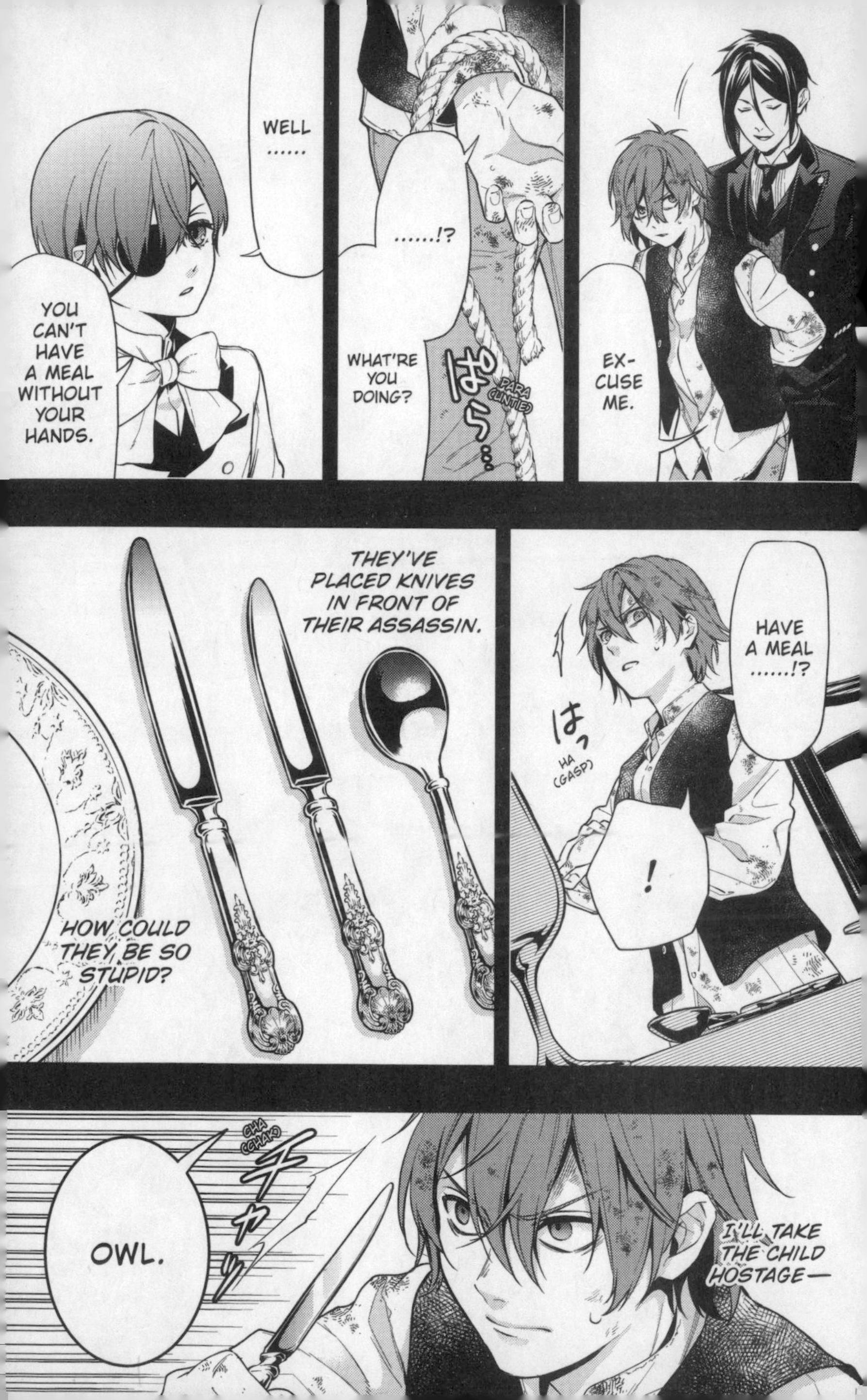
EX-
CUSE
ME.
......!?
ぱら..
PARA (UNTIED)
WHAT'RE YOU DOING?
WELL ......
YOU CAN'T HAVE A MEAL WITHOUT YOUR HANDS.
HAVE A MEAL ......!?
はっ
HA (GASP)
!
THEY'VE PLACED KNIVES IN FRONT OF THEIR ASSASSIN.
HOW COULD THEY BE SO STUPID?
I'LL TAKE THE CHILD HOSTAGE—
チャッ
CHA (CHAK)
OWL.

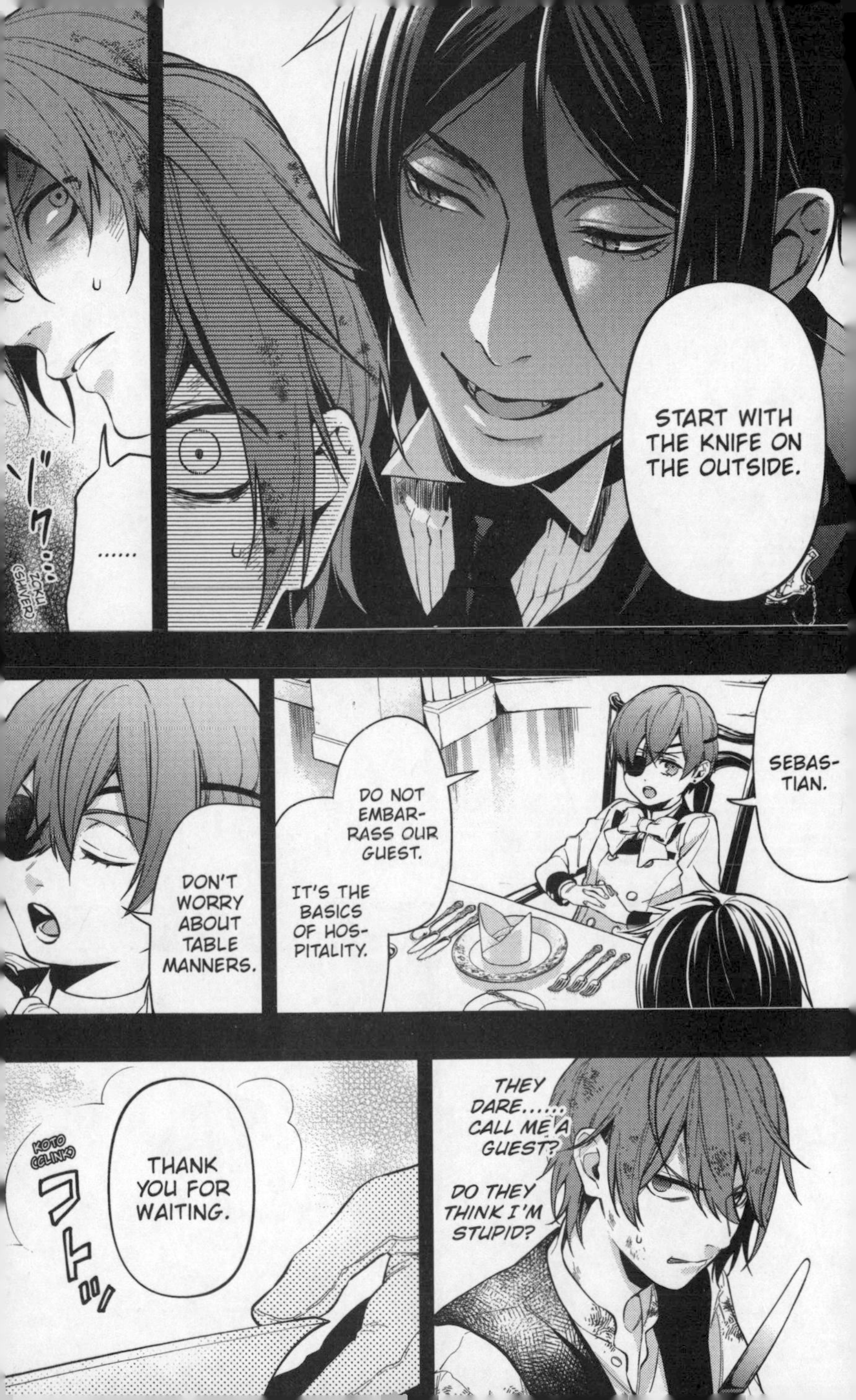
START WITH THE KNIFE ON THE OUTSIDE.
......
ZOKU
(SHIVER)
SEBASTIAN.
DO NOT EMBARRASS OUR GUEST.
IT'S THE BASICS OF HOSPITALITY.
DON'T WORRY ABOUT TABLE MANNERS.
THEY DARE...... CALL ME A GUEST?
DO THEY THINK I'M STUPID?
THANK YOU FOR WAITING.
KOTO
(CLINK)

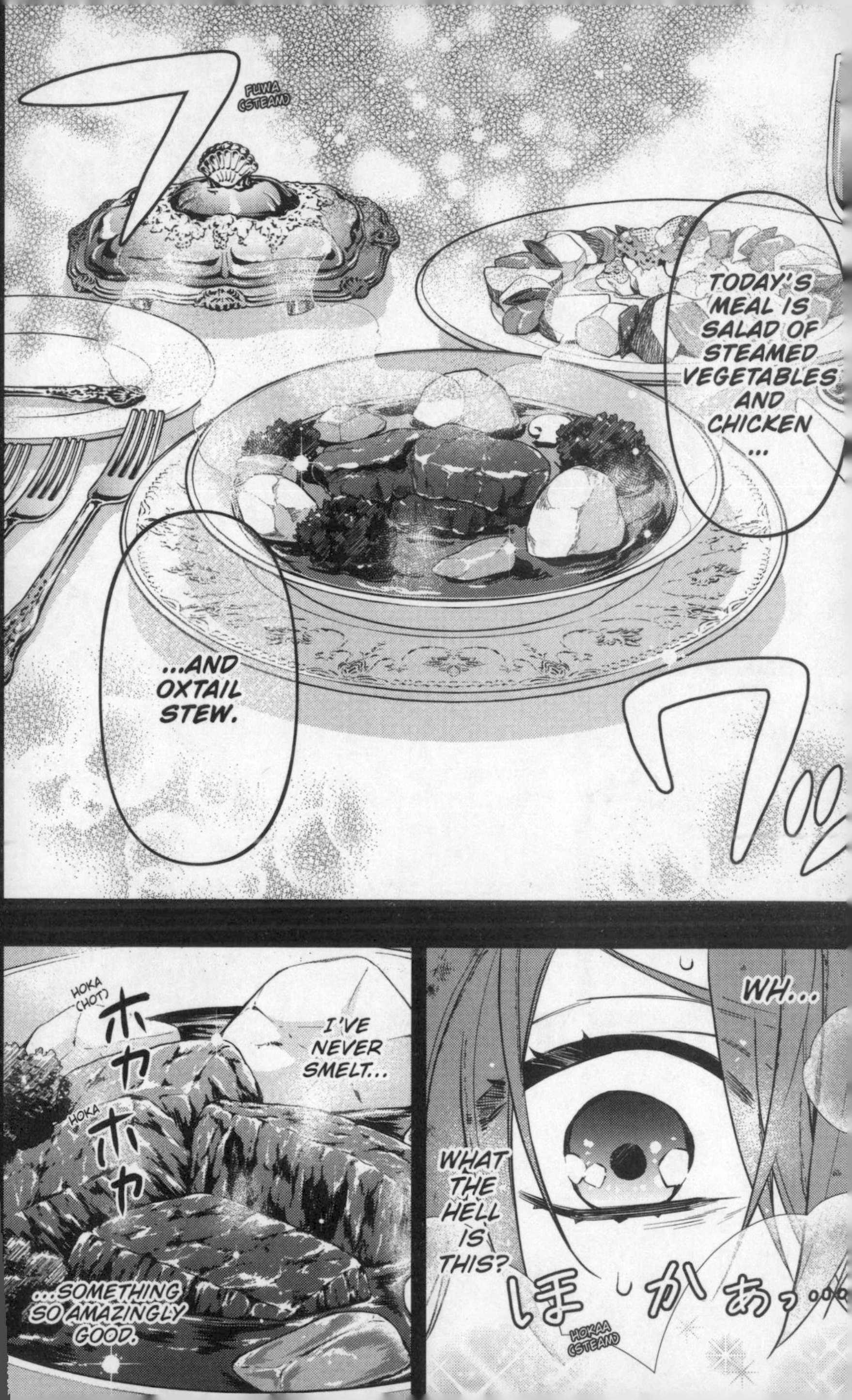
FUWA (STEAM)
TODAY'S MEAL IS SALAD OF STEAMED VEGETABLES AND CHICKEN ...
...AND OXTAIL STEW.
WH...
WHAT THE HELL IS THIS?
HOKAA (STEAM)
HOKA (HOT)
HOKA
I'VE NEVER SMELT...
...SOMETHING SO AMAZINGLY GOOD.

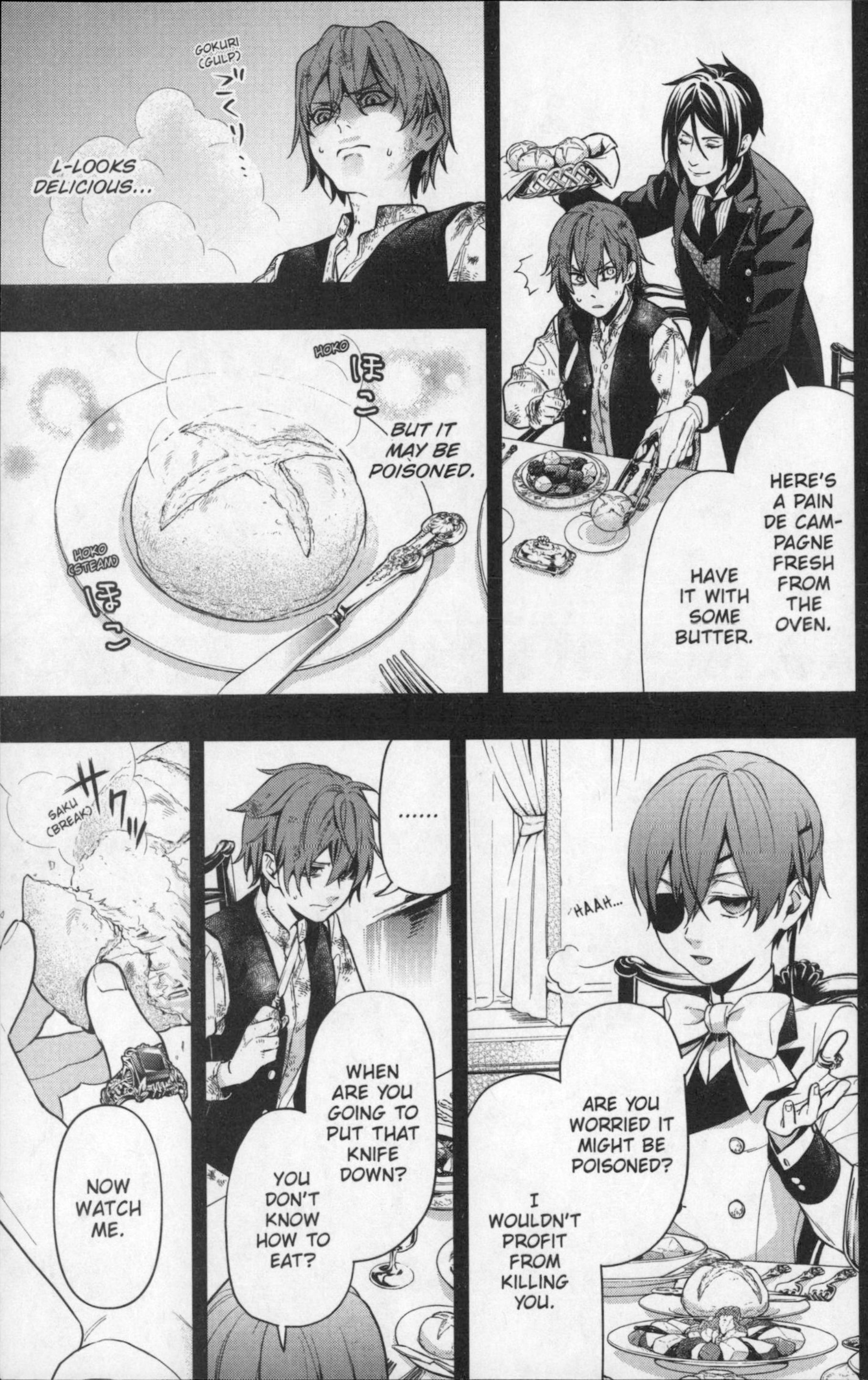
HERE'S A PAIN DE CAMPAGNE FRESH FROM THE OVEN.
HAVE IT WITH SOME BUTTER.
GOKURI (GULP)
L-LOOKS DELICIOUS...
HOKO
BUT IT MAY BE POISONED.
HOKO (STEAM)
HAAH...
ARE YOU WORRIED IT MIGHT BE POISONED?
I WOULDN'T PROFIT FROM KILLING YOU.
......
WHEN ARE YOU GOING TO PUT THAT KNIFE DOWN?
YOU DON'T KNOW HOW TO EAT?
SAKU (BREAK)
NOW WATCH ME.

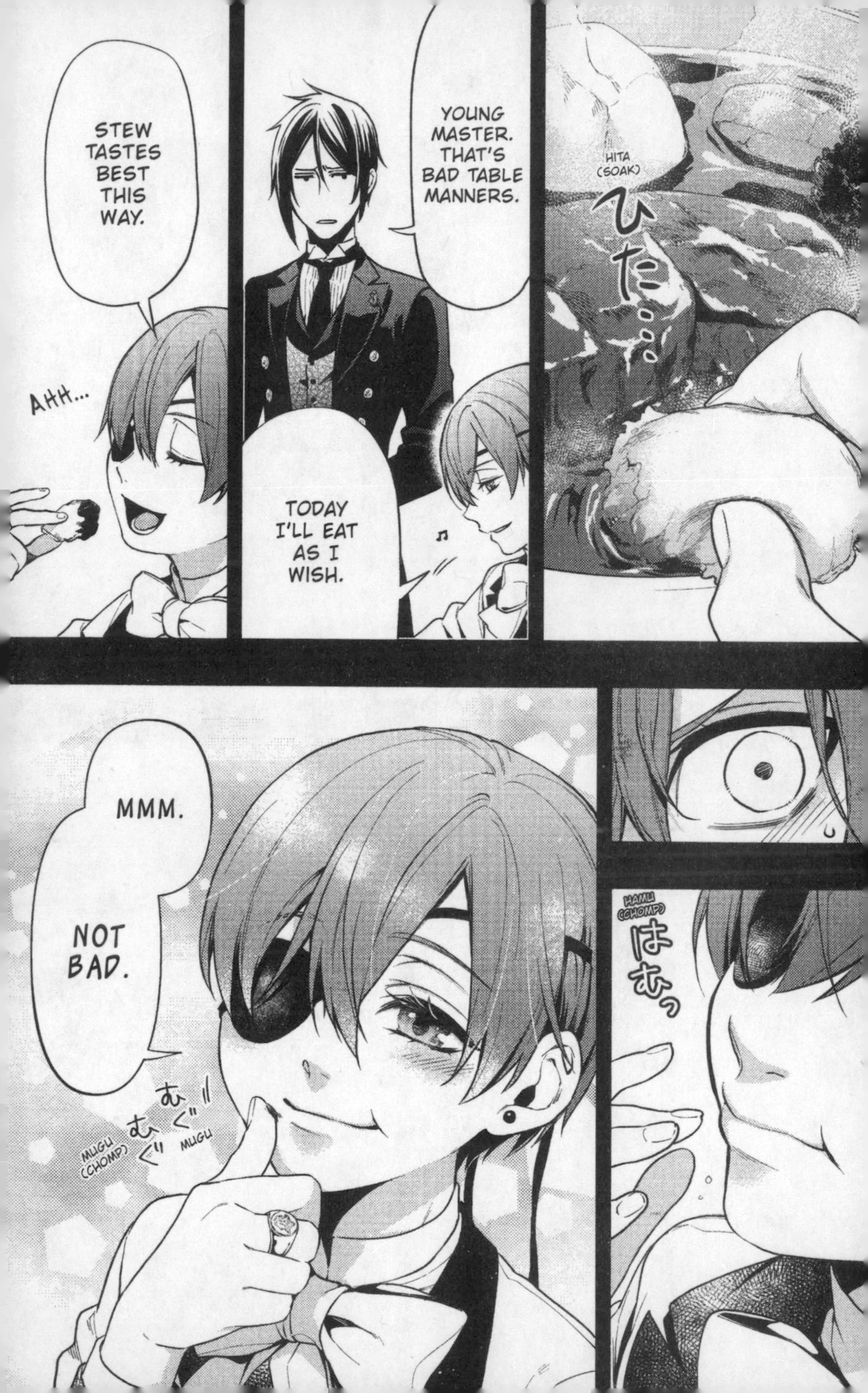
HITA (SOAK)
ひた…
YOUNG MASTER. THAT'S BAD TABLE MANNERS.
TODAY I'LL EAT AS I WISH.
STEW TASTES BEST THIS WAY.
AHH...
HAMU (CHOMP)
はむっ
MMM.
NOT BAD.
むぐ むぐ
MUGU (CHOMP) MUGU

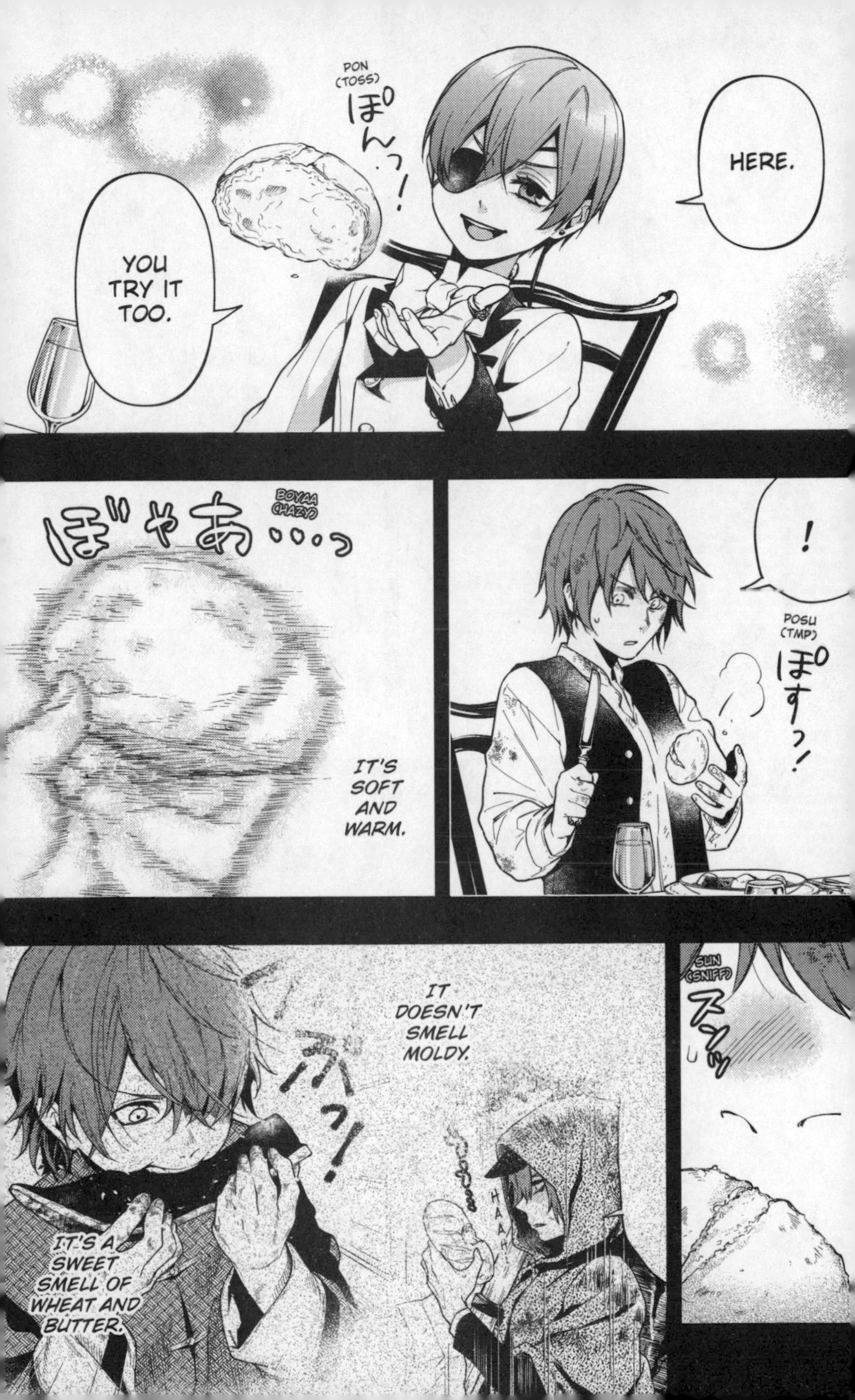
HERE.
PON (TOSS)
ぽんっ!
YOU TRY IT TOO.
!
POSU (TMP)
ぽすっ!
BOYAA (HAZY)
ぼやぁ…っ
IT'S SOFT AND WARM.
SUN (SNIFF)
スンッ
IT DOESN'T SMELL MOLDY.
HAAH
IT'S A SWEET SMELL OF WHEAT AND BUTTER.

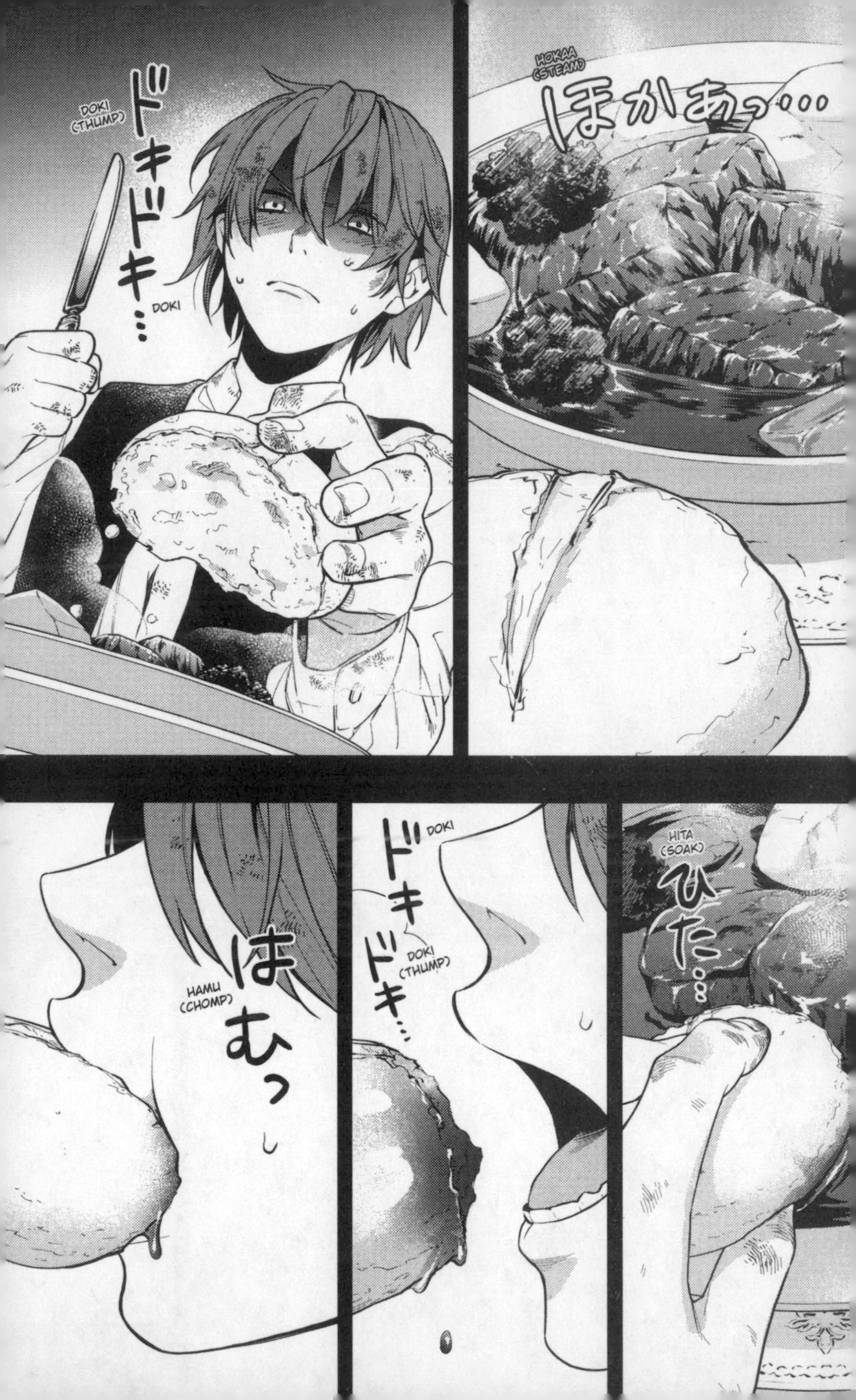
HOKAA (STEAM)
ほかあっ・・・
DOKI (THUMP)
ドキドキ…
DOKI
HITA (SOAK)
ひた…
DOKI
ドキドキ…
DOKI (THUMP)
HAMU (CHOMP)
はむっ

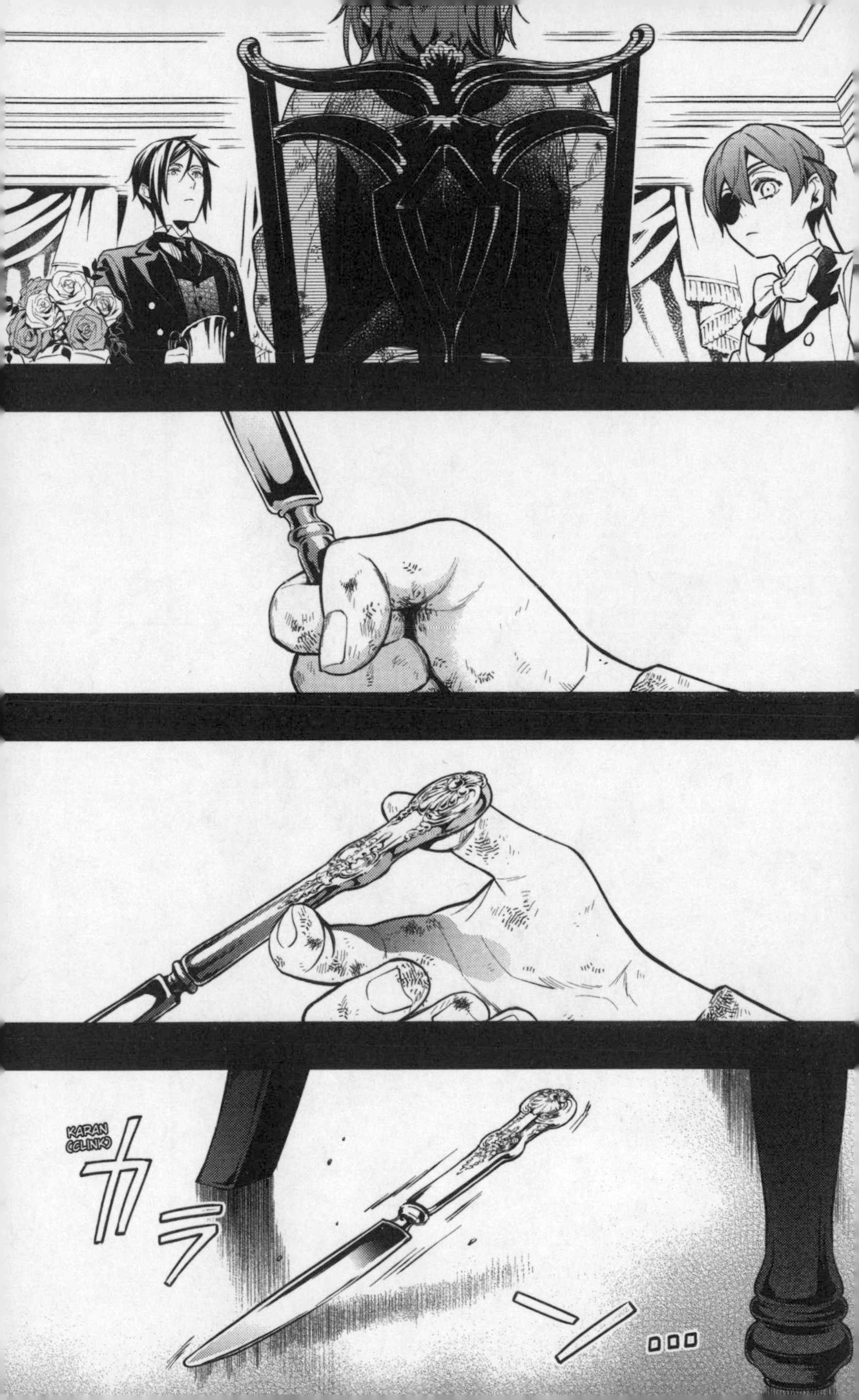

KARAN (CLINK)
カラーン
...

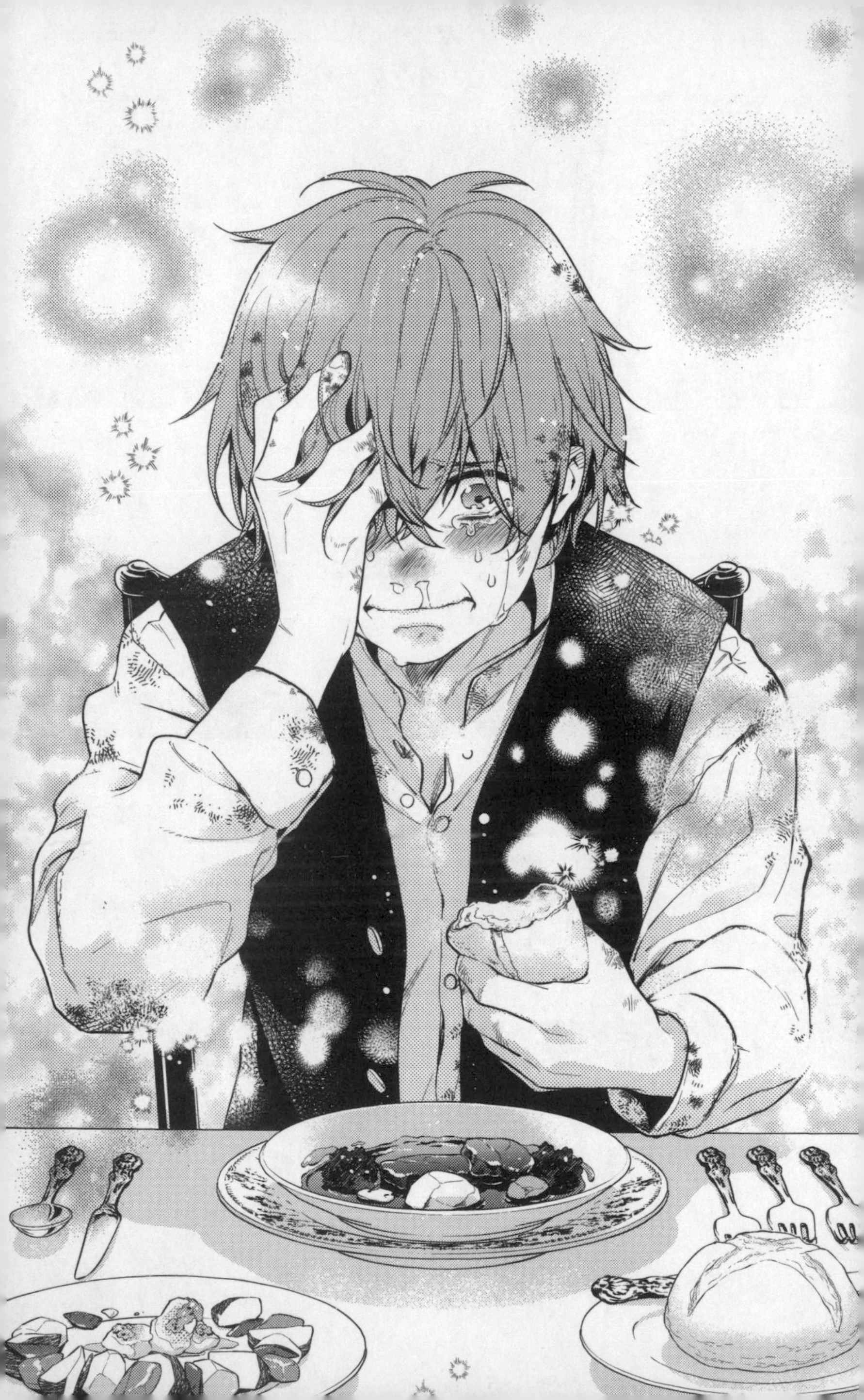

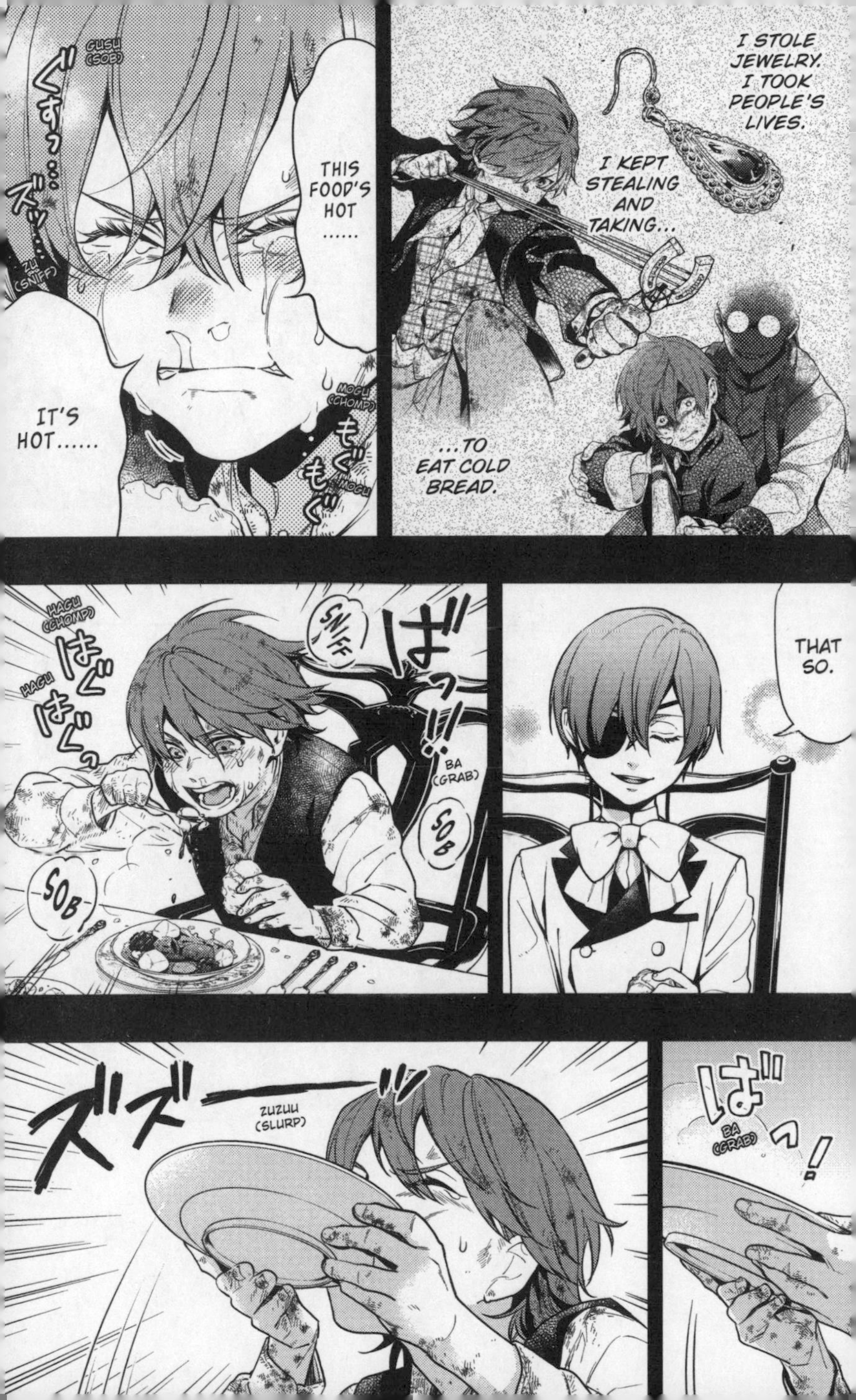
I STOLE JEWELRY. I TOOK PEOPLE'S LIVES.
I KEPT STEALING AND TAKING...
...TO EAT COLD BREAD.
ぐすっ…
GUSU (SOB)
ズッ…
ZU (SNIFF)
THIS FOOD'S HOT ......
IT'S HOT......
もぐもぐ
MOGU (CHOMP)
MOGU
THAT SO.
ばっ!!
BA (GRAB)
SNIFF
SOB
はぐはぐっ
HAGU (CHOMP)
HAGU
SOB
ばっ!
BA (GRAB)
ズズーーッ
ZUZUU (SLURP)

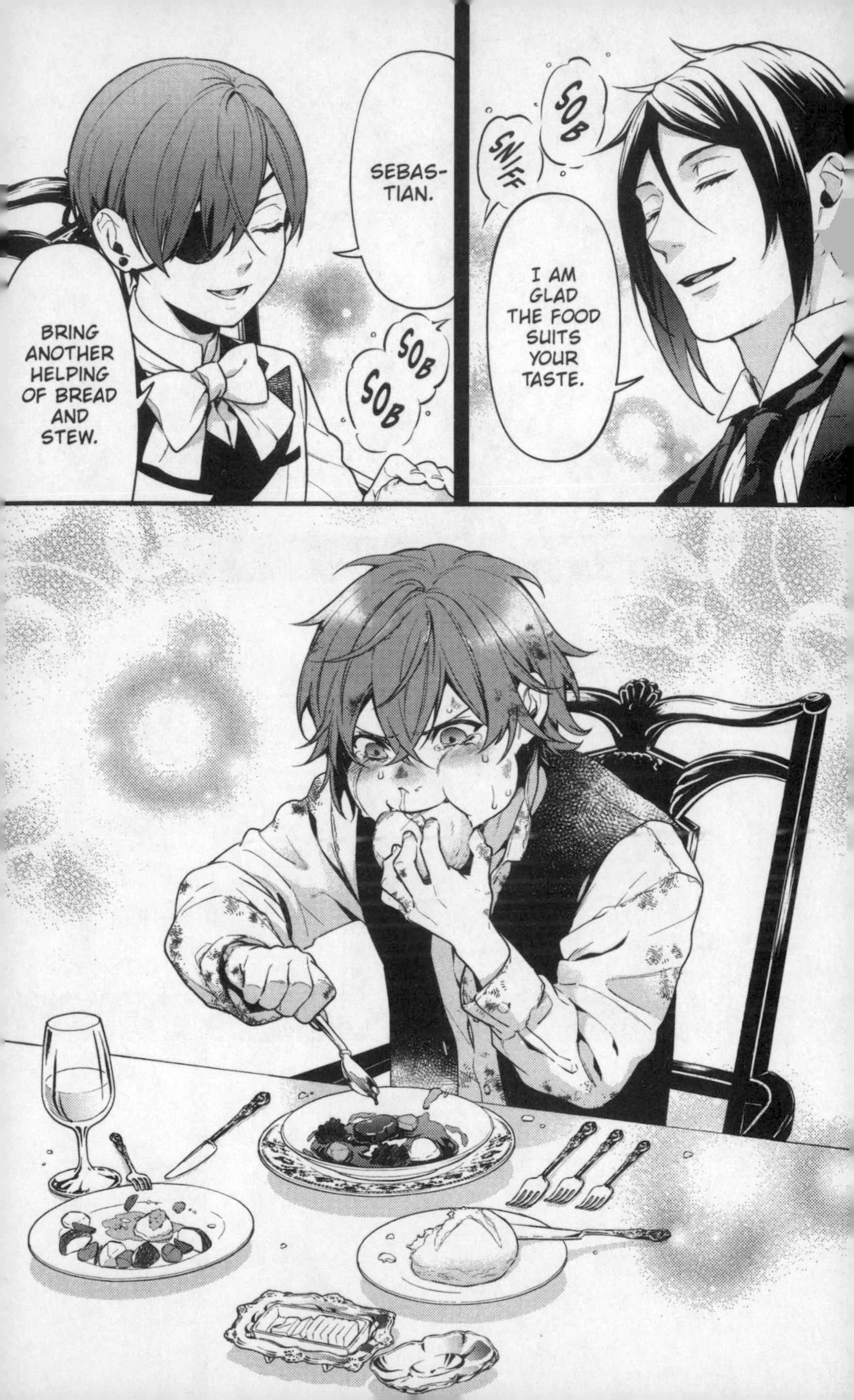
SOB
SNIFF
I AM GLAD THE FOOD SUITS YOUR TASTE.
SEBAS-TIAN.
SOB SOB
BRING ANOTHER HELPING OF BREAD AND STEW.

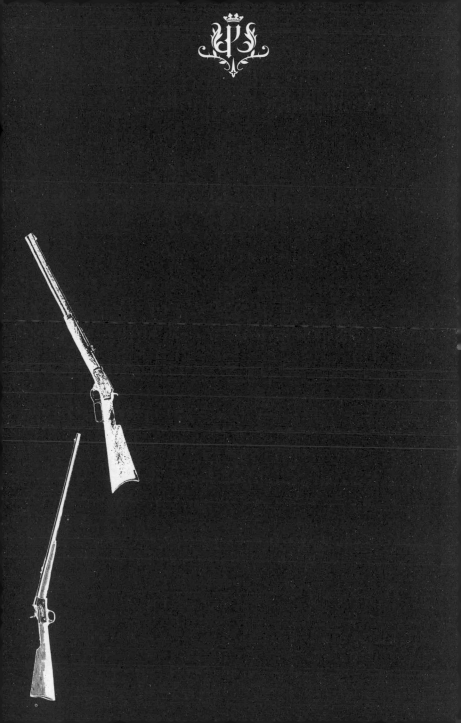

Black Butler

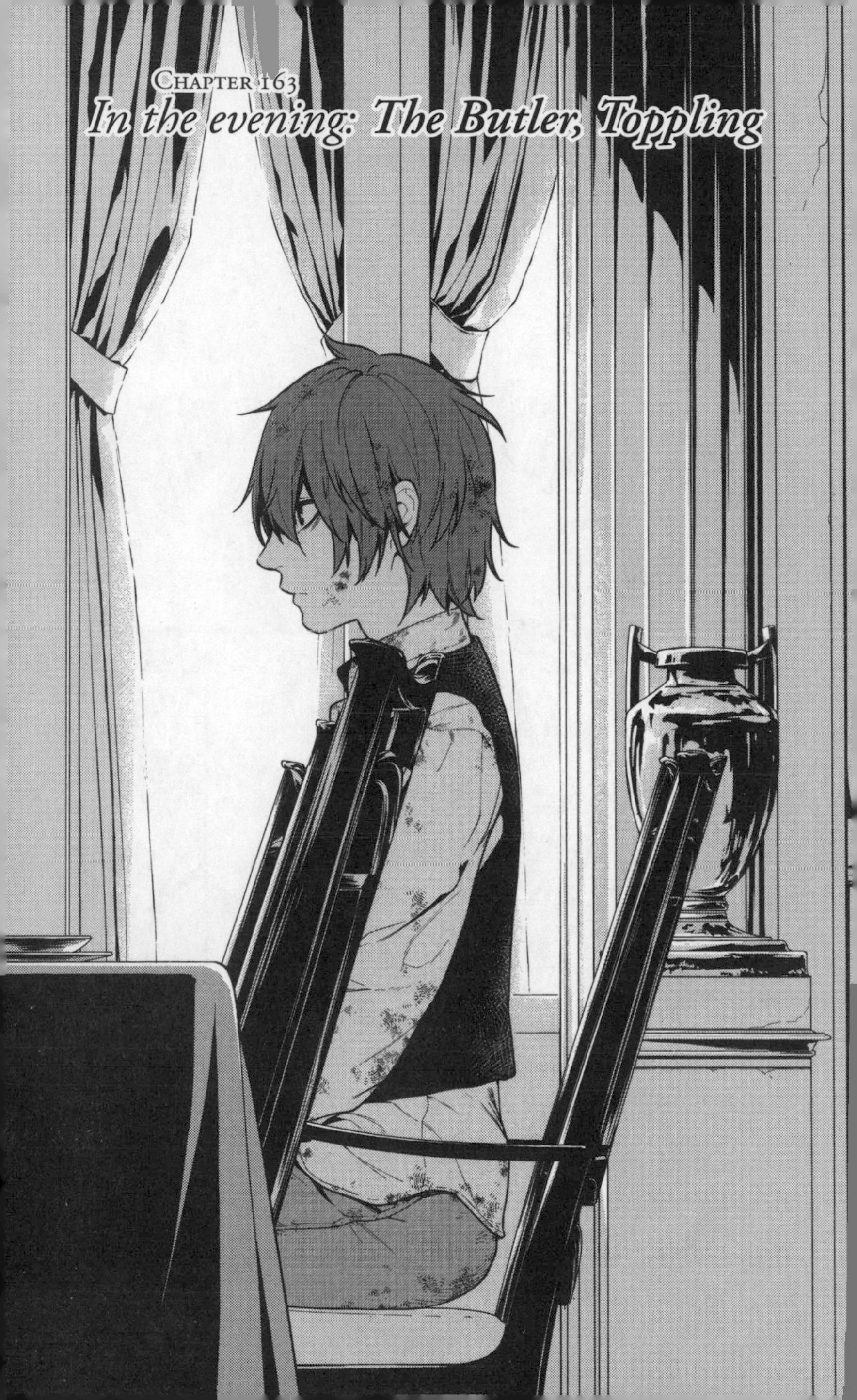
Chapter 163
In the evening: The Butler, Toppling

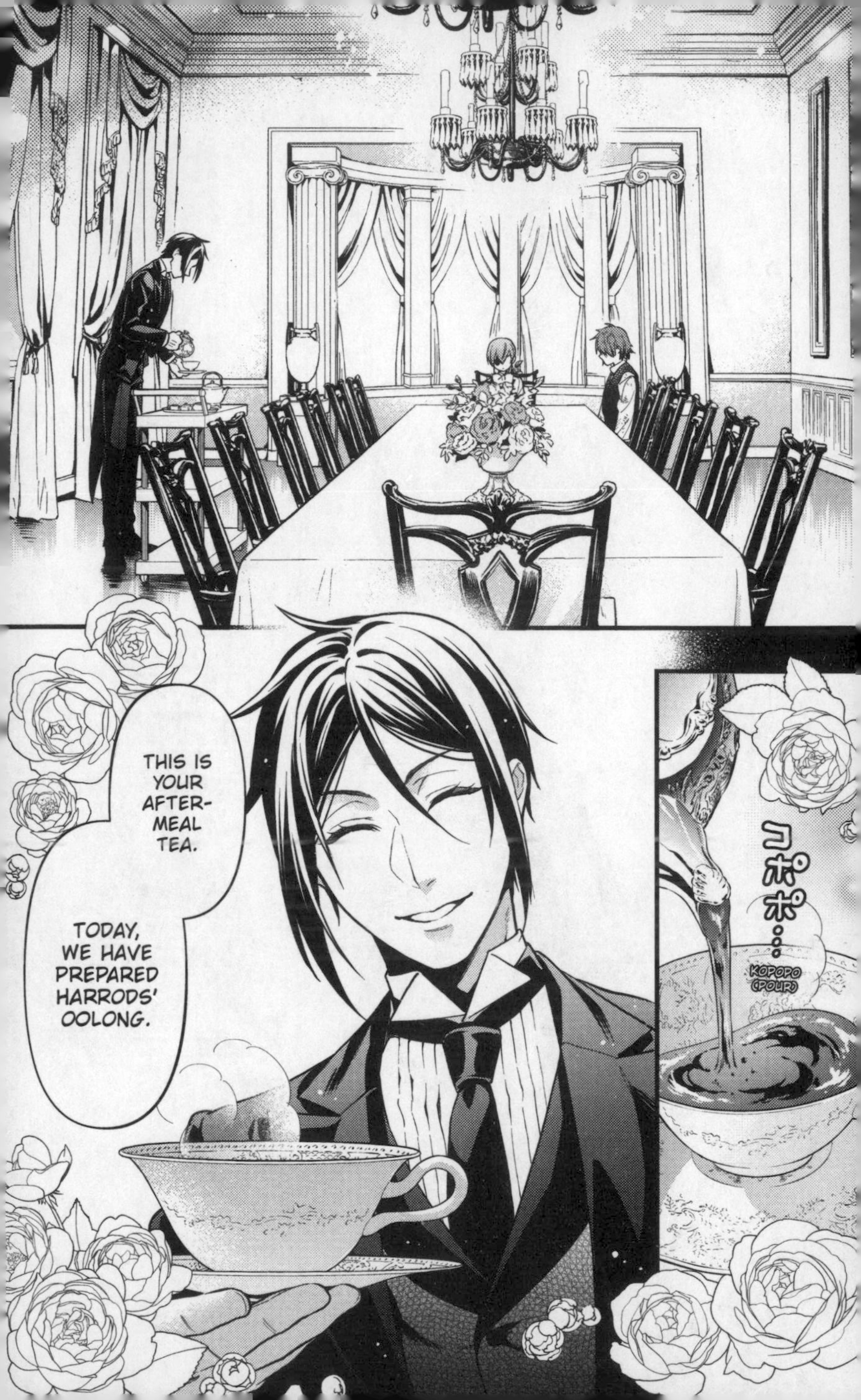
コポポ…
KOPOPO (POUR)
THIS IS YOUR AFTER-MEAL TEA.
TODAY, WE HAVE PREPARED HARRODS' OOLONG.

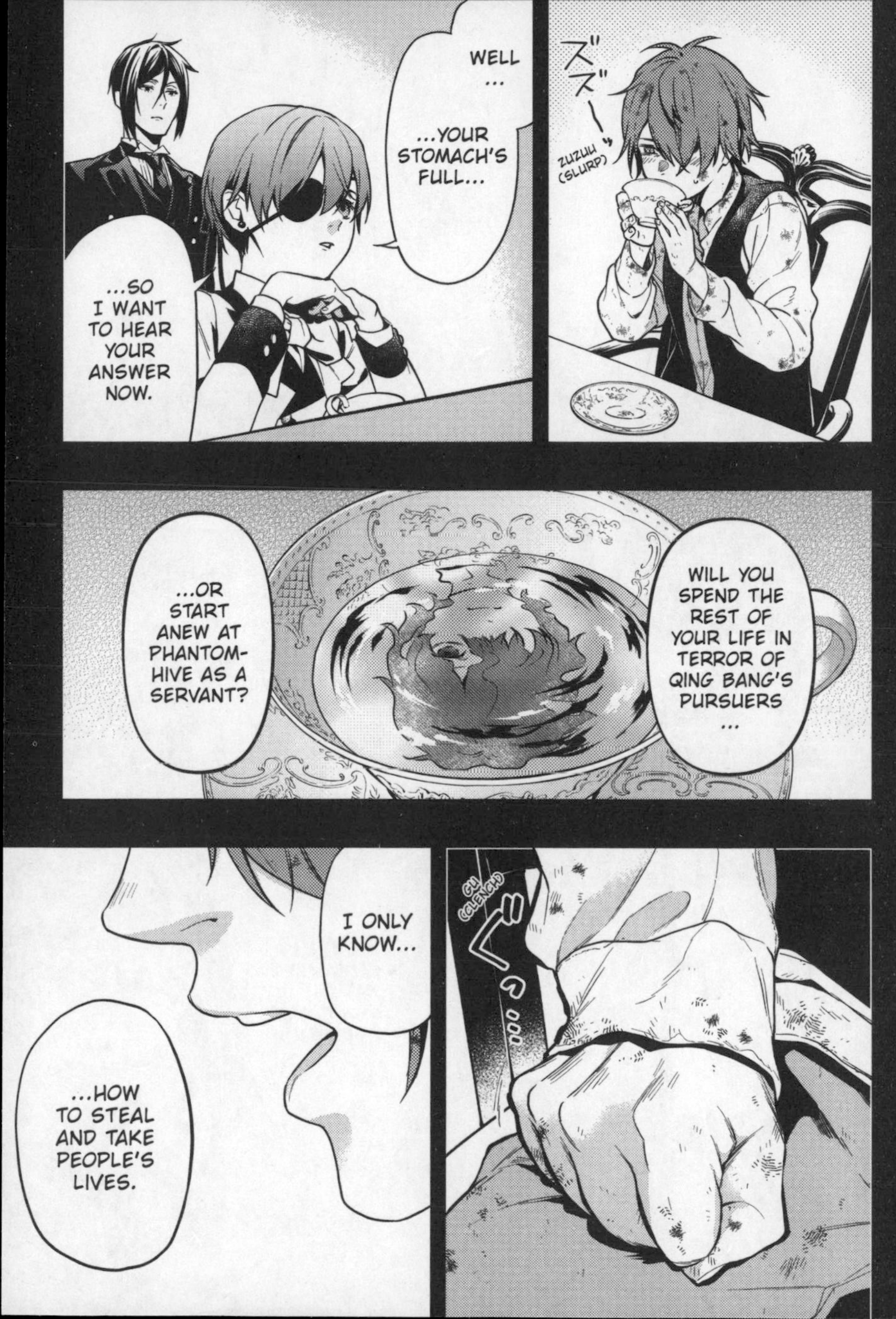
ズズー
ZUZUU (SLURP)
WELL ...
...YOUR STOMACH'S FULL...
...SO I WANT TO HEAR YOUR ANSWER NOW.
WILL YOU SPEND THE REST OF YOUR LIFE IN TERROR OF QING BANG'S PURSUERS ...
...OR START ANEW AT PHANTOM-HIVE AS A SERVANT?
GU (CLENCH)
I ONLY KNOW...
...HOW TO STEAL AND TAKE PEOPLE'S LIVES.

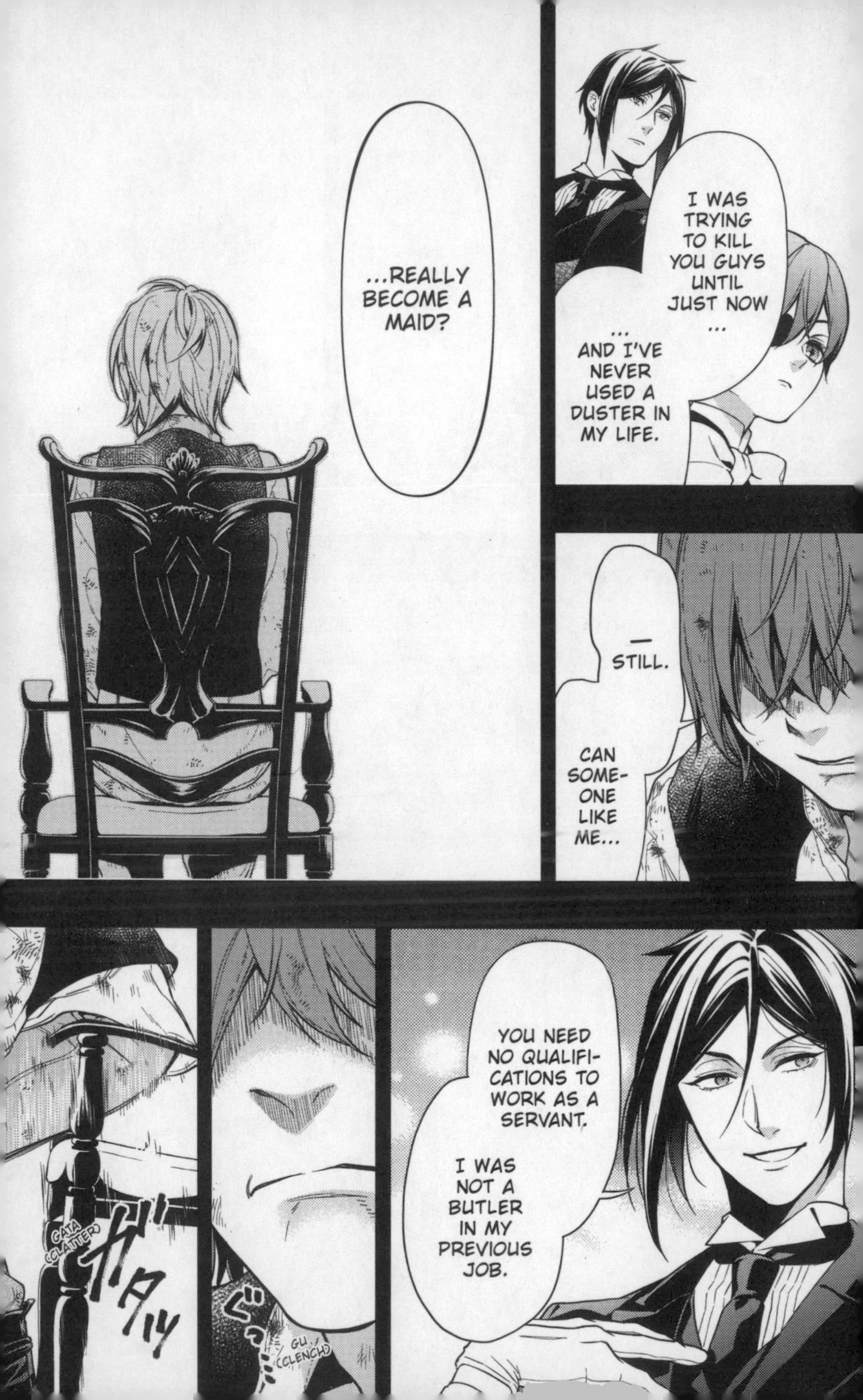
I WAS TRYING TO KILL YOU GUYS UNTIL JUST NOW ...
... AND I'VE NEVER USED A DUSTER IN MY LIFE.
— STILL.
CAN SOME-ONE LIKE ME...
...REALLY BECOME A MAID?
YOU NEED NO QUALIFI-CATIONS TO WORK AS A SERVANT.
I WAS NOT A BUTLER IN MY PREVIOUS JOB.
GU (CLENCH)
GATA (CLATTER)

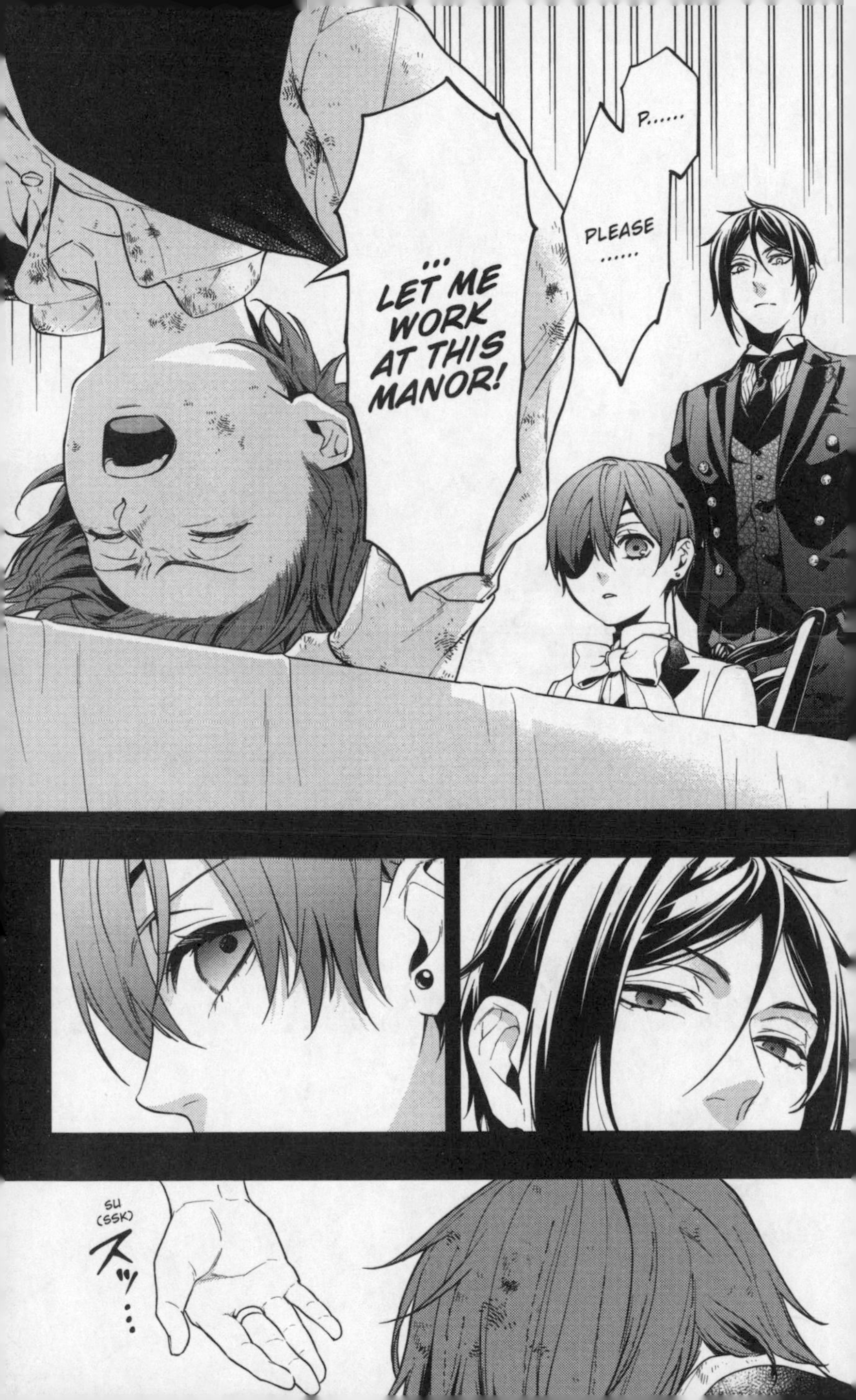
P......
PLEASE ......
...LET ME WORK AT THIS MANOR!
SU (SSK)

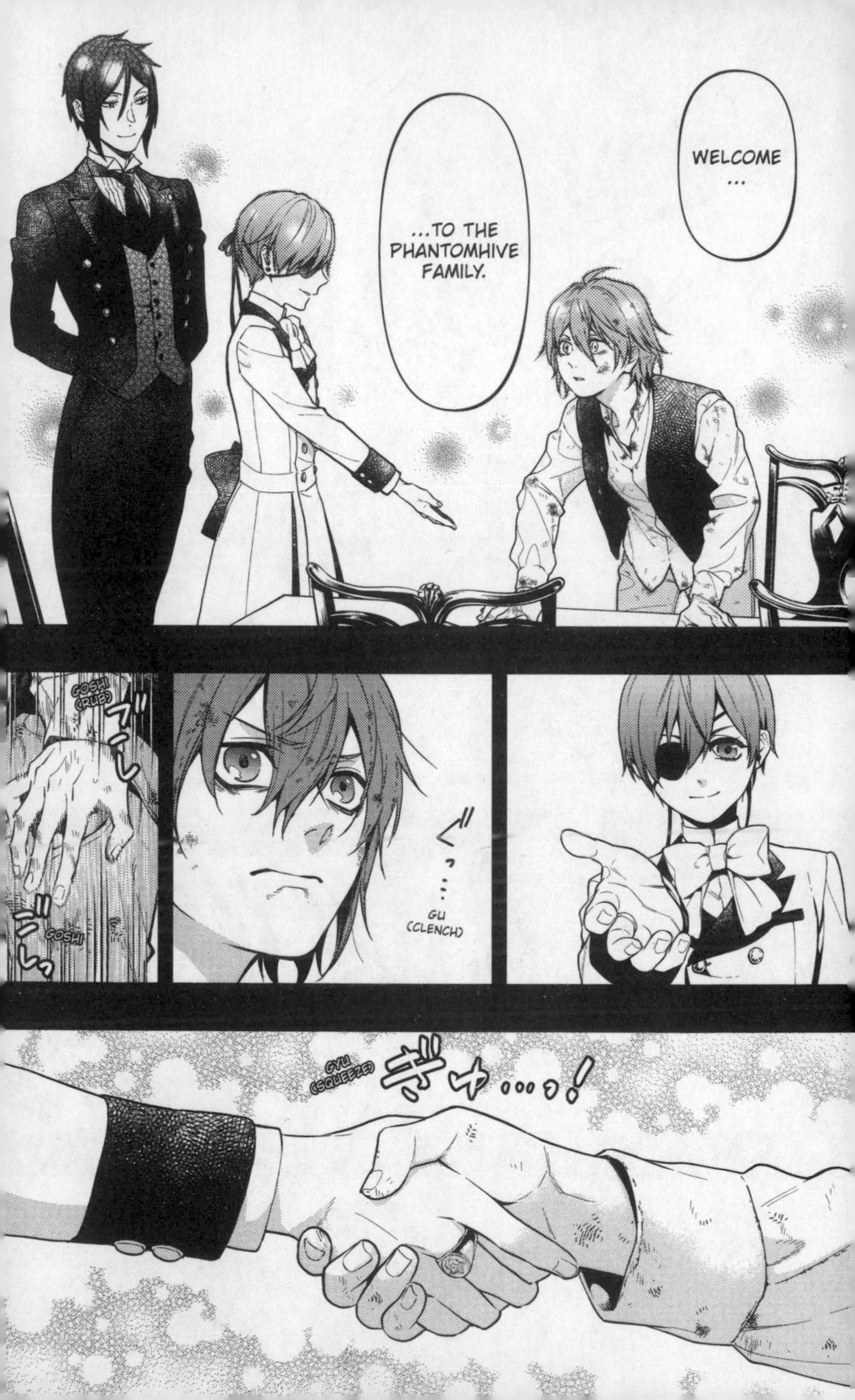
WELCOME ...
...TO THE PHANTOMHIVE FAMILY.
GU (CLENCH)
GOSHI (RUB)
GOSHI
GYU (SQUEEZE)

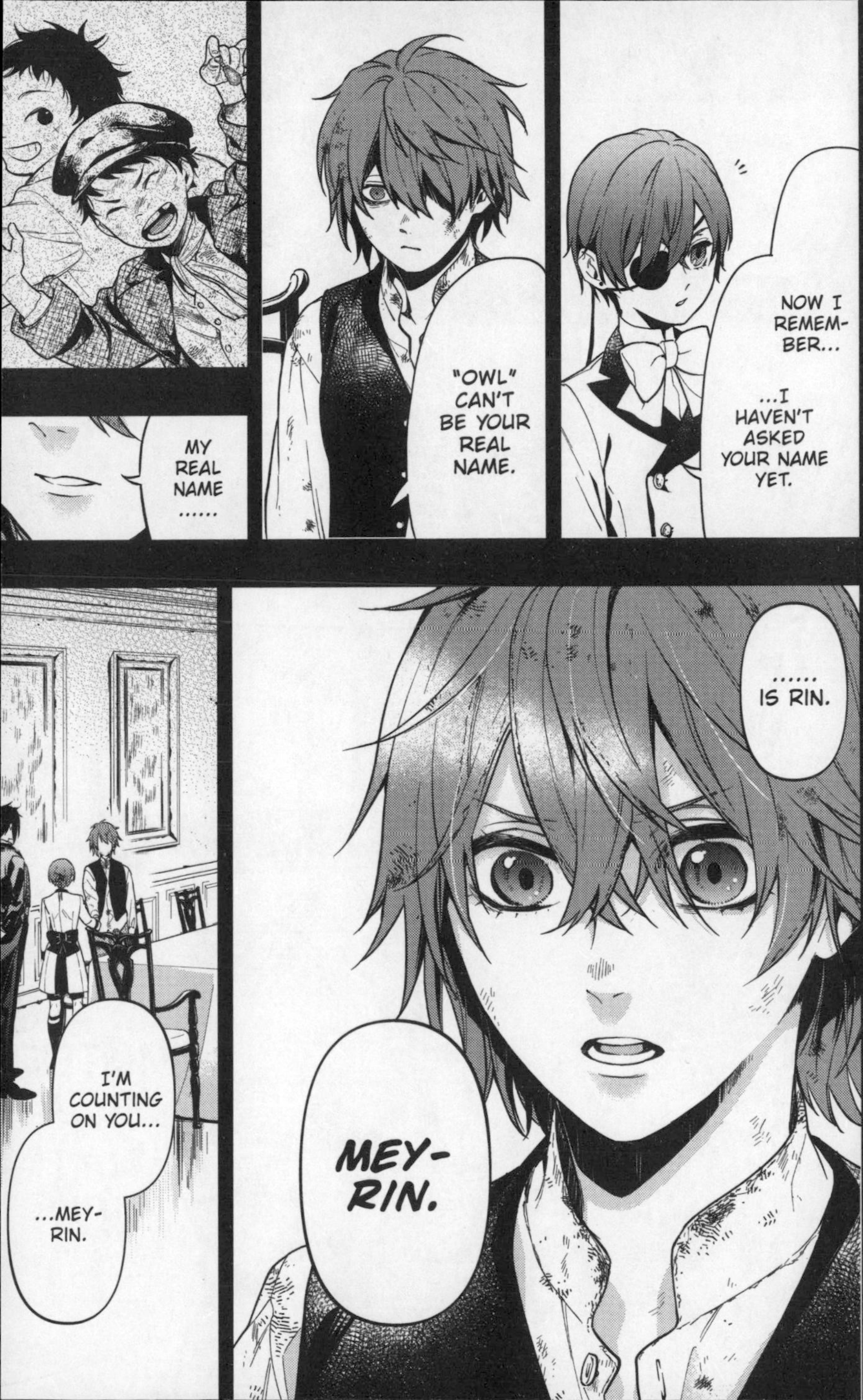
NOW I REMEMBER...
...I HAVEN'T ASKED YOUR NAME YET.
"OWL" CAN'T BE YOUR REAL NAME.
MY REAL NAME ......
...... IS RIN.
MEY-RIN.
I'M COUNTING ON YOU...
...MEY-RIN.

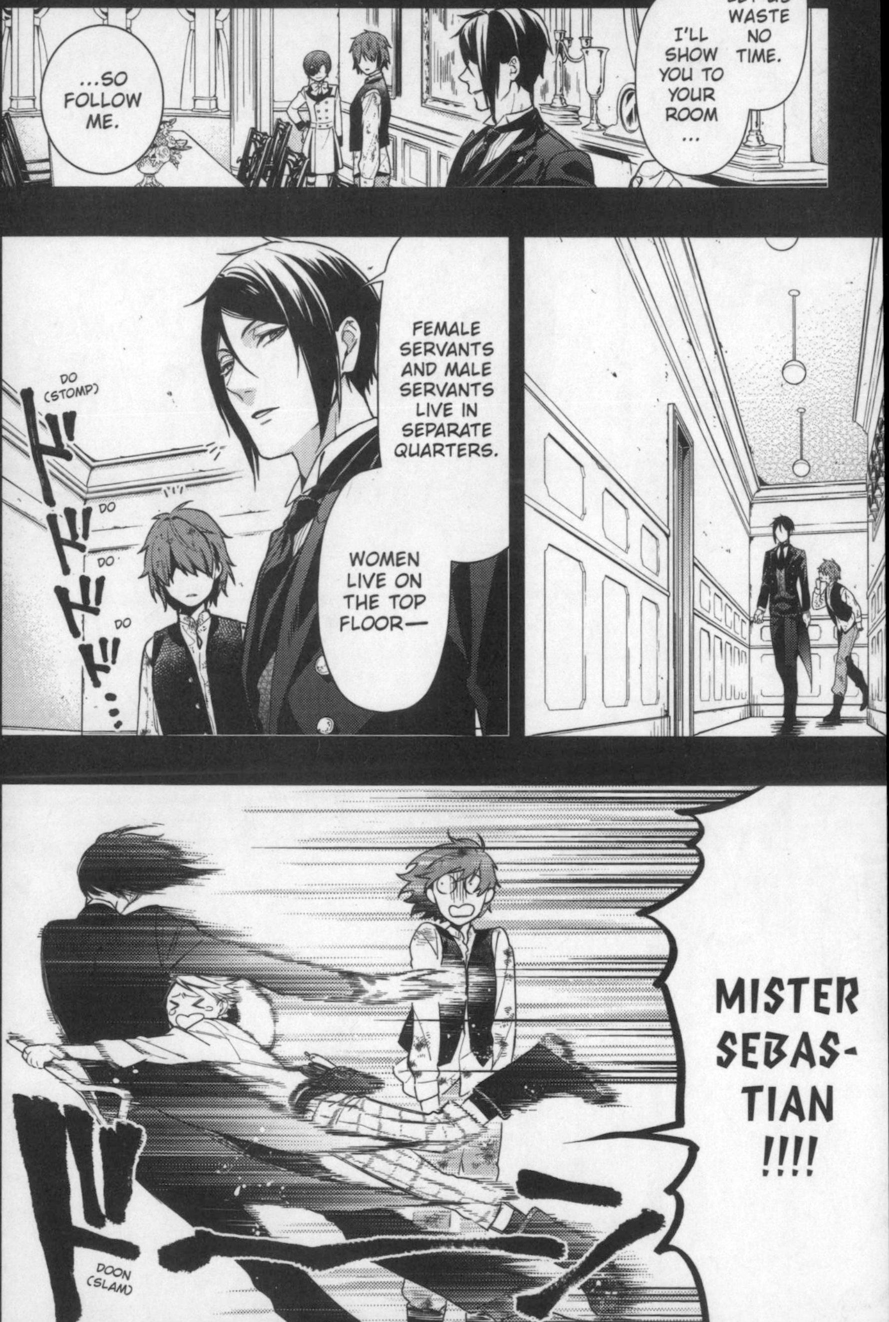
THEN LET US WASTE NO TIME.
I'LL SHOW YOU TO YOUR ROOM ...
...SO FOLLOW ME.
FEMALE SERVANTS AND MALE SERVANTS LIVE IN SEPARATE QUARTERS.
WOMEN LIVE ON THE TOP FLOOR—
DO (STOMP)
DO
DO
DO
MISTER SEBAS-TIAN !!!!
DOON (SLAM)

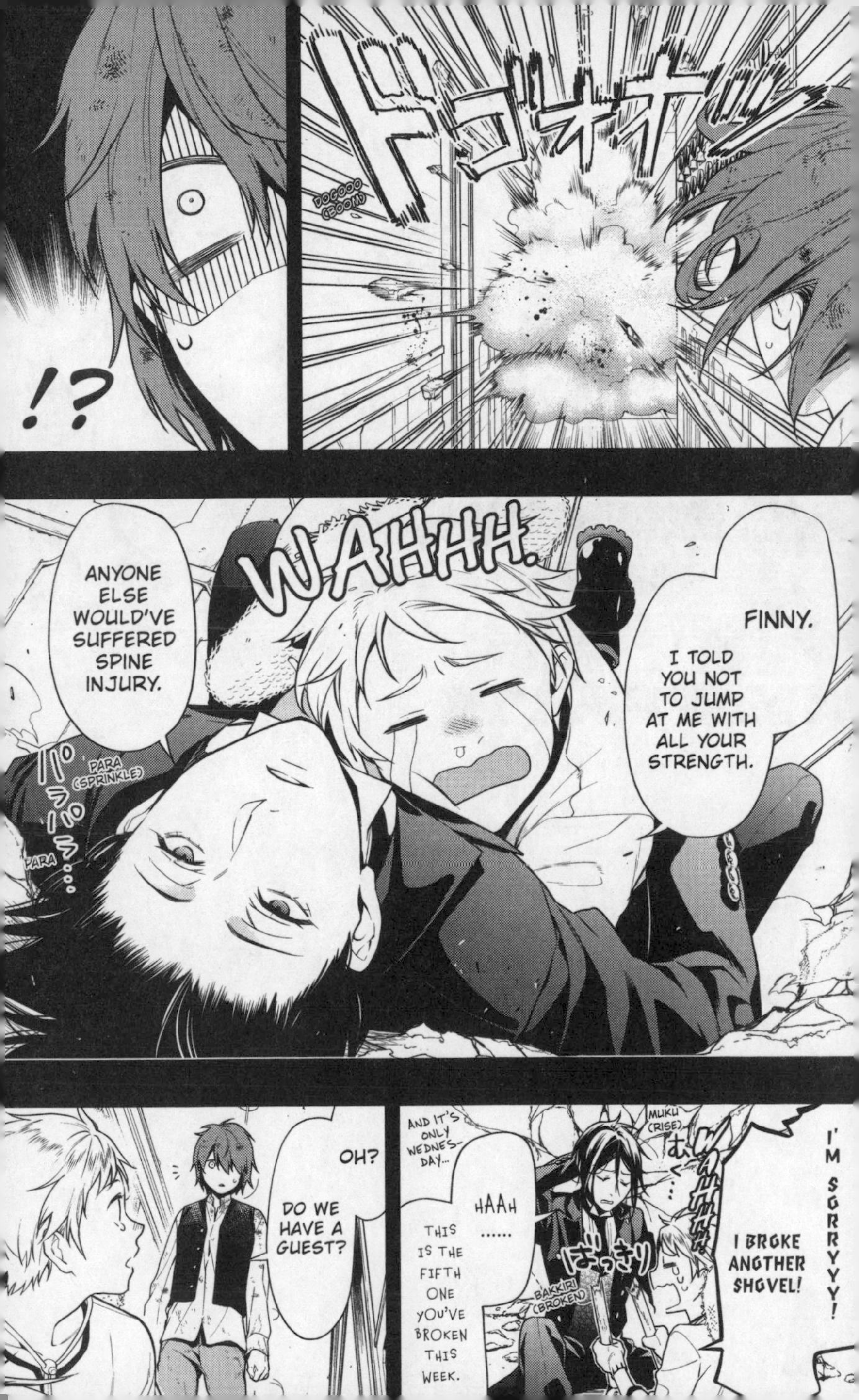
DOGOOO (ZOOM)
!?
FINNY. I TOLD YOU NOT TO JUMP AT ME WITH ALL YOUR STRENGTH.
WAHHH.
ANYONE ELSE WOULD'VE SUFFERED SPINE INJURY.
PARA (SPRINKLE)
PARA
I'M SORRYYY!
I BROKE ANOTHER SHOVEL!
MUKU (RISE)
BAKKIRI (BROKEN)
HAAH ......
THIS IS THE FIFTH ONE YOU'VE BROKEN THIS WEEK.
AND IT'S ONLY WEDNES-DAY...
OH?
DO WE HAVE A GUEST?

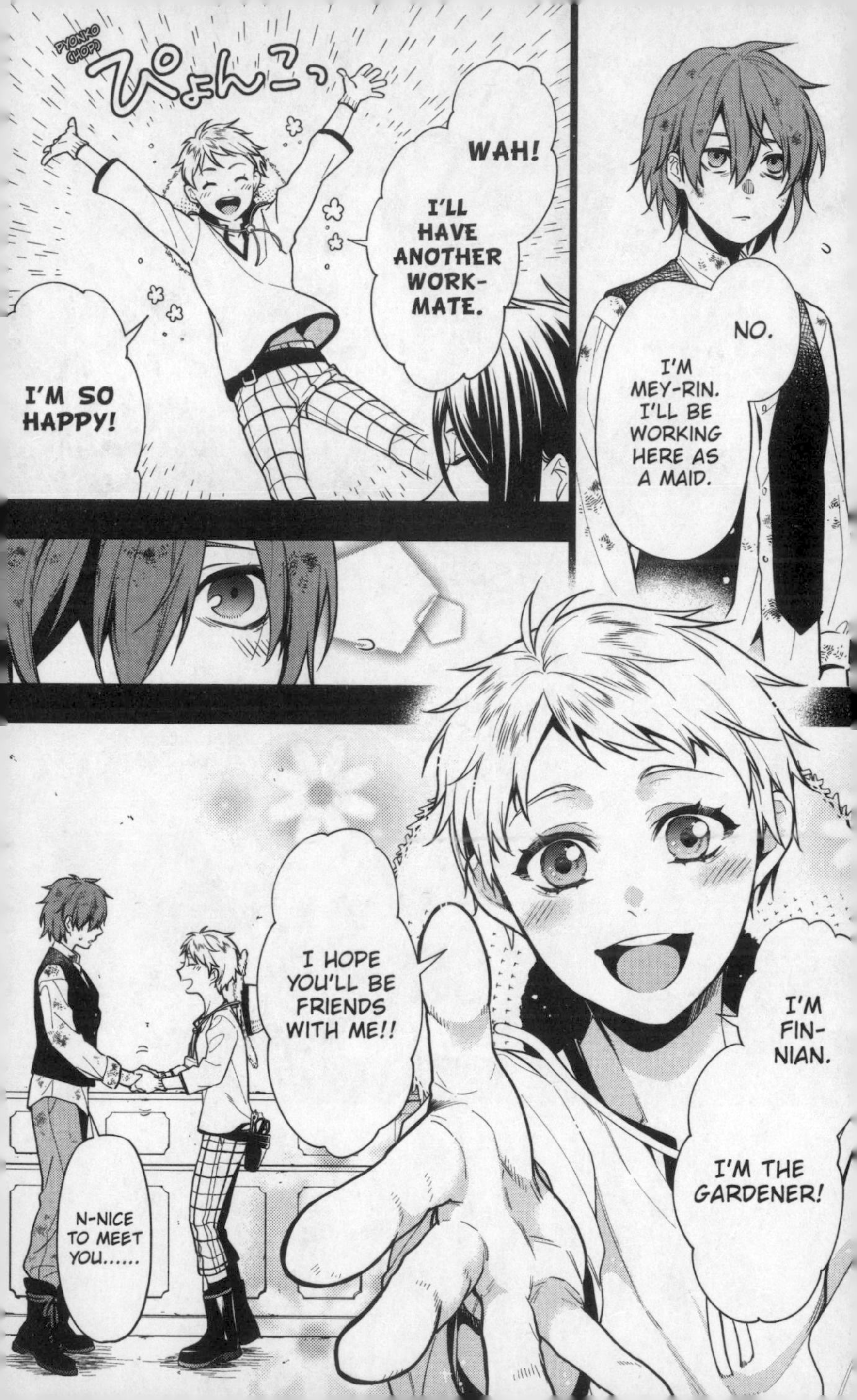
NO.
I'M MEY-RIN. I'LL BE WORKING HERE AS A MAID.
WAH!
I'LL HAVE ANOTHER WORK-MATE.
ぴょんこっ
PYONKO (HOP)
I'M SO HAPPY!
I'M FIN-NIAN.
I'M THE GARDENER!
I HOPE YOU'LL BE FRIENDS WITH ME!!
N-NICE TO MEET YOU......

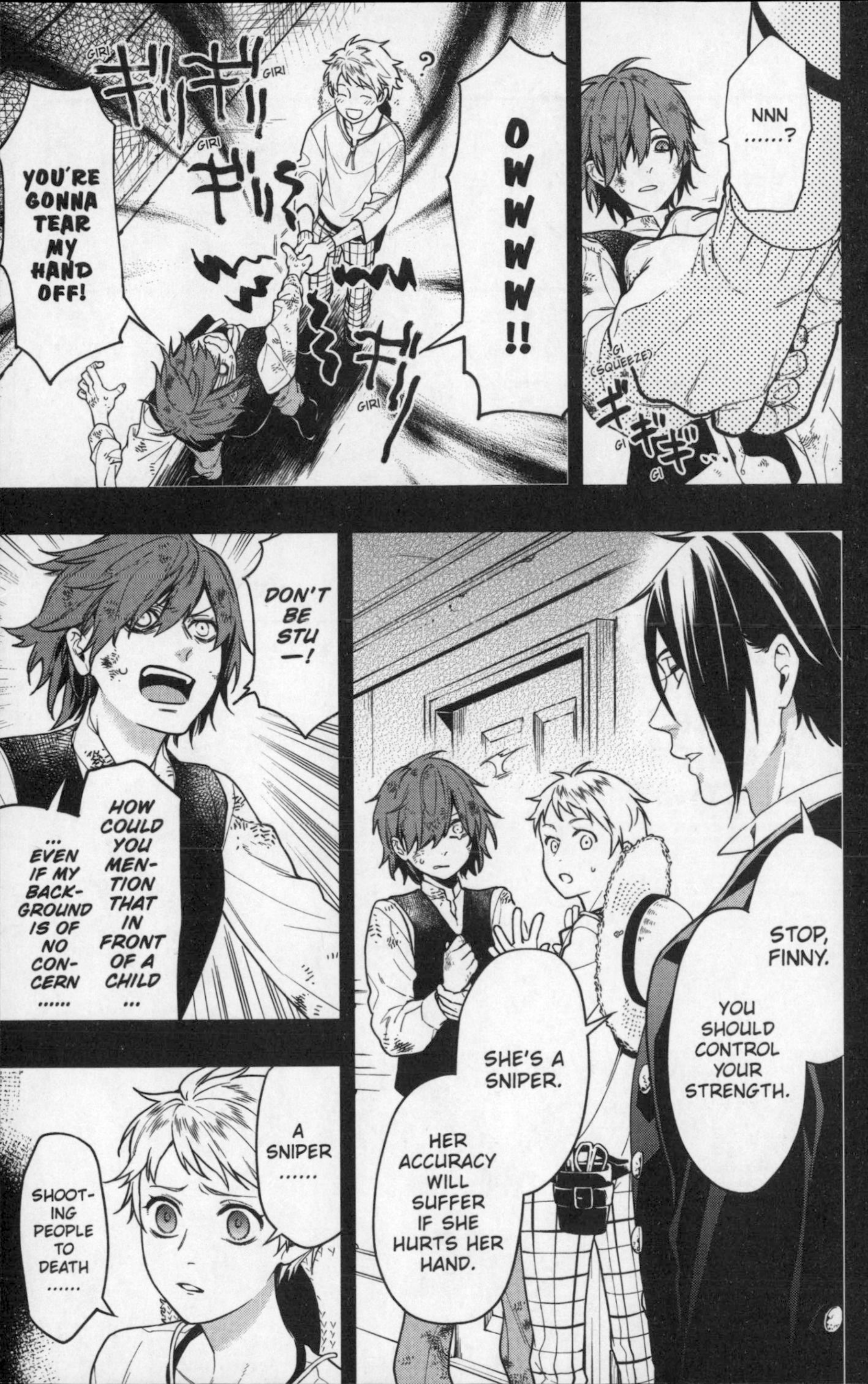
NNN ......?
GI (SQUEEZE)
GI
GI
GIRI
GIRI
GIRI
GIRI
OWWWWW!!
YOU'RE GONNA TEAR MY HAND OFF!
STOP, FINNY.
YOU SHOULD CONTROL YOUR STRENGTH.
SHE'S A SNIPER.
HER ACCURACY WILL SUFFER IF SHE HURTS HER HAND.
DON'T BE STU—!
HOW COULD YOU MENTION THAT IN FRONT OF A CHILD ...
... EVEN IF MY BACKGROUND IS OF NO CONCERN ......
A SNIPER ......
SHOOTING PEOPLE TO DEATH ......

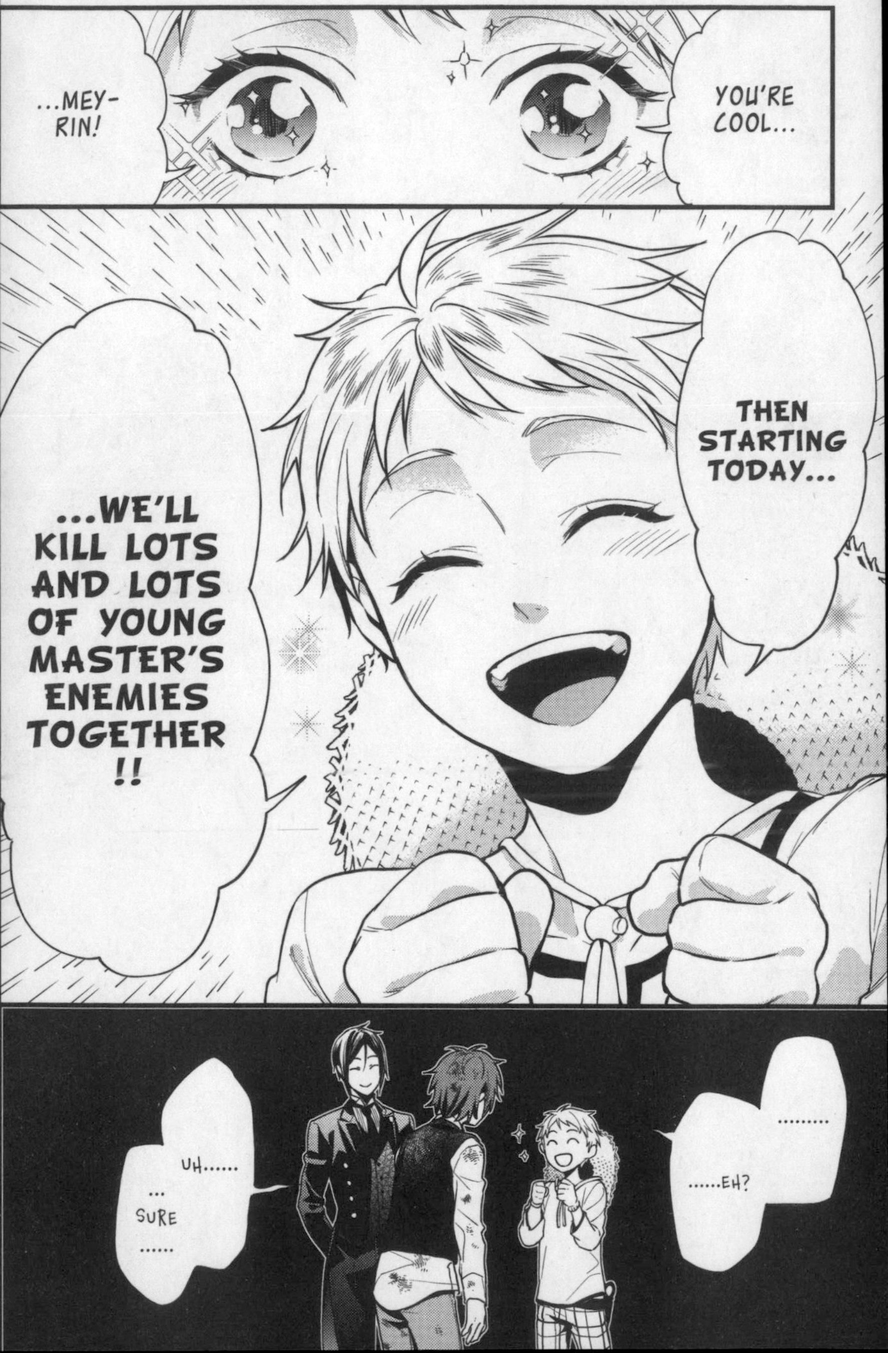
YOU'RE COOL...
...MEY-RIN!
THEN STARTING TODAY...
...WE'LL KILL LOTS AND LOTS OF YOUNG MASTER'S ENEMIES TOGETHER!!
....
......EH?
UH......
...SURE......

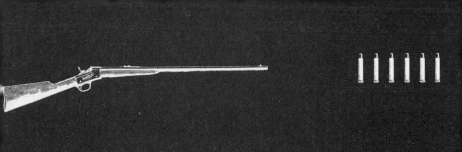

Black Butler

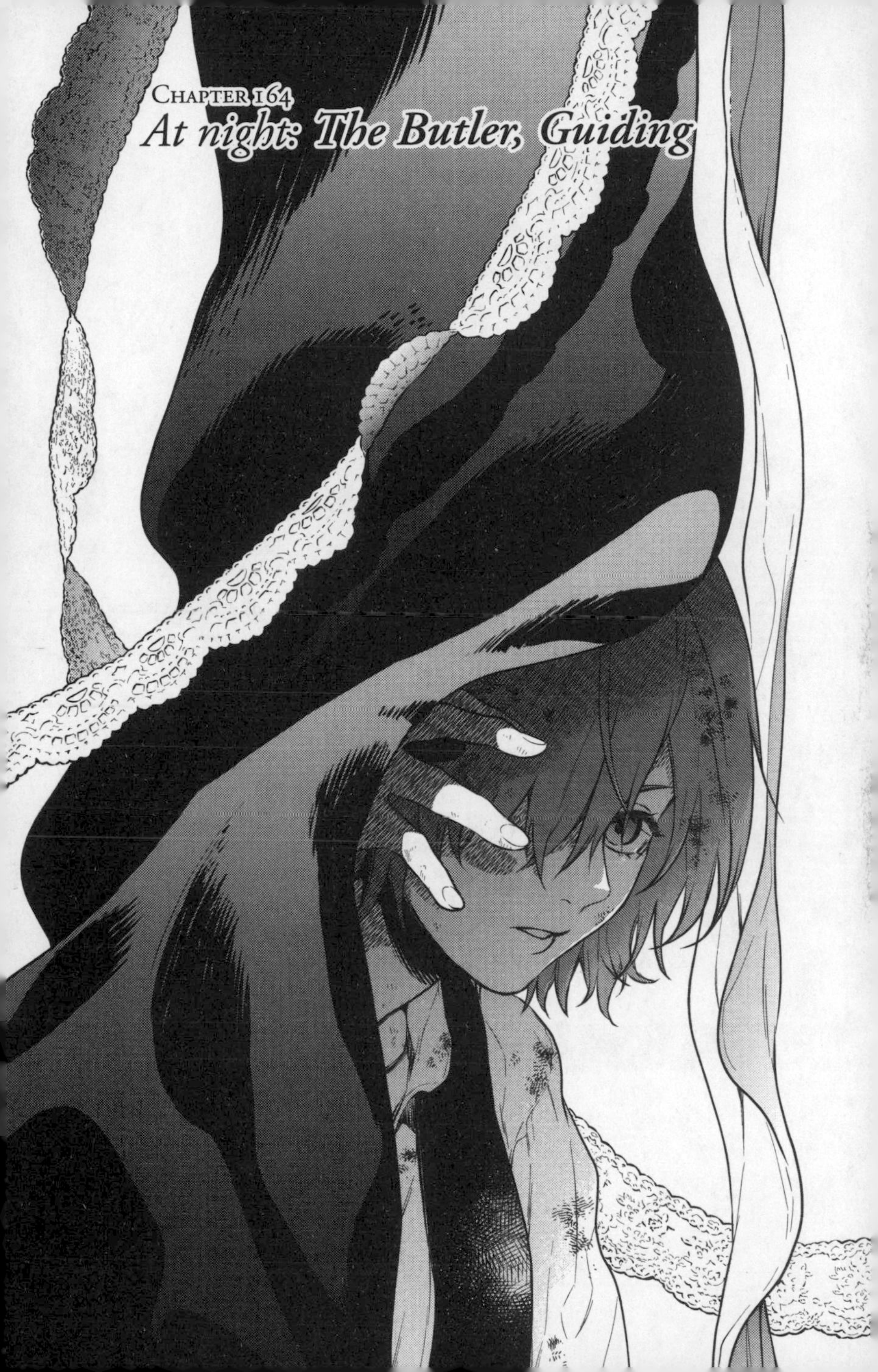
Chapter 164
At night: The Butler, Guiding

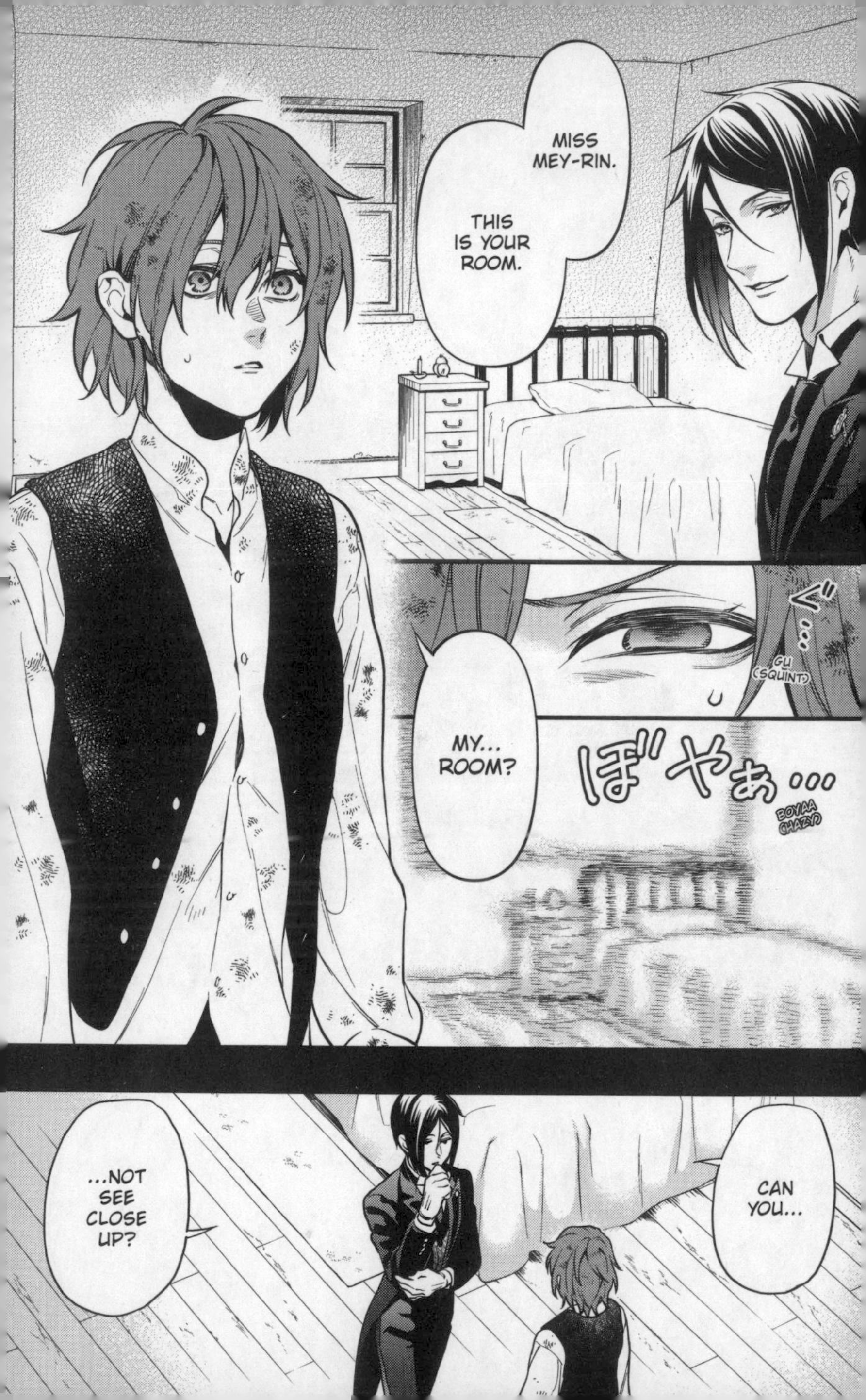

MISS MEY-RIN.
THIS IS YOUR ROOM.
ぐ…
GU (SQUINT)
MY... ROOM?
ぼやぁ…
BOYAA (HAZY)
CAN YOU...
...NOT SEE CLOSE UP?

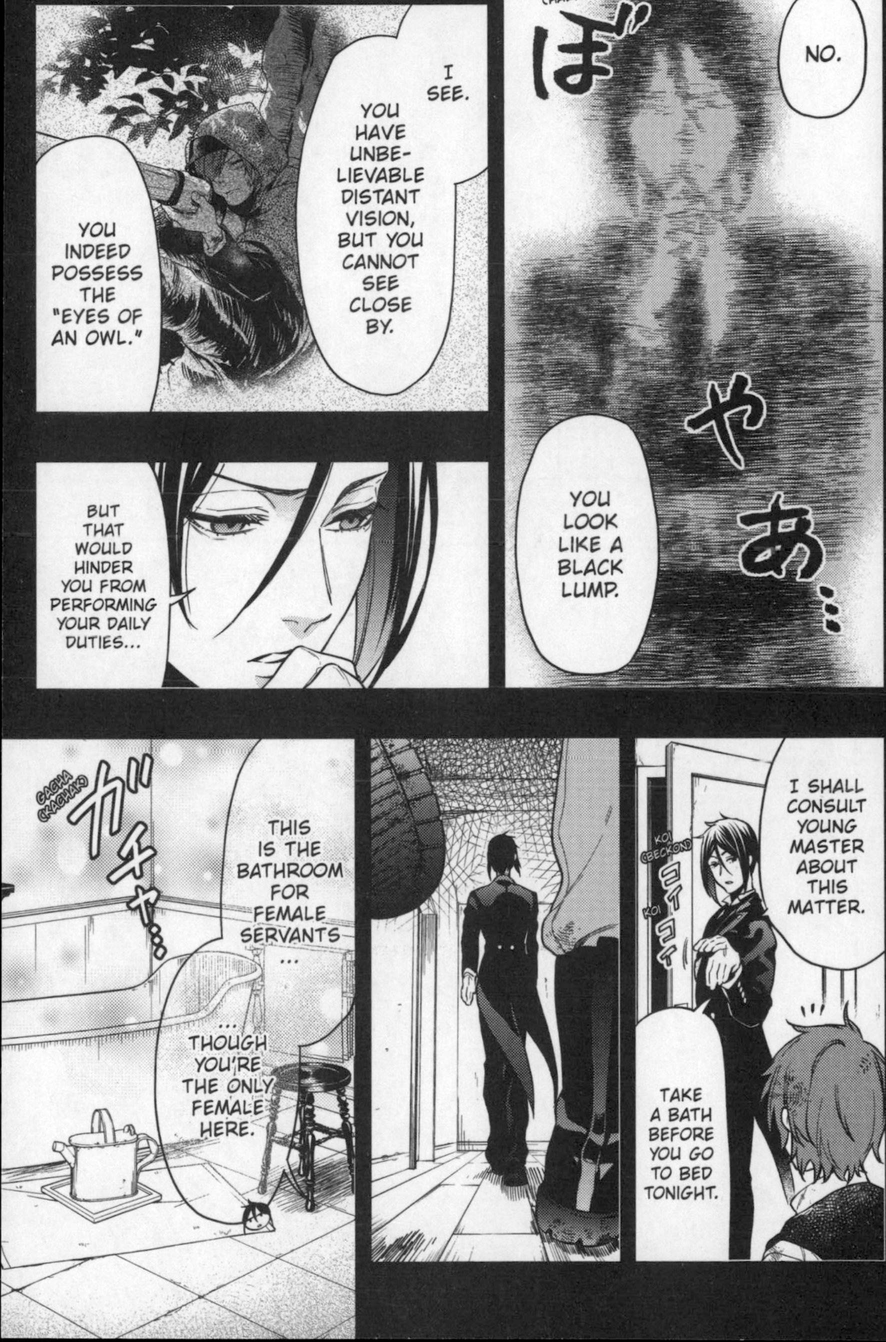

BOYAA (HAZY)
ぼやぁ…
NO.
YOU LOOK LIKE A BLACK LUMP.
I SEE.
YOU HAVE UNBE-LIEVABLE DISTANT VISION, BUT YOU CANNOT SEE CLOSE BY.
YOU INDEED POSSESS THE "EYES OF AN OWL."
BUT THAT WOULD HINDER YOU FROM PERFORMING YOUR DAILY DUTIES...
I SHALL CONSULT YOUNG MASTER ABOUT THIS MATTER.
KOI (BECKON) KOI
コイコイ
TAKE A BATH BEFORE YOU GO TO BED TONIGHT.
GACHA (KACHA)
ガチャ…
THIS IS THE BATHROOM FOR FEMALE SERVANTS...
...THOUGH YOU'RE THE ONLY FEMALE HERE.

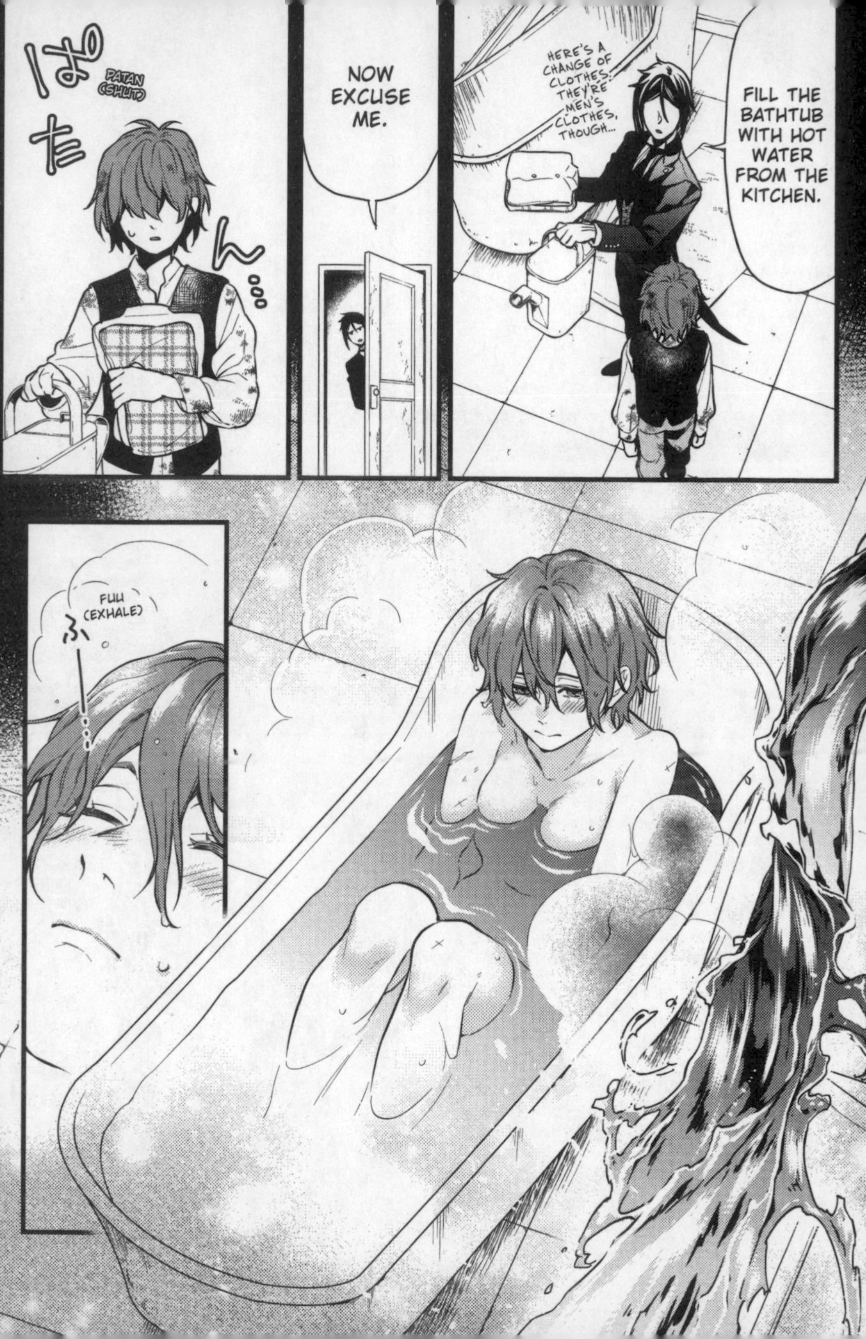
FILL THE BATHTUB WITH HOT WATER FROM THE KITCHEN.
HERE'S A CHANGE OF CLOTHES. THEY'RE MEN'S CLOTHES, THOUGH...
NOW EXCUSE ME.
ぱたん
PATAN (SHUT)
ふ
FUU (EXHALE)

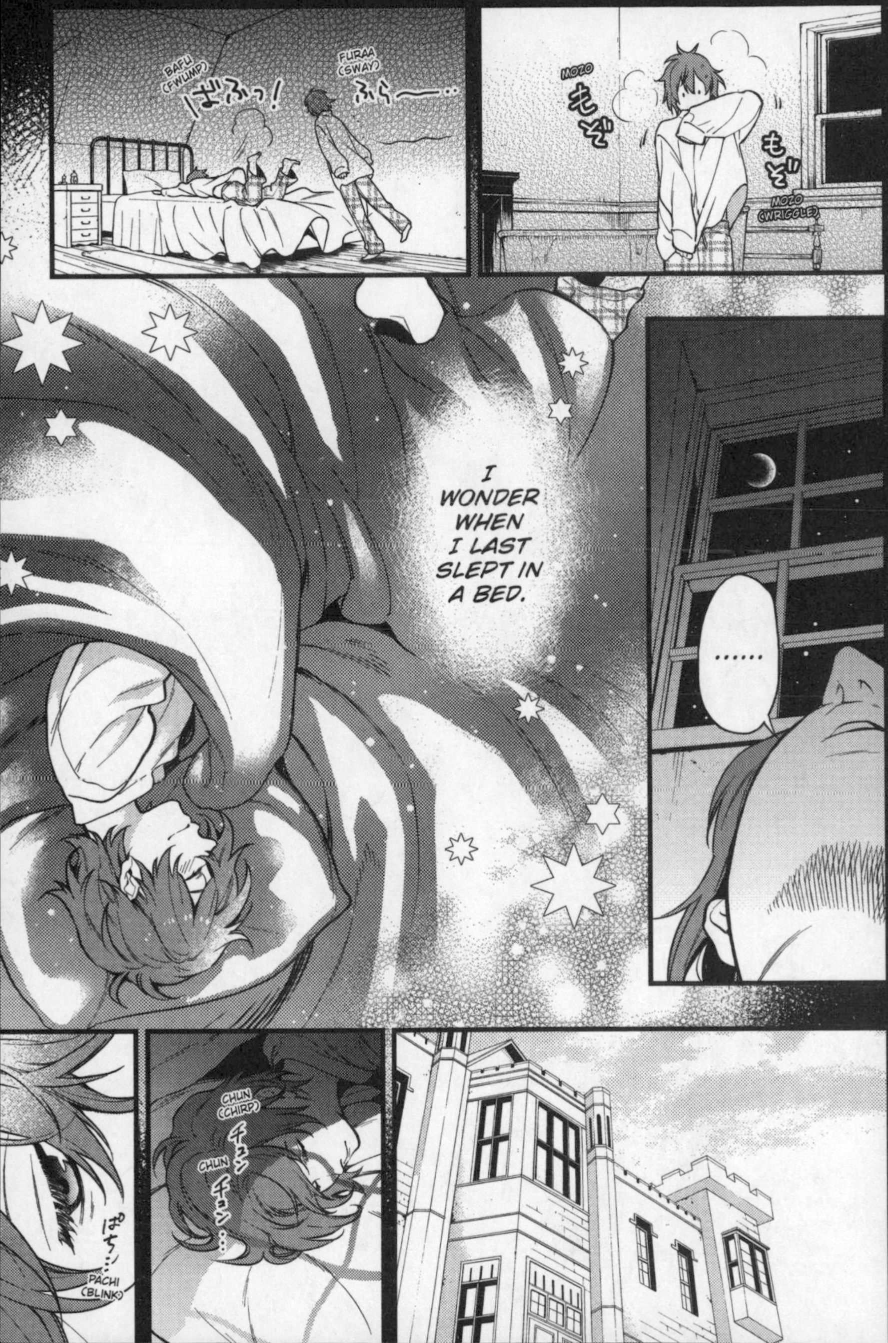
MOZO
もぞ
もぞ
MOZO (WRIGGLE)
FURAA (SWAY)
ふら〜…
BAFU (FWUMP)
ばふっ!
......
I WONDER WHEN I LAST SLEPT IN A BED.
CHUN (CHIRP)
チュン
CHUN
チュン…
ぱち…
PACHI (BLINK)

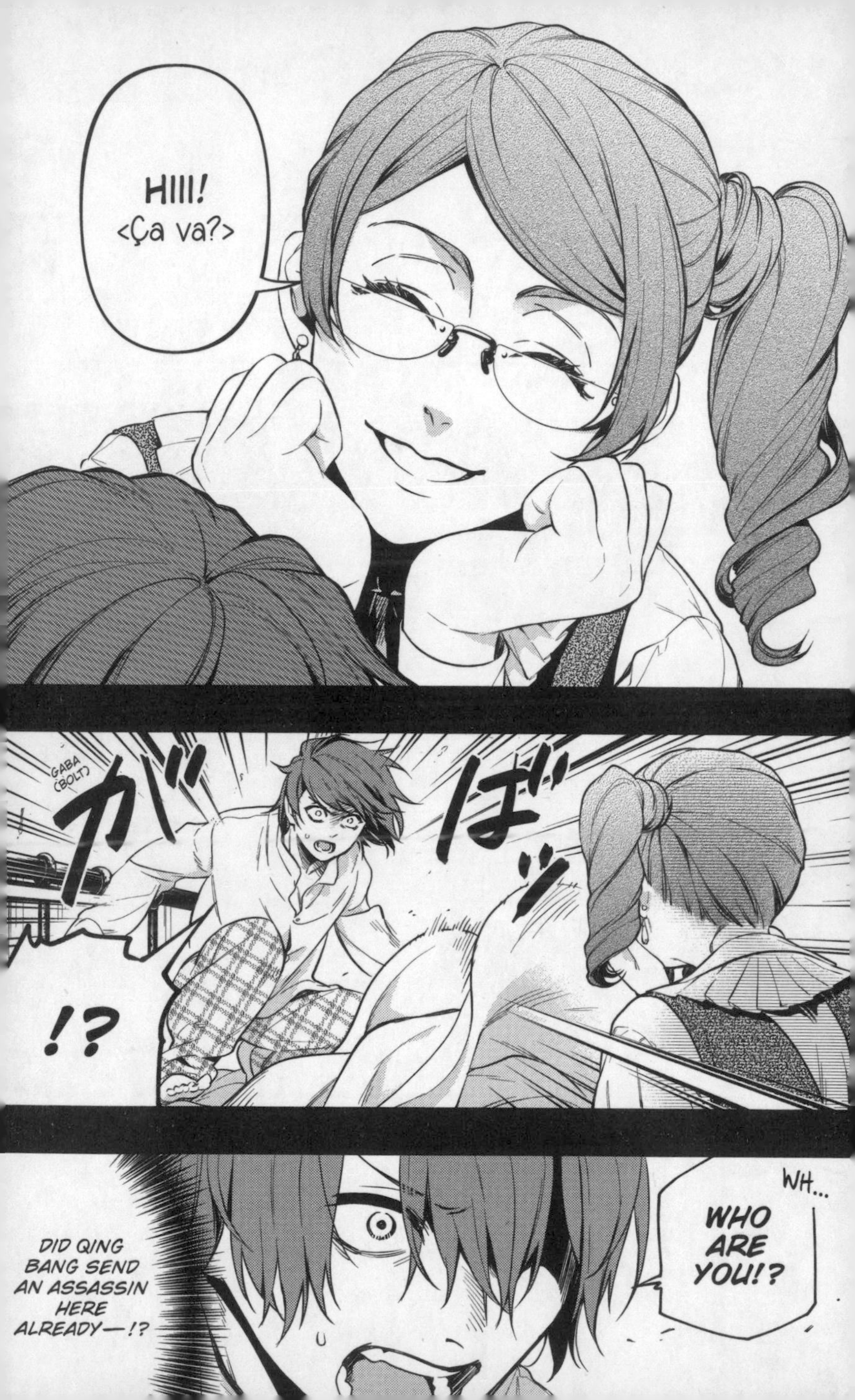
HIII!
<Ça va?>
GABA (BOLT)
!?
WH...
WHO ARE YOU!?
DID QING BANG SEND AN ASSASSIN HERE ALREADY—!?

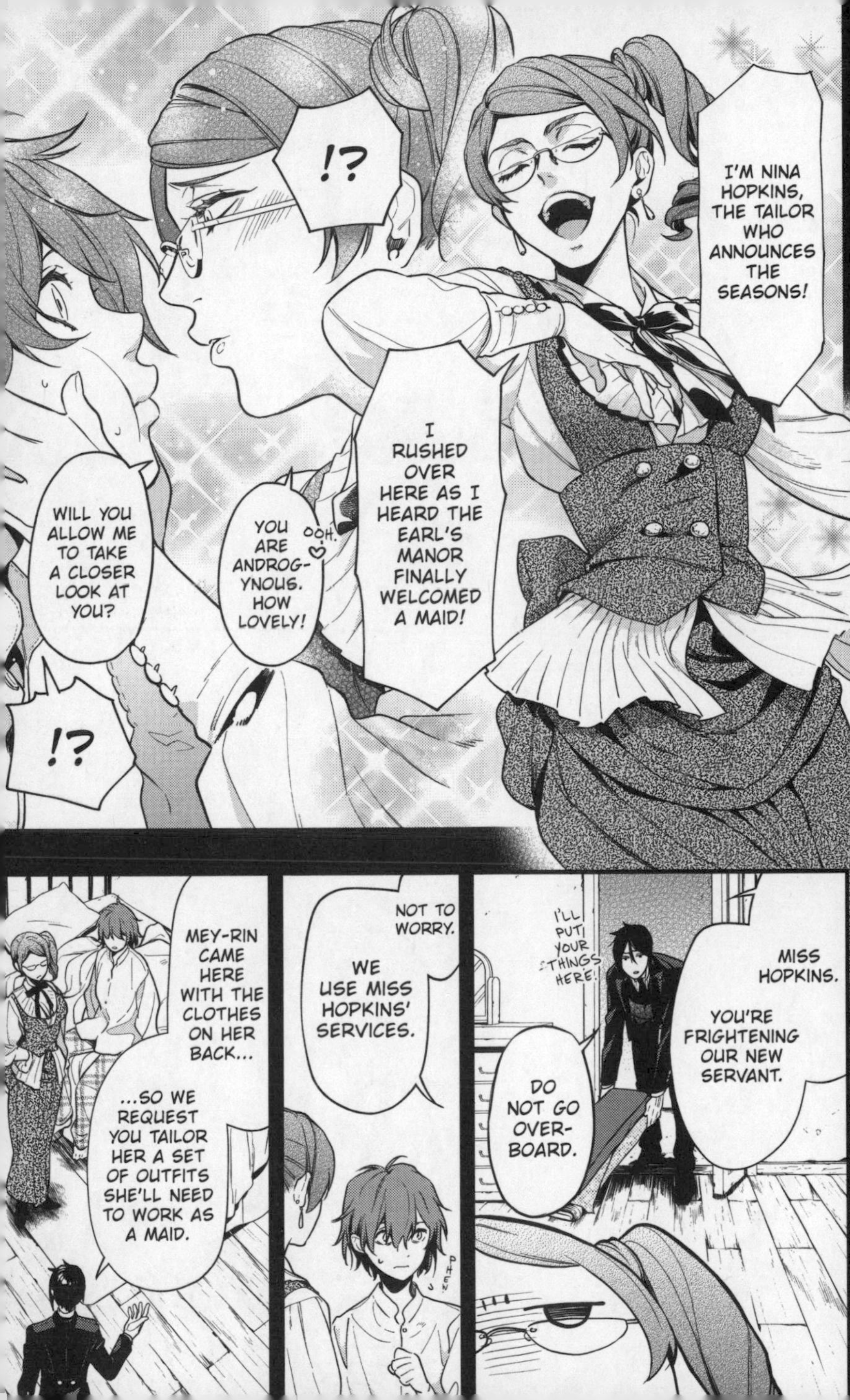
I'M NINA HOPKINS, THE TAILOR WHO ANNOUNCES THE SEASONS!
!?
I RUSHED OVER HERE AS I HEARD THE EARL'S MANOR FINALLY WELCOMED A MAID!
OOH.
YOU ARE ANDROGYNOUS. HOW LOVELY!
WILL YOU ALLOW ME TO TAKE A CLOSER LOOK AT YOU?
!?
MISS HOPKINS.
YOU'RE FRIGHTENING OUR NEW SERVANT.
I'LL PUT YOUR THINGS HERE!
DO NOT GO OVER-BOARD.
NOT TO WORRY.
WE USE MISS HOPKINS' SERVICES.
PHEN.
MEY-RIN CAME HERE WITH THE CLOTHES ON HER BACK...
...SO WE REQUEST YOU TAILOR HER A SET OF OUTFITS SHE'LL NEED TO WORK AS A MAID.

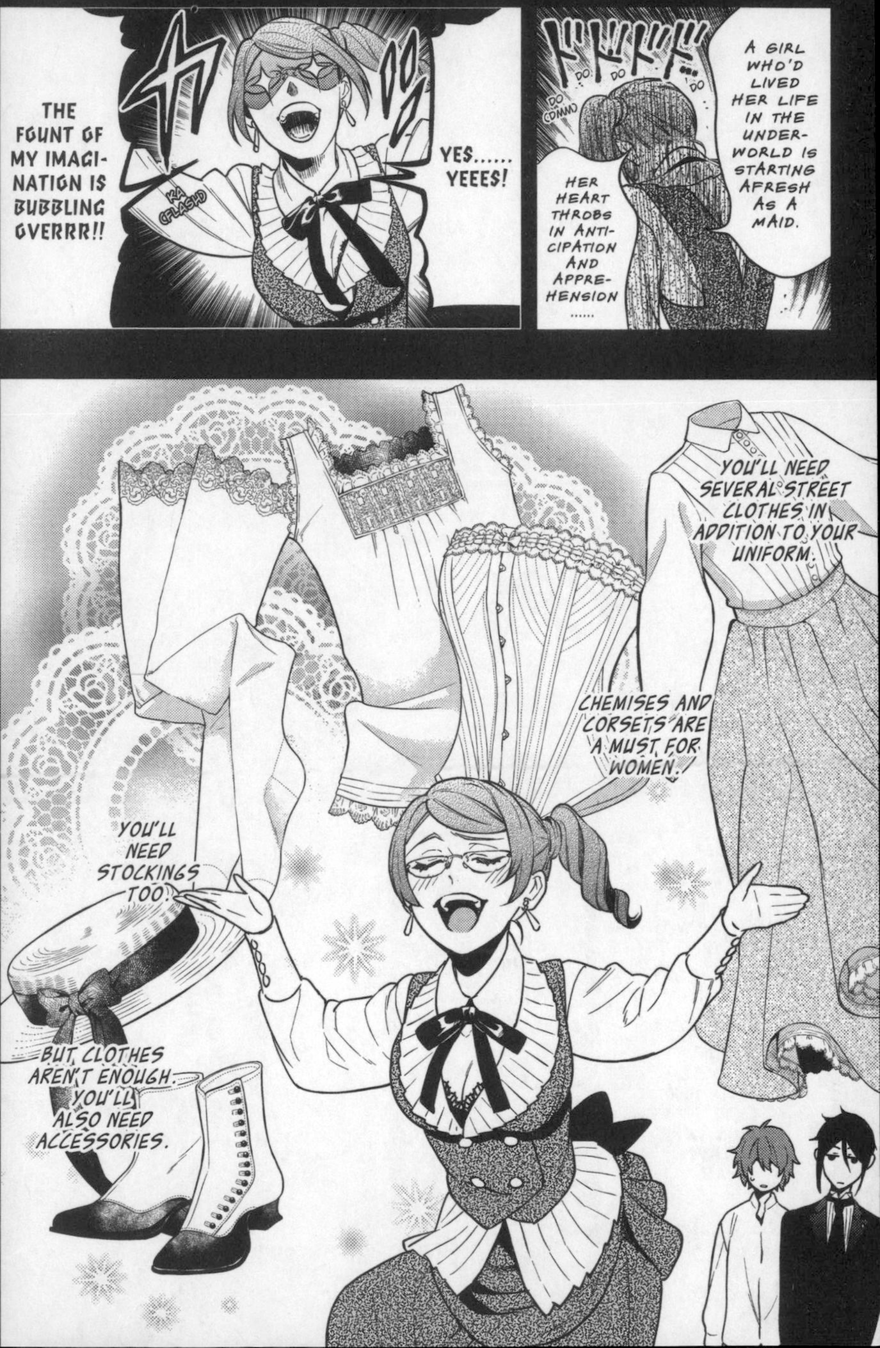
DO DO DO DO (DMM)
A GIRL WHO'D LIVED HER LIFE IN THE UNDER-WORLD IS STARTING AFRESH AS A MAID.
HER HEART THROBS IN ANTI-CIPATION AND APPRE-HENSION ......
YES...... YEEES!
KA (FLASH)
THE FOUNT OF MY IMAGI-NATION IS BUBBLING OVERRR!!
YOU'LL NEED SEVERAL STREET CLOTHES IN ADDITION TO YOUR UNIFORM.
CHEMISES AND CORSETS ARE A MUST FOR WOMEN.
YOU'LL NEED STOCKINGS TOO.
BUT CLOTHES AREN'T ENOUGH. YOU'LL ALSO NEED ACCESSORIES.

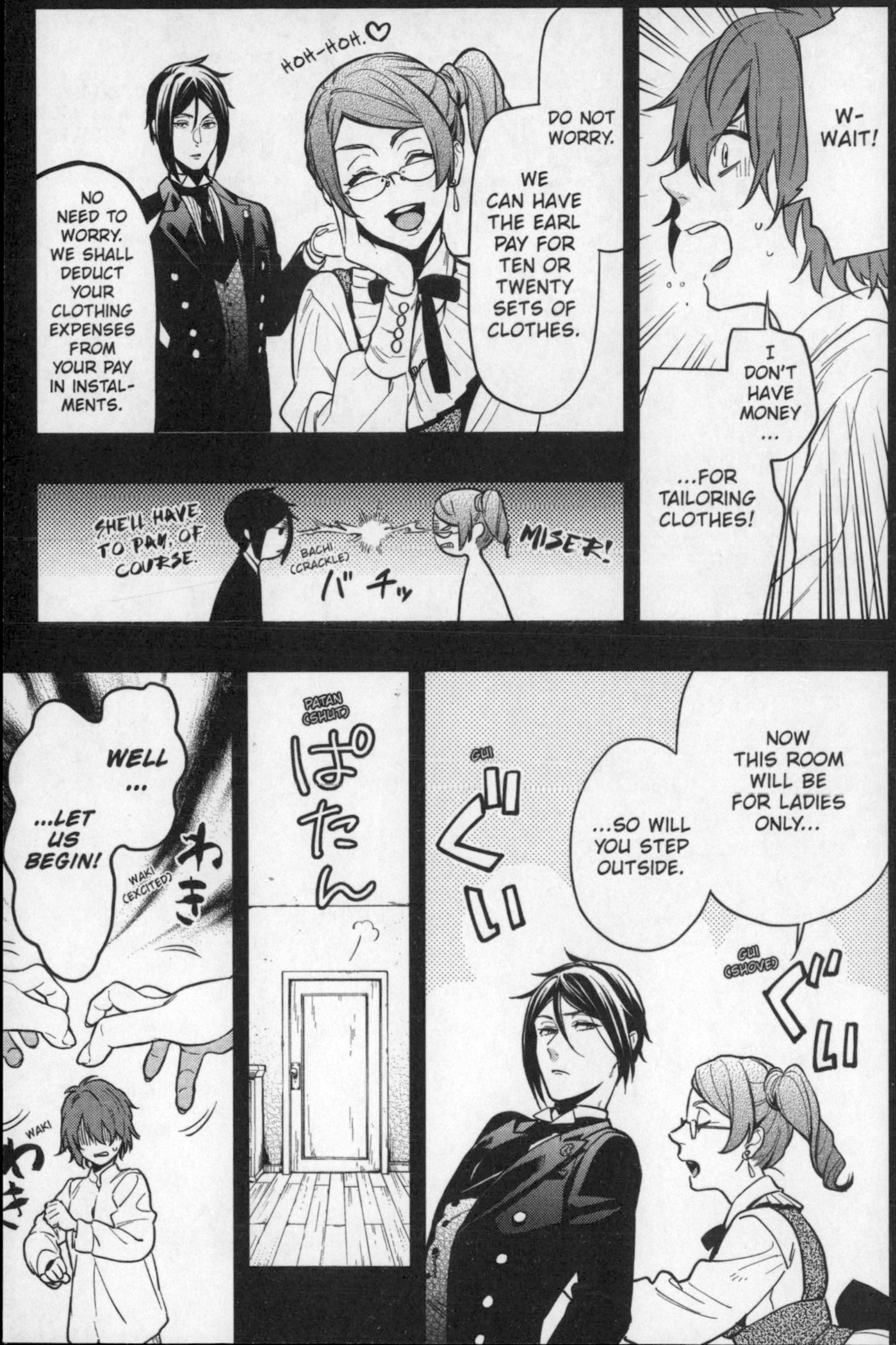

W-WAIT!
I DON'T HAVE MONEY...
...FOR TAILORING CLOTHES!
HOH-HOH.♡
DO NOT WORRY.
WE CAN HAVE THE EARL PAY FOR TEN OR TWENTY SETS OF CLOTHES.
NO NEED TO WORRY. WE SHALL DEDUCT YOUR CLOTHING EXPENSES FROM YOUR PAY IN INSTALMENTS.
MISER!
BACHI (CRACKLE)
バチッ
SHE'LL HAVE TO PAY, OF COURSE.
NOW THIS ROOM WILL BE FOR LADIES ONLY...
...SO WILL YOU STEP OUTSIDE.
GUI
ぐい
GUI (SHOVE)
ぐい
PATAN (SHUT)
ぱたん
WELL...
...LET US BEGIN!
WAKI (EXCITED)
わき
WAKI
わき

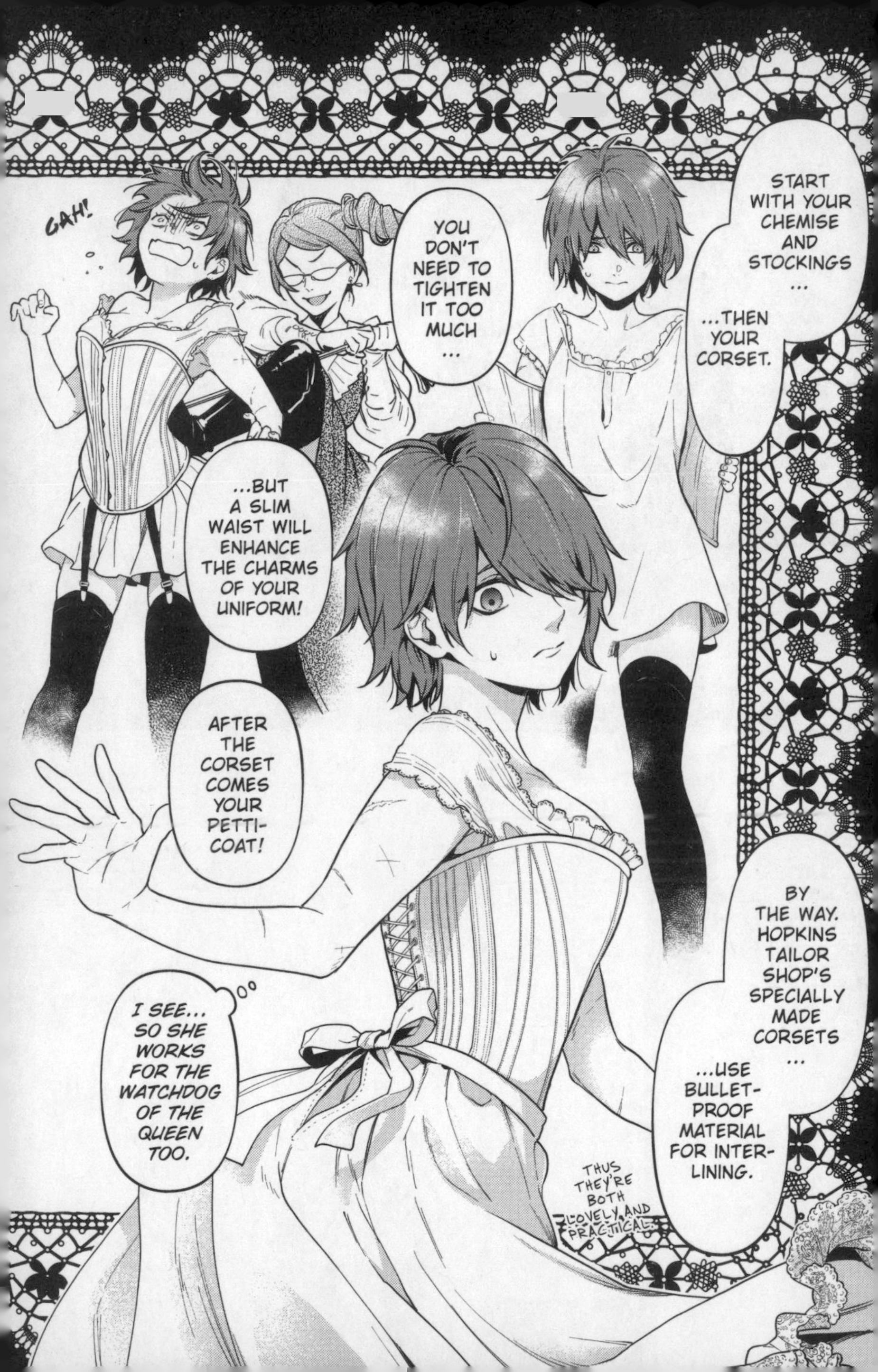
START WITH YOUR CHEMISE AND STOCKINGS...
...THEN YOUR CORSET.
YOU DON'T NEED TO TIGHTEN IT TOO MUCH...
GAH!
...BUT A SLIM WAIST WILL ENHANCE THE CHARMS OF YOUR UNIFORM!
AFTER THE CORSET COMES YOUR PETTI-COAT!
BY THE WAY. HOPKINS TAILOR SHOP'S SPECIALLY MADE CORSETS...
...USE BULLET-PROOF MATERIAL FOR INTER-LINING.
THUS THEY'RE BOTH LOVELY AND PRACTICAL.
I SEE... SO SHE WORKS FOR THE WATCHDOG OF THE QUEEN TOO.

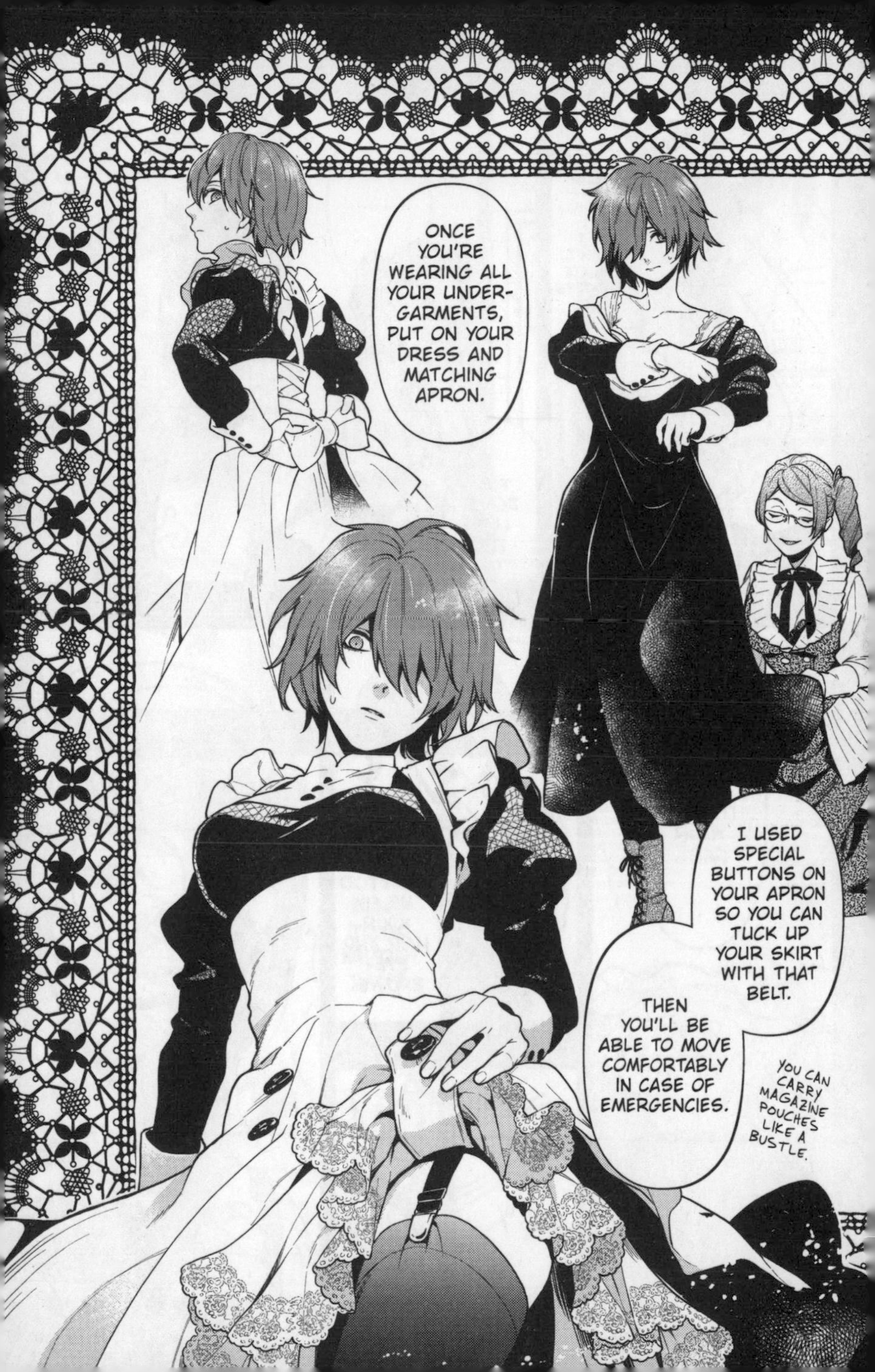
ONCE YOU'RE WEARING ALL YOUR UNDER-GARMENTS, PUT ON YOUR DRESS AND MATCHING APRON.
I USED SPECIAL BUTTONS ON YOUR APRON SO YOU CAN TUCK UP YOUR SKIRT WITH THAT BELT.
THEN YOU'LL BE ABLE TO MOVE COMFORTABLY IN CASE OF EMERGENCIES.
YOU CAN CARRY MAGAZINE POUCHES LIKE A BUSTLE.

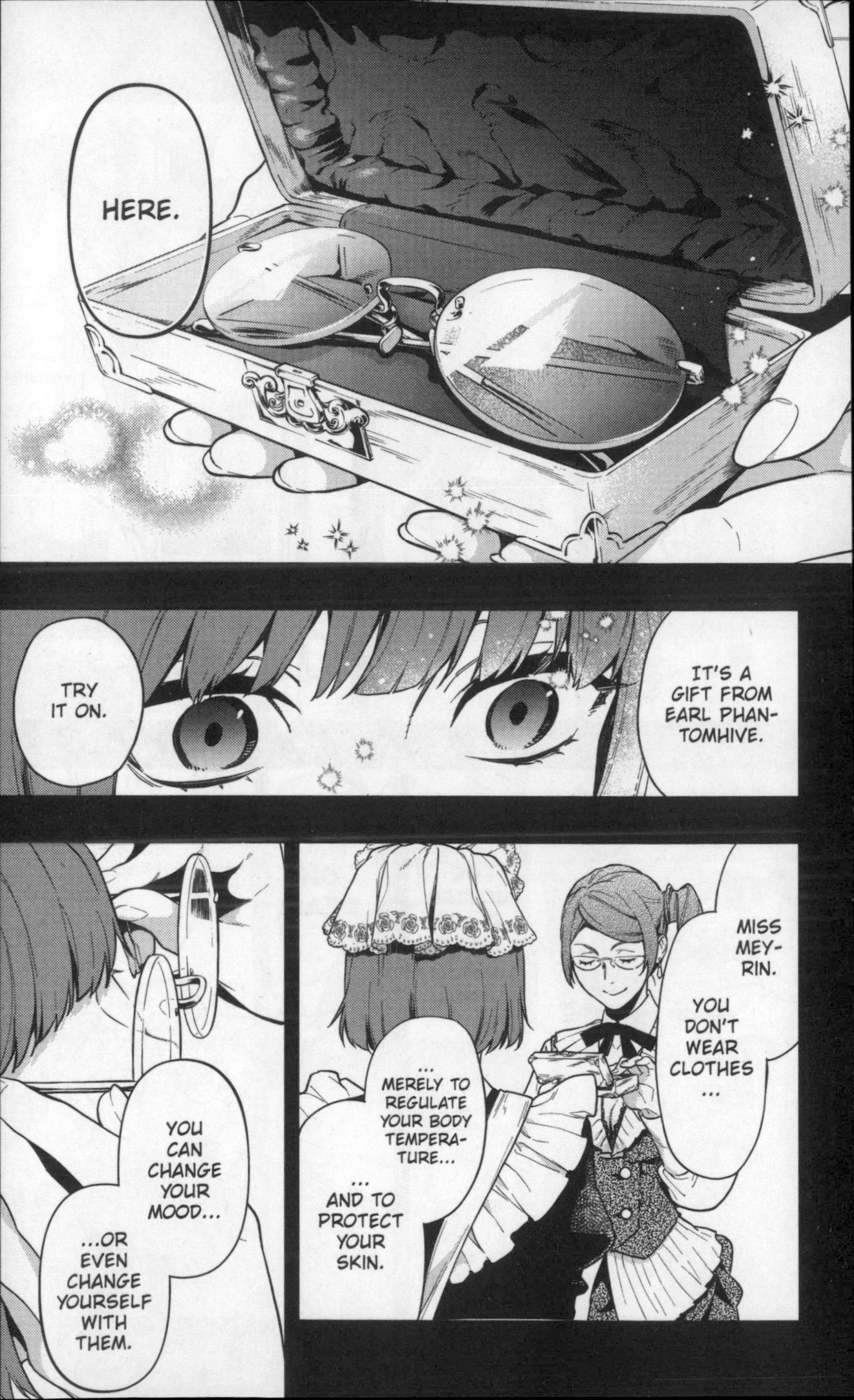
HERE.
IT'S A GIFT FROM EARL PHANTOMHIVE.
TRY IT ON.
MISS MEYRIN.
YOU DON'T WEAR CLOTHES...
...MERELY TO REGULATE YOUR BODY TEMPERATURE...
...AND TO PROTECT YOUR SKIN.
YOU CAN CHANGE YOUR MOOD...
...OR EVEN CHANGE YOURSELF WITH THEM.

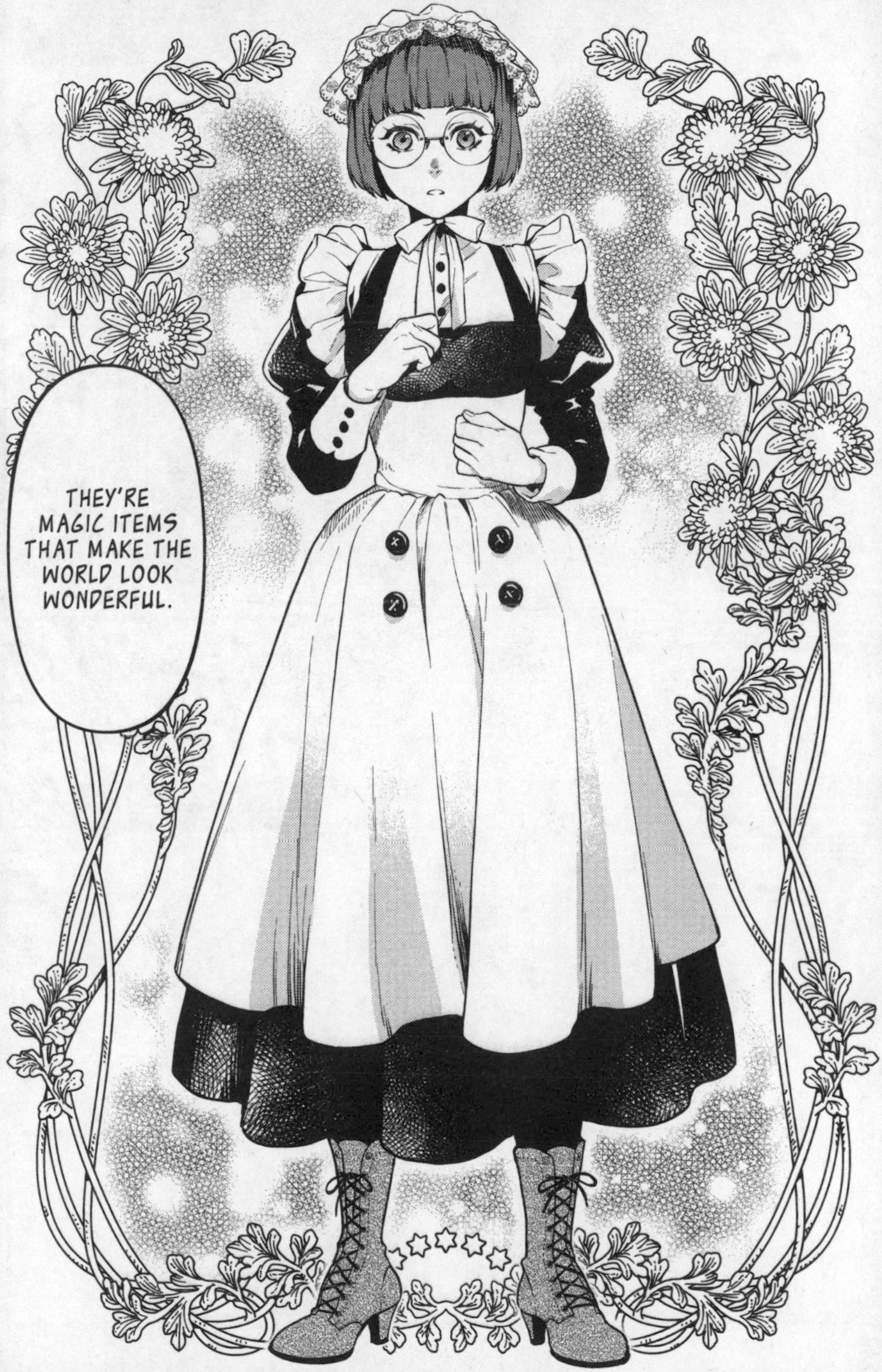
THEY'RE MAGIC ITEMS THAT MAKE THE WORLD LOOK WONDERFUL.

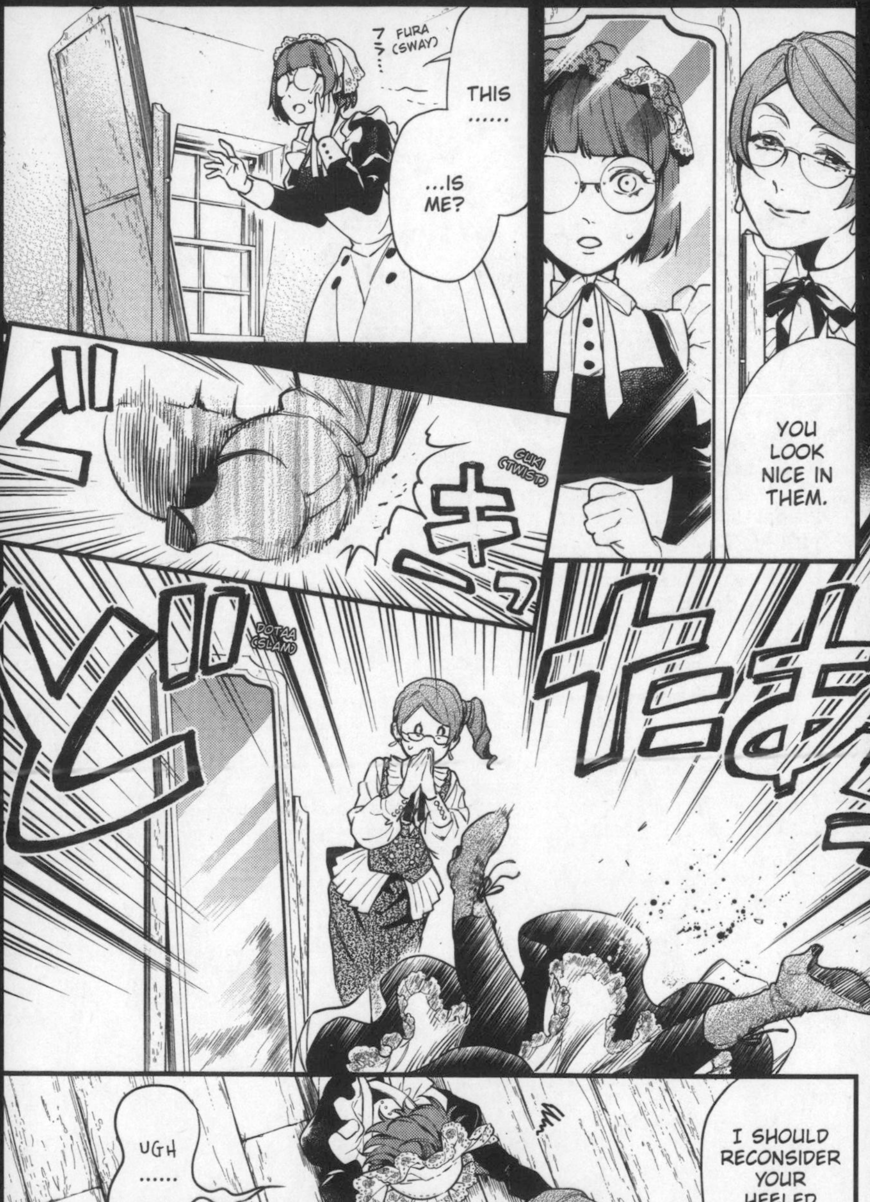
YOU LOOK NICE IN THEM.
FURA (SWAY)
THIS ......
...IS ME?
GUKI (TWIST)
DOTAA (SLAM)
I SHOULD RECONSIDER YOUR HEELED BOOTS.
UGH ......

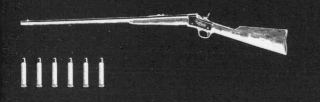

Black Butler

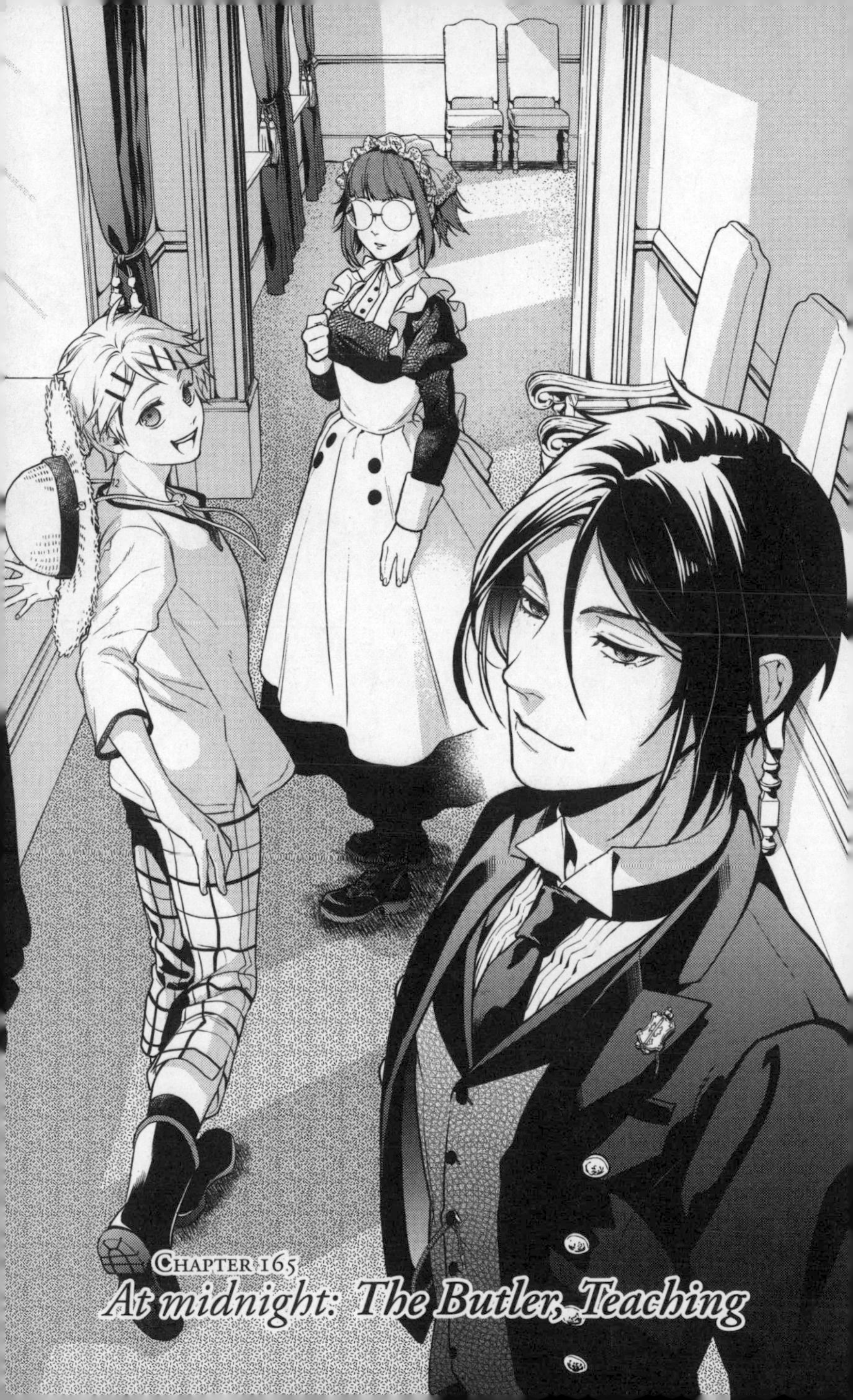
Chapter 165
At midnight: The Butler, Teaching

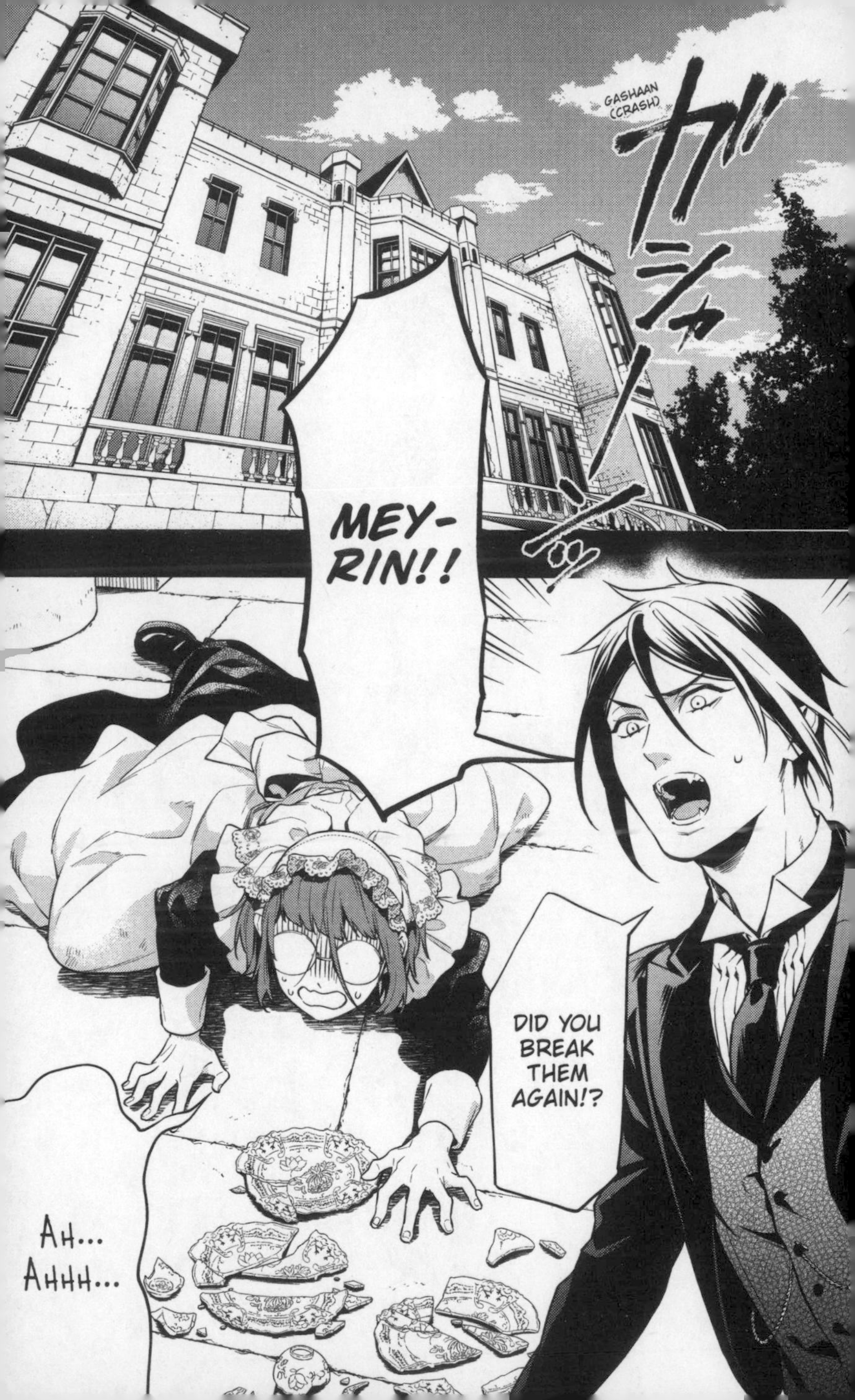
GASHAAN (CRASH)
MEY-RIN!!
DID YOU BREAK THEM AGAIN!?
AH... AHHH...

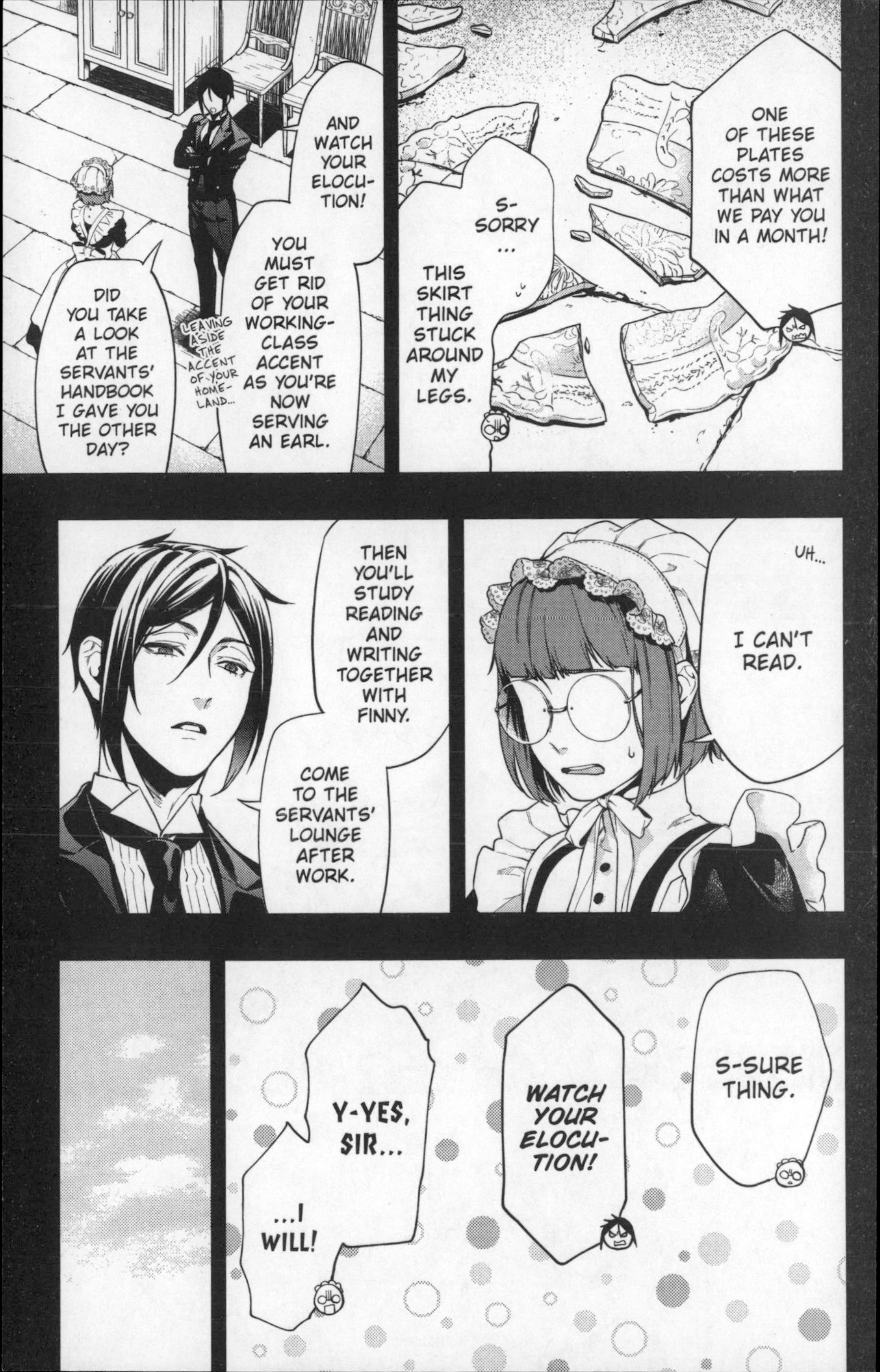
ONE OF THESE PLATES COSTS MORE THAN WHAT WE PAY YOU IN A MONTH!
S-SORRY...
THIS SKIRT THING STUCK AROUND MY LEGS.
AND WATCH YOUR ELOCU-TION!
YOU MUST GET RID OF YOUR WORKING-CLASS ACCENT AS YOU'RE NOW SERVING AN EARL.
LEAVING ASIDE THE ACCENT OF YOUR HOME-LAND...
DID YOU TAKE A LOOK AT THE SERVANTS' HANDBOOK I GAVE YOU THE OTHER DAY?
UH...
I CAN'T READ.
THEN YOU'LL STUDY READING AND WRITING TOGETHER WITH FINNY.
COME TO THE SERVANTS' LOUNGE AFTER WORK.
S-SURE THING.
WATCH YOUR ELOCU-TION!
Y-YES, SIR...
...I WILL!

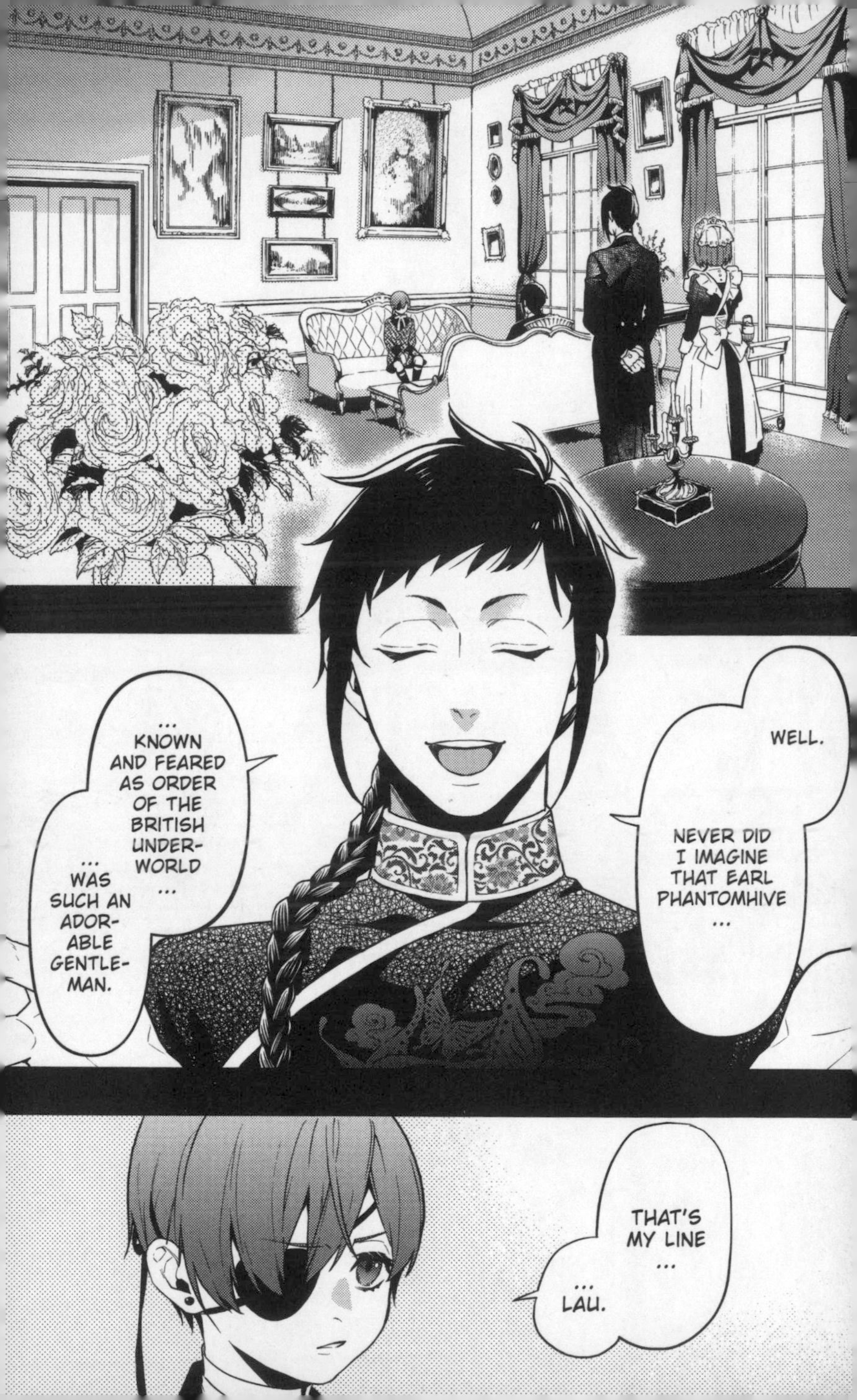
WELL.
NEVER DID I IMAGINE THAT EARL PHANTOMHIVE ...
... KNOWN AND FEARED AS ORDER OF THE BRITISH UNDER-WORLD ...
... WAS SUCH AN ADOR-ABLE GENTLE-MAN.
THAT'S MY LINE ...
... LAU.

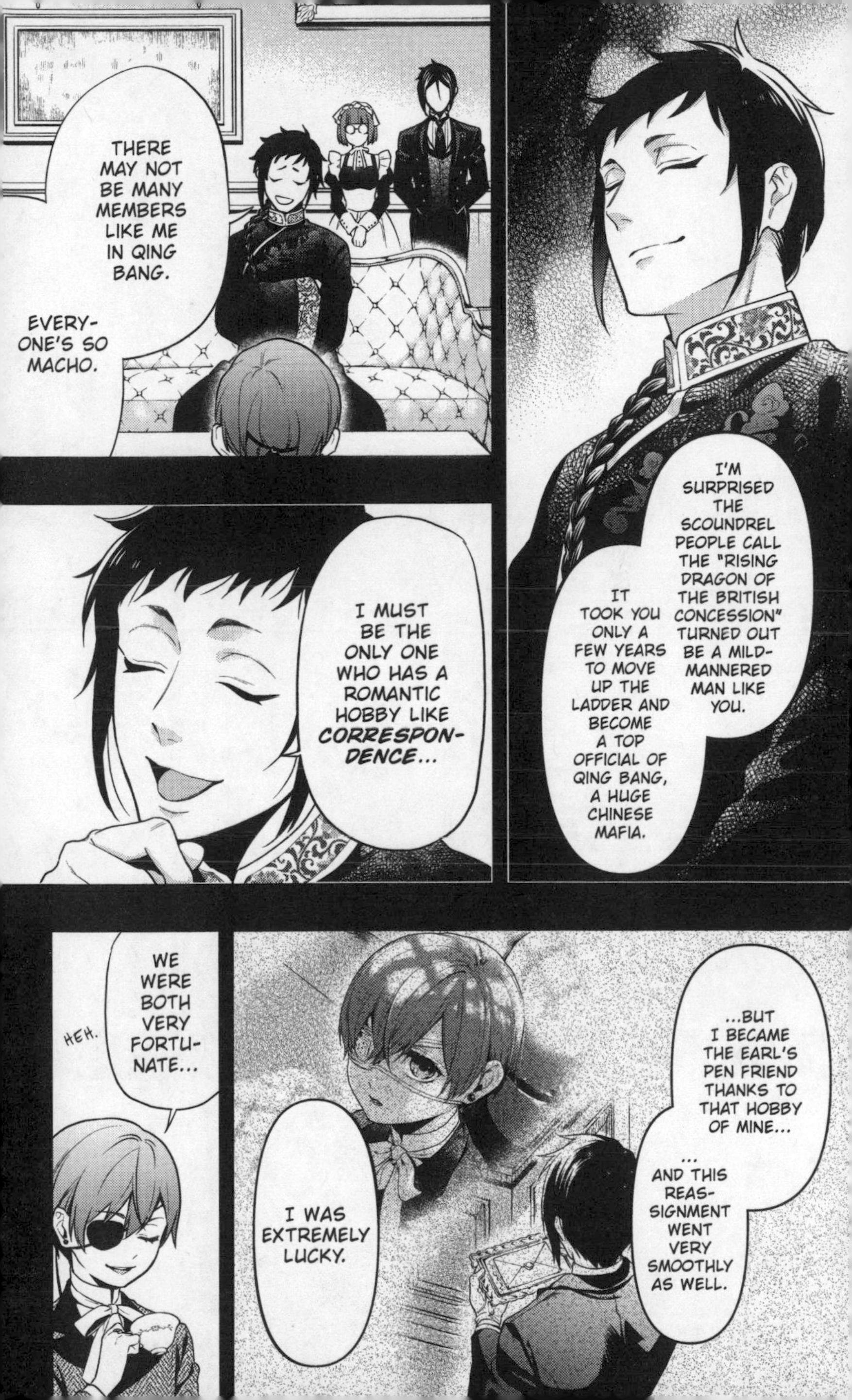
I'M SURPRISED THE SCOUNDREL PEOPLE CALL THE "RISING DRAGON OF THE BRITISH CONCESSION" TURNED OUT BE A MILD-MANNERED MAN LIKE YOU.
IT TOOK YOU ONLY A FEW YEARS TO MOVE UP THE LADDER AND BECOME A TOP OFFICIAL OF QING BANG, A HUGE CHINESE MAFIA.
THERE MAY NOT BE MANY MEMBERS LIKE ME IN QING BANG.
EVERY-ONE'S SO MACHO.
I MUST BE THE ONLY ONE WHO HAS A ROMANTIC HOBBY LIKE ***CORRESPON-DENCE***...
...BUT I BECAME THE EARL'S PEN FRIEND THANKS TO THAT HOBBY OF MINE...
...AND THIS REAS-SIGNMENT WENT VERY SMOOTHLY AS WELL.
I WAS EXTREMELY LUCKY.
WE WERE BOTH VERY FORTU-NATE...
HEH.

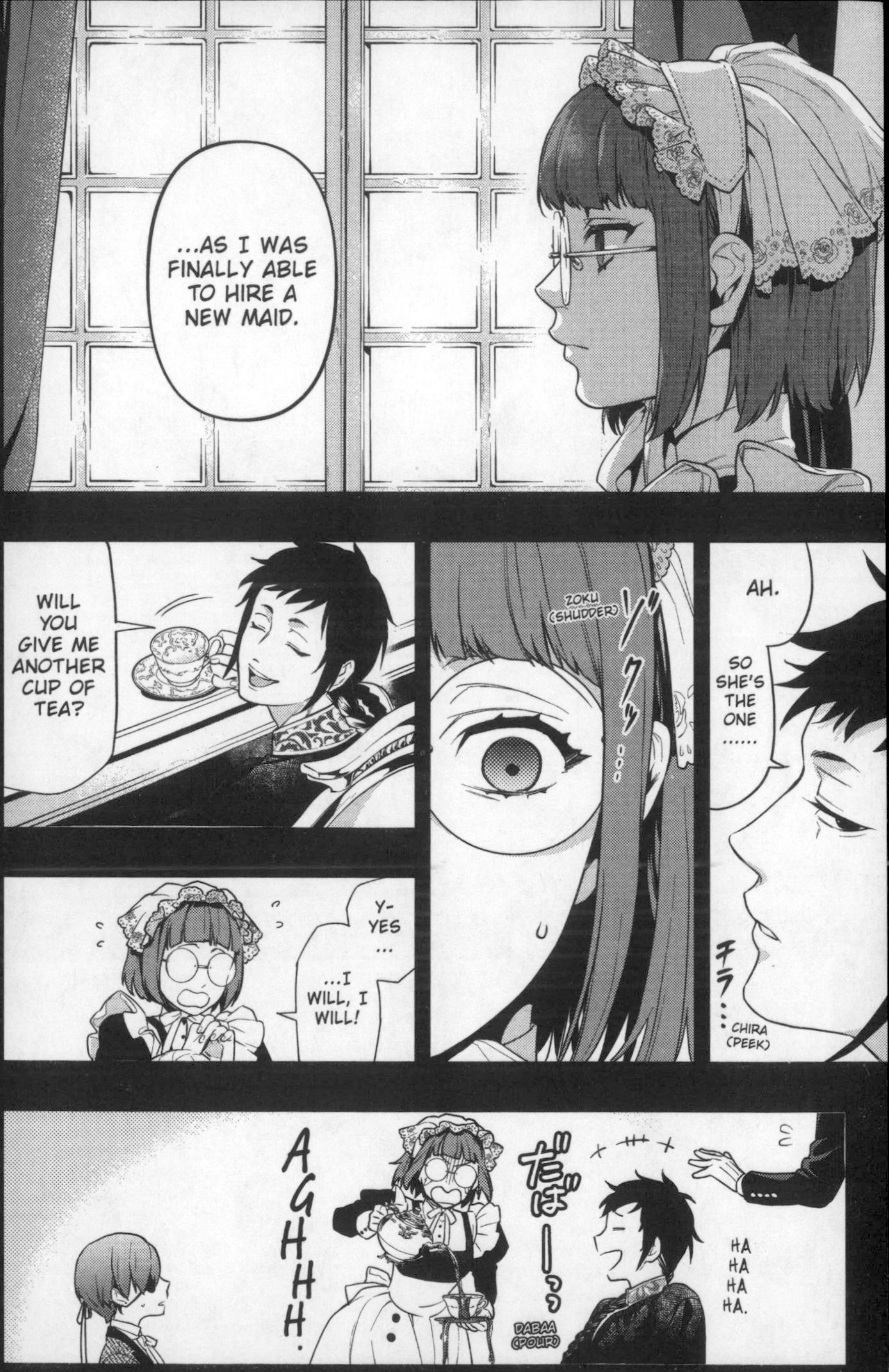
...AS I WAS FINALLY ABLE TO HIRE A NEW MAID.
AH.
SO SHE'S THE ONE......
チラ…
CHIRA (PEEK)
ゾクッ…
ZOKU (SHUDDER)
WILL YOU GIVE ME ANOTHER CUP OF TEA?
Y-YES...
...I WILL, I WILL!
HA HA HA HA.
だばーっっ
DABAA (POUR)
AGHHH.

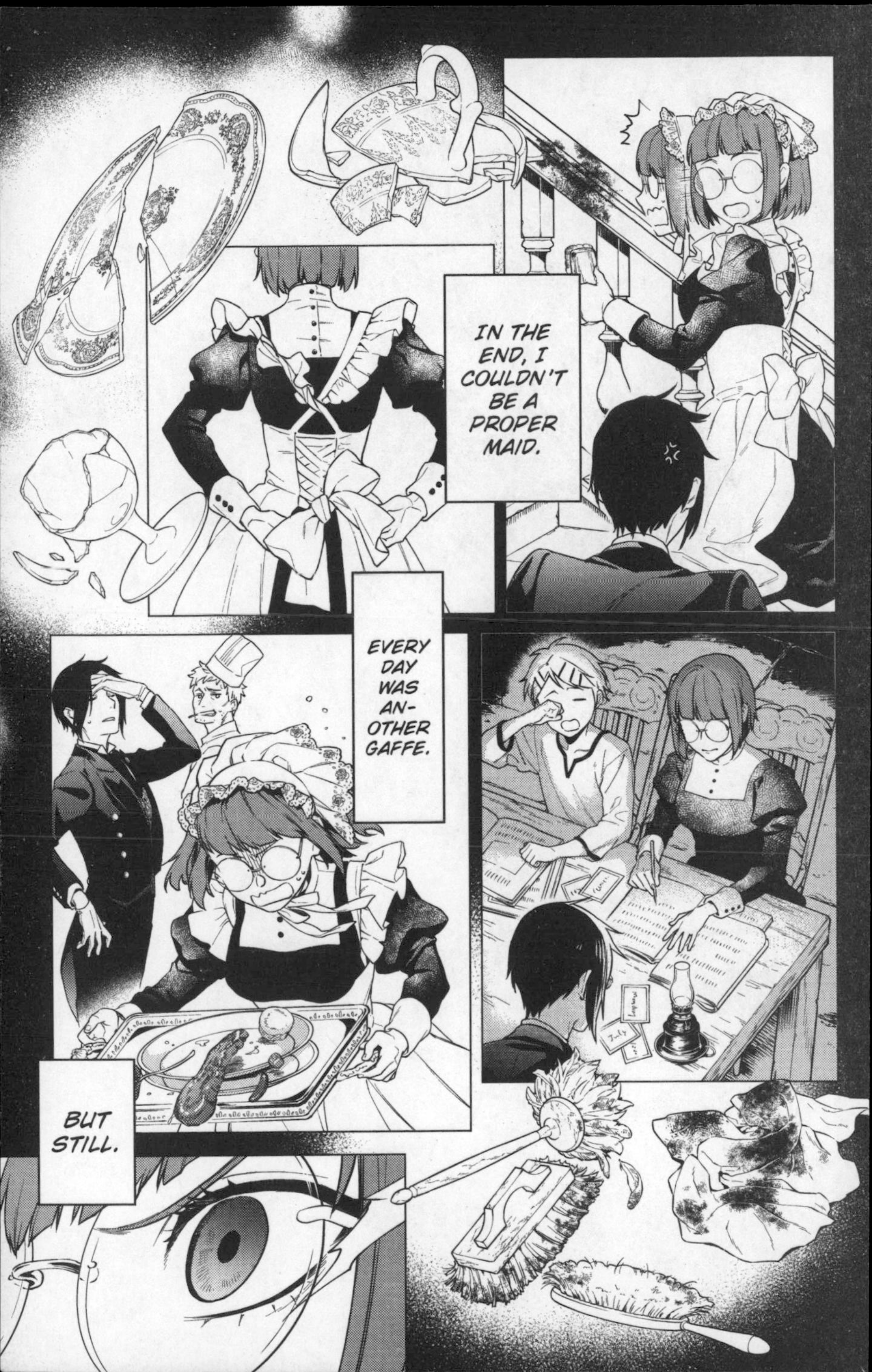
IN THE END, I COULDN'T BE A PROPER MAID.
EVERY DAY WAS AN-OTHER GAFFE.
BUT STILL.

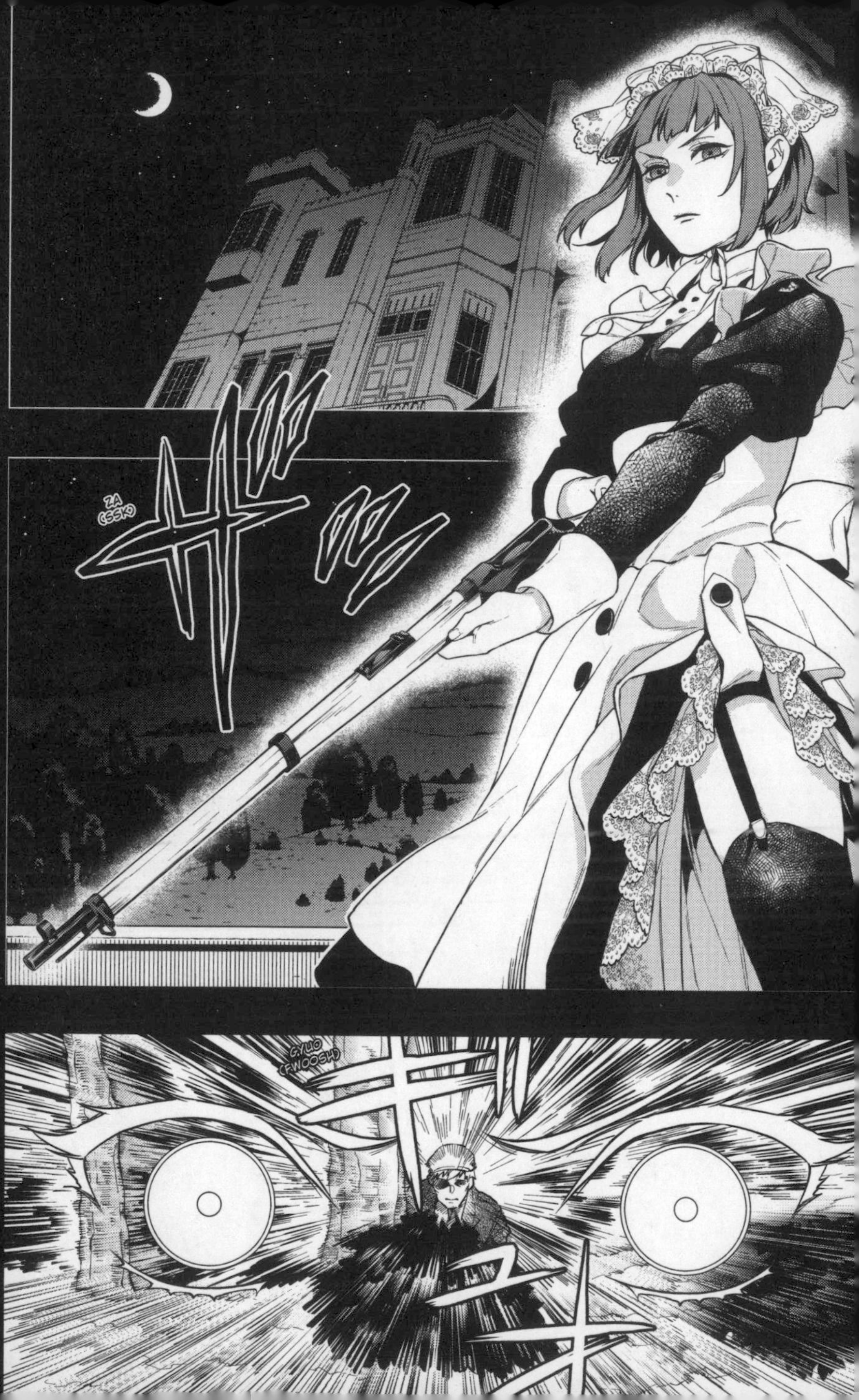
ZA (SSK)
GYUO (FWOOSH)

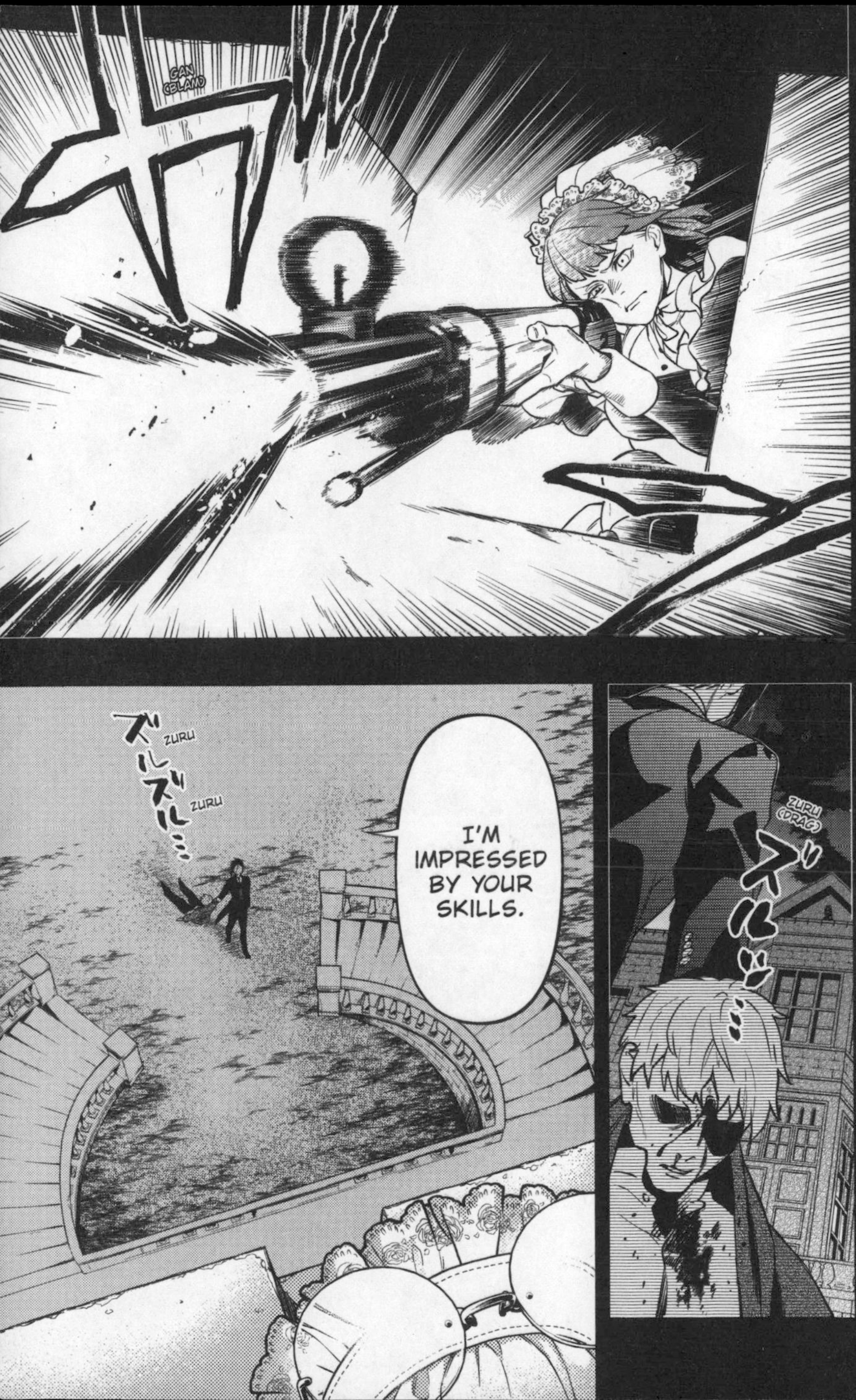
GAN (BLAM)
ZURU (DRAG)
ZURU
ZURU
I'M IMPRESSED BY YOUR SKILLS.

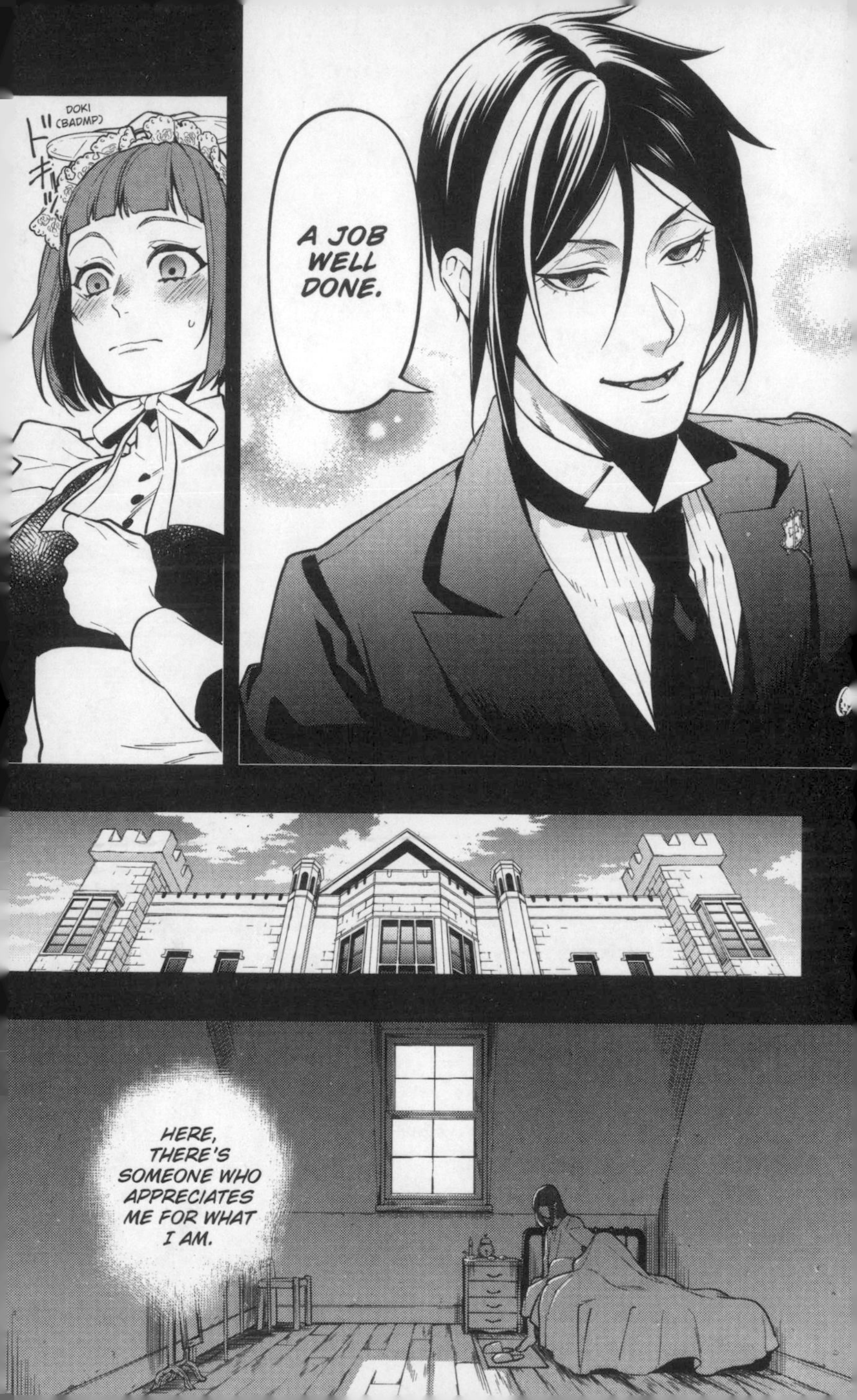
A JOB WELL DONE.
ドキッ
DOKI (BADMP)
HERE, THERE'S SOMEONE WHO APPRECIATES ME FOR WHAT I AM.

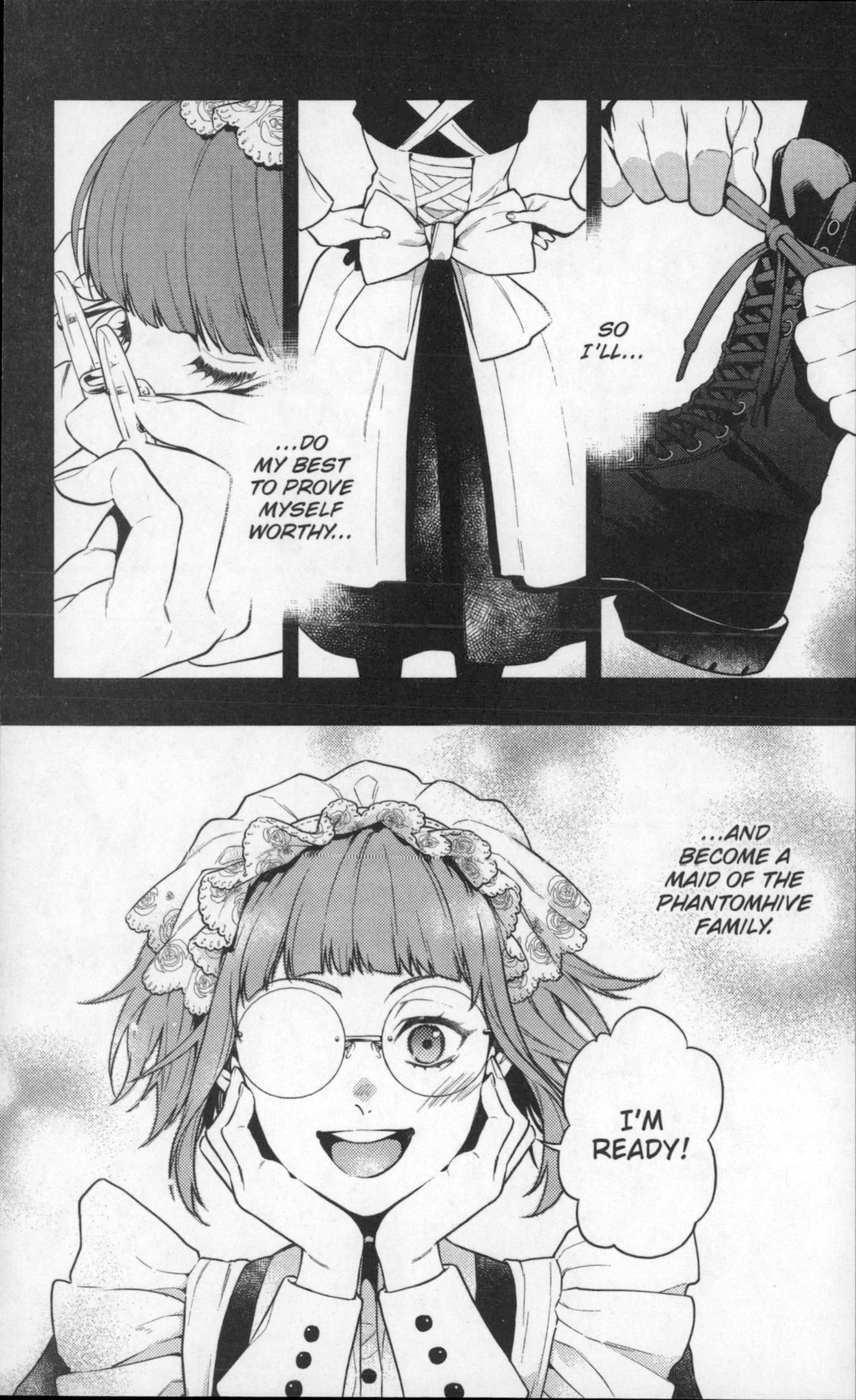
SO I'LL...
...DO MY BEST TO PROVE MYSELF WORTHY...
...AND BECOME A MAID OF THE PHANTOMHIVE FAMILY.
I'M READY!

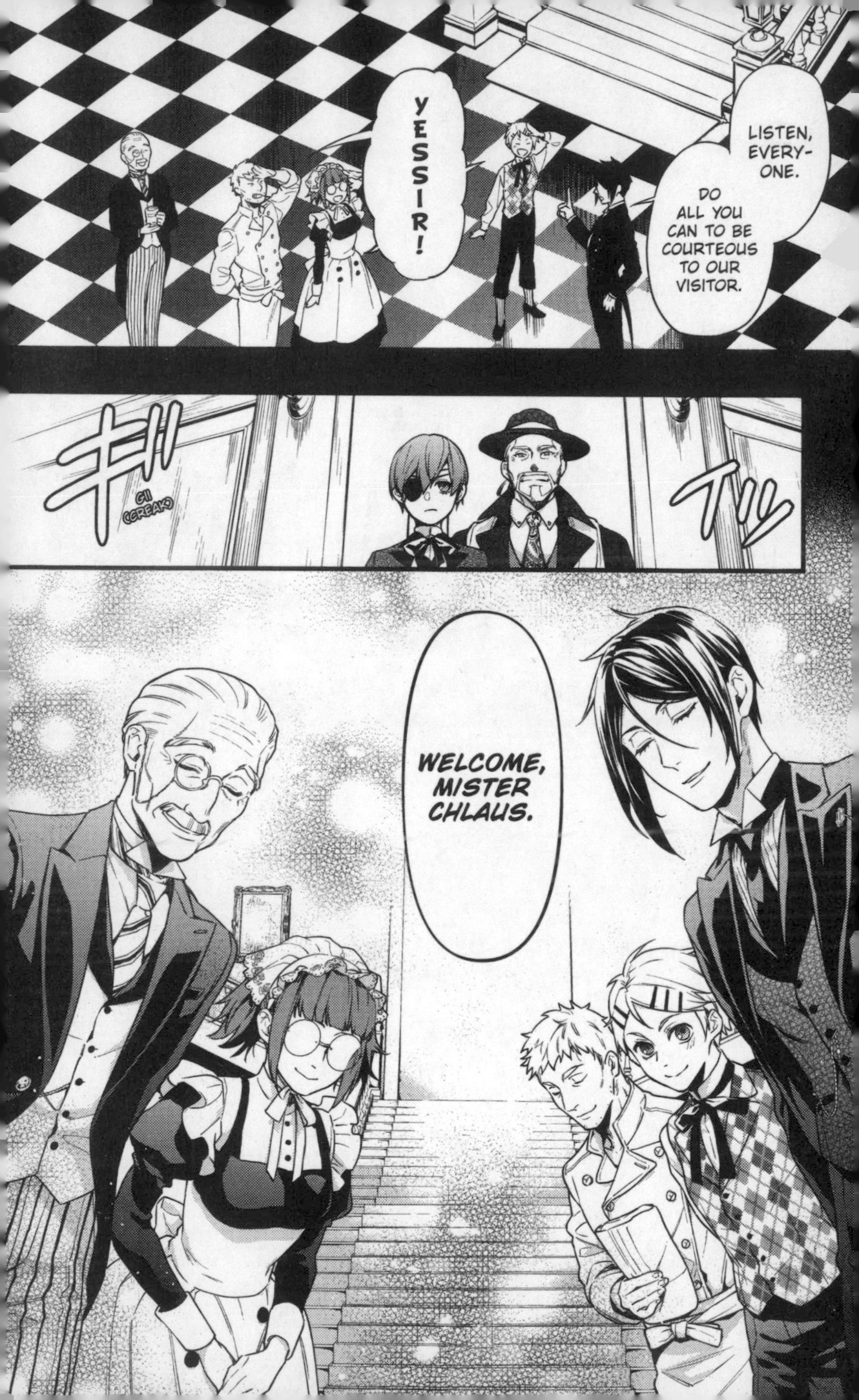
LISTEN, EVERY-ONE.
DO ALL YOU CAN TO BE COURTEOUS TO OUR VISITOR.
YESSIR!
GII (CREAK)
WELCOME, MISTER CHLAUS.

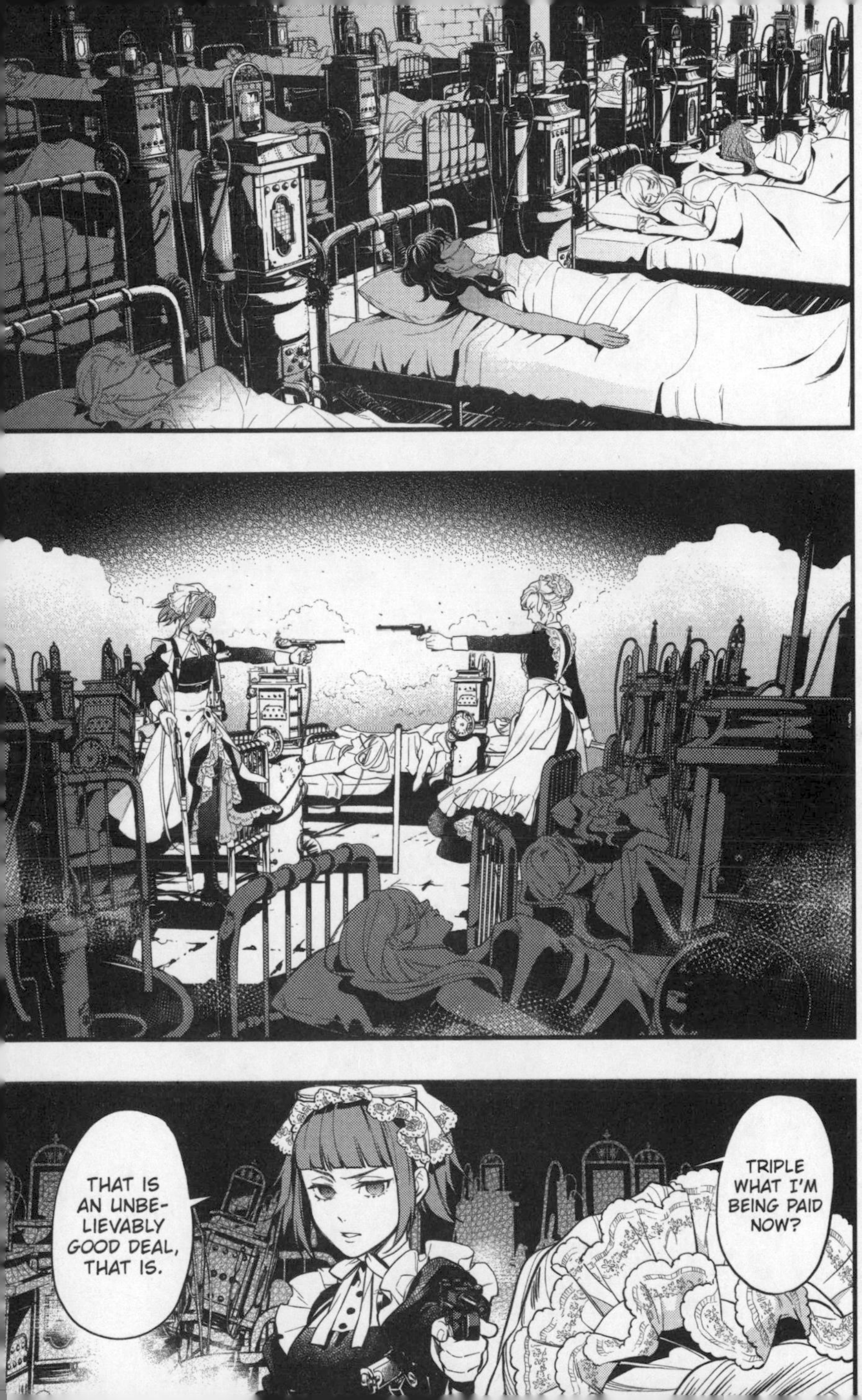
TRIPLE WHAT I'M BEING PAID NOW?
THAT IS AN UNBE-LIEVABLY GOOD DEAL, THAT IS.

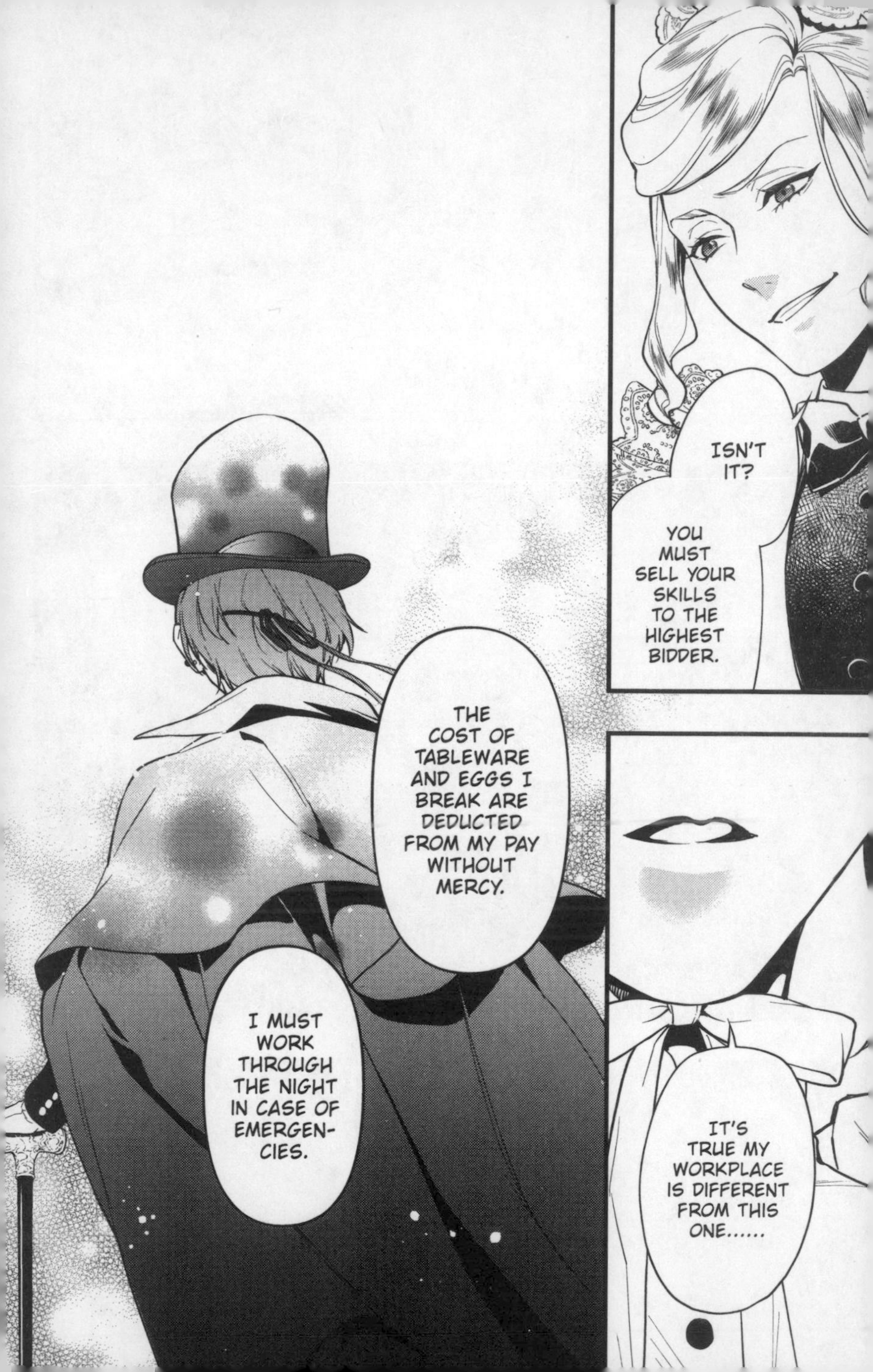
ISN'T IT?
YOU MUST SELL YOUR SKILLS TO THE HIGHEST BIDDER.
IT'S TRUE MY WORKPLACE IS DIFFERENT FROM THIS ONE......
THE COST OF TABLEWARE AND EGGS I BREAK ARE DEDUCTED FROM MY PAY WITHOUT MERCY.
I MUST WORK THROUGH THE NIGHT IN CASE OF EMERGEN-CIES.

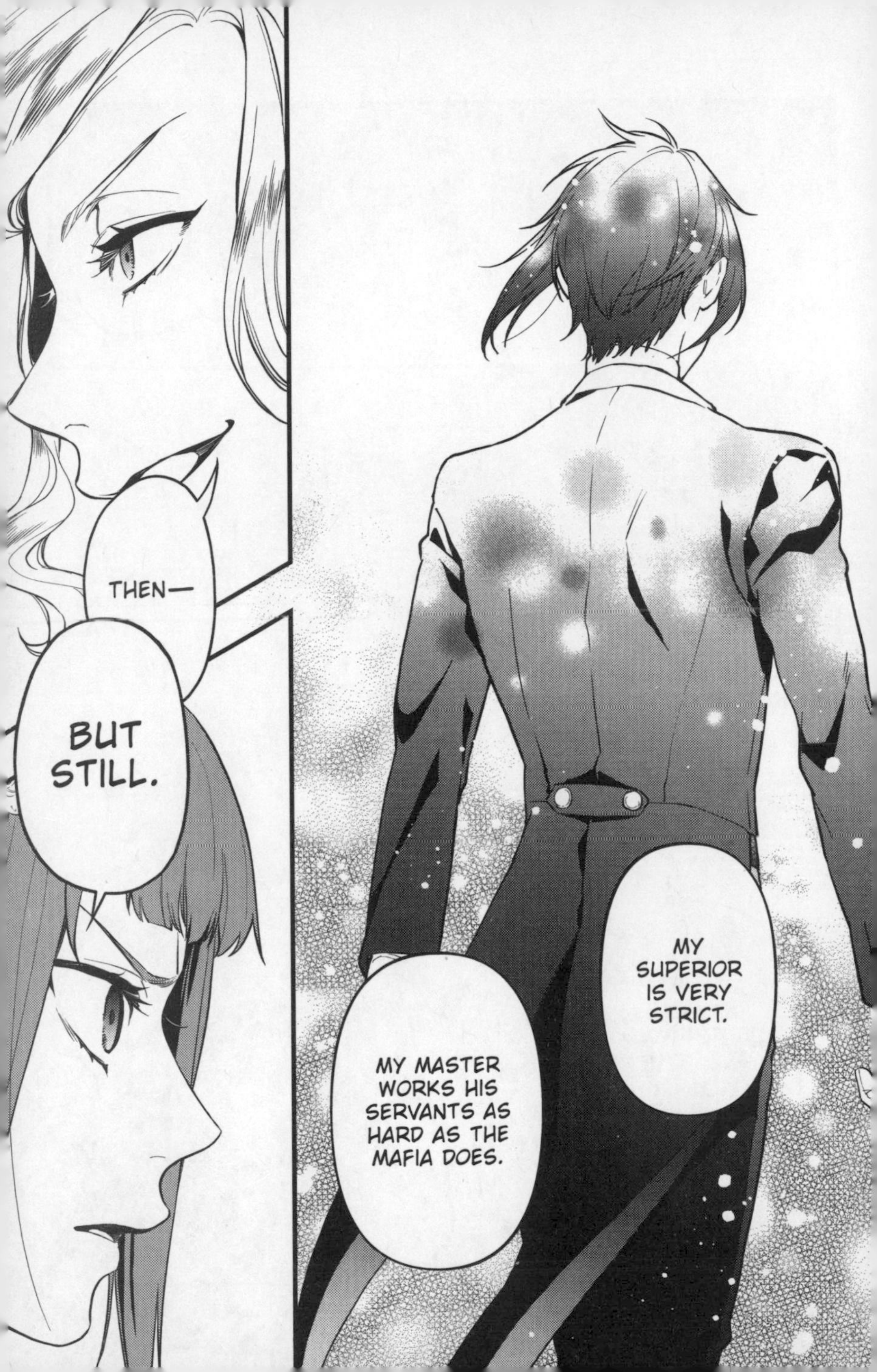
MY SUPERIOR IS VERY STRICT.
MY MASTER WORKS HIS SERVANTS AS HARD AS THE MAFIA DOES.
THEN—
BUT STILL.

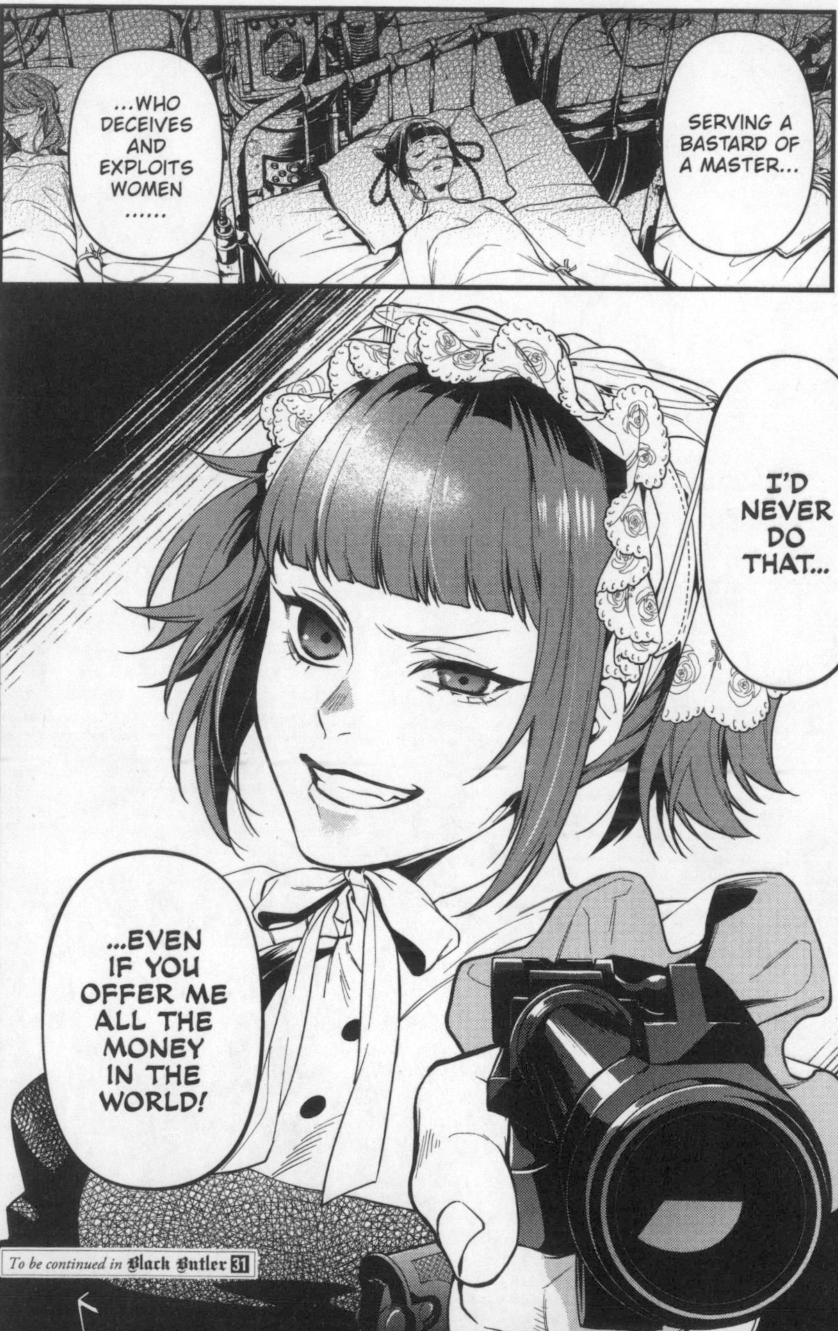
SERVING A BASTARD OF A MASTER...
...WHO DECEIVES AND EXPLOITS WOMEN ......
I'D NEVER DO THAT...
...EVEN IF YOU OFFER ME ALL THE MONEY IN THE WORLD!
To be continued in Black Butler 31

Black Butler

黒執事

Downstairs

Wakana Haduki
7
Tsuki Sorano
Sumire Kowono
Jun Hioki
Mine
Sanihiko/Kumako/KG/Tastu

*

Takeshi Kuma

*

Yana Toboso

Adviser

Rico Murakami

Special thanks to You!

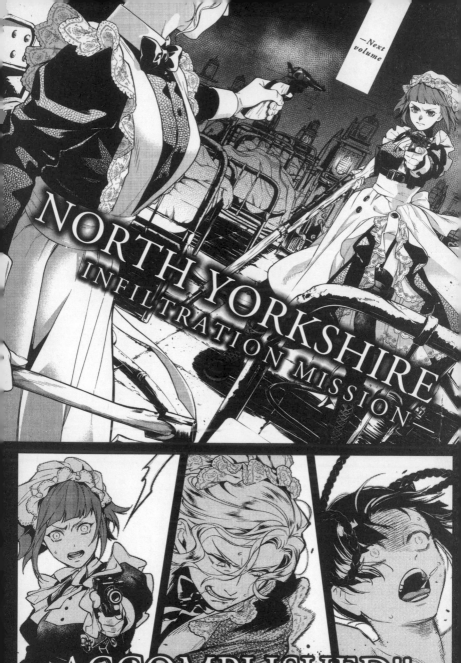

—Next volume

NORTH YORKSHIRE
INFILTRATION MISSION

ACCOMPLISHED!!

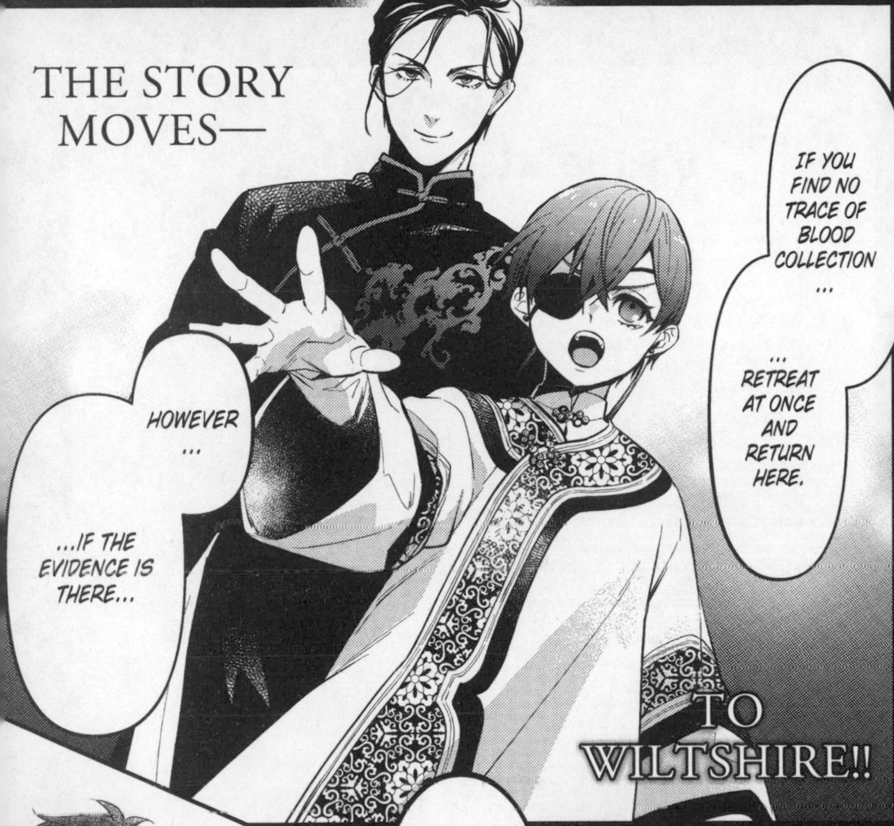
THE STORY MOVES—
IF YOU FIND NO TRACE OF BLOOD COLLECTION ...
... RETREAT AT ONCE AND RETURN HERE.
HOWEVER ...
...IF THE EVIDENCE IS THERE...
TO WILTSHIRE!!

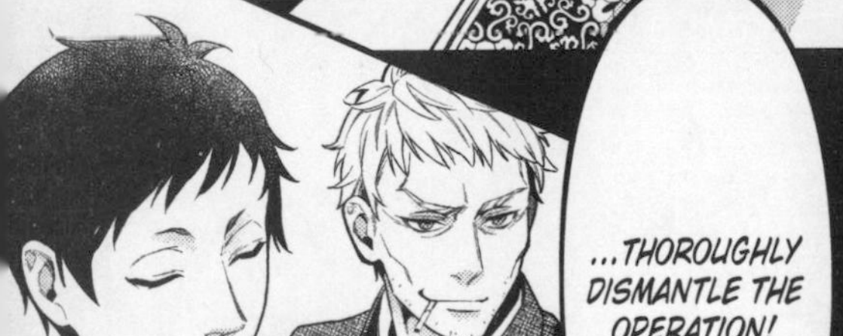
...THOROUGHLY DISMANTLE THE OPERATION!

While Mey-Rin and Ran-Mao were on their mission at Baron Heathfield's manor, Baldo and Lau were at a sanatorium for ex-servicemen.

The two encounter a nurse who guides soldiers wounded in conflicts and thought to be beyond hope back to society......

Is the "miracle healer" providing medical care or casting spells?

Black Butler 31

Coming soon!

Translation Notes

PAGE 36
Gelaohui
The "Elder Brothers Society," an actual Chinese syndicate that was active in Shanghai in the late nineteenth and early twentieth centuries. Also known as "The Red Gang." *Gelaohui* and *Qing Bang* were rival syndicates.

PAGE 49
The Bund
The Bund is a stretch of riverfront along the Huangpu River that was part of the Shanghai International Settlement. Also known as *Waitan*, which means "the foreigners' riverfront."

INSIDE BACK COVER
Tea Squad
Ciel and the servants of Phantomhive Manor are cosplaying the immensely popular long-running kids' television franchise *Super Sentai*. Known more commonly as *Power Rangers* to English-speaking audiences, every new season features a squad that uses their weapons to transform into leotard-wearing superheroes.

The show title for each season makes the unifying theme of their outfits and weapons clear—in this case, they are Patriciangers, or "Aristocrat-rangers." The enemies also usually have a unifying theme with names that utilize puns or wordplay, similar to Grill Reaper here. Weapons, like Sebastian's sword, are often designed with children in mind.

Gunpowder
Super Sentai and other similar shows like *Kamen Rider* are known for their continued reliance on practical effects, especially pyrotechnics.

Yana Toboso

AUTHOR'S NOTE

This is the thirtieth time I'm writing this inside flap text.

Black Butler started out as a lighthearted butler comedy, but......I feel like we've come pretty far as the butler fought, sang, and danced his way here.

And so, this is Volume 30.

Black Butler

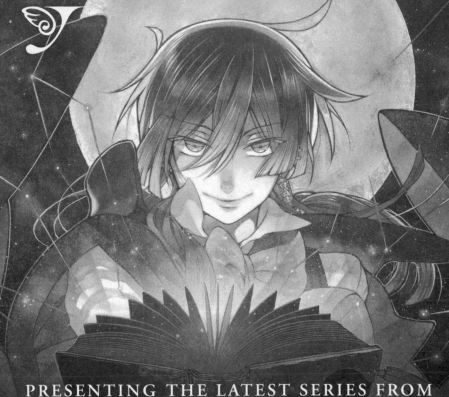

BLACK BUTLER ㉚

YANA TOBOSO

Translation: Tomo Kimura
Lettering: Bianca Pistillo

KUROSHITSUJI Vol. 30 © 2020 Yana Toboso / SQUARE ENIX CO., LTD. First published in Japan in 2020 by SQUARE ENIX CO., LTD. English translation rights arranged with SQUARE ENIX CO., LTD. and Yen Press, LLC through Tuttle-Mori Agency, Inc.

English translation © 2021 by SQUARE ENIX CO., LTD.

Yen Press
150 West 30th Street, 19th Floor
New York, NY 10001

Visit us!
† yenpress.com
† facebook.com/yenpress
† twitter.com/yenpress
† yenpress.tumblr.com
† instagram.com/yenpress

First Yen Press Edition: August 2021
The chapters in this volume were originally published as ebooks by Yen Press.

Yen Press is an imprint of Yen Press, LLC.
The Yen Press name and logo are trademarks of Yen Press, LLC.

The publisher is not responsible for websites (or their content) that are not owned by the publisher.

Library of Congress Control Number: 2010525567

ISBNs: 978-1-9753-2485-8 (paperback)
       978-1-9753-2486-5 (ebook)

10 9 8 7 6 5 4 3 2 1

WOR

Printed in the United States of America